A SEASON IN HELL

THE DEFENCE OF THE LUCKNOW RESIDENCY

A SEASON IN HELL

MICHAEL EDWARDES

Ever the day with its traitorous
      death from the loopholes around,
Ever the night with its coffinless
      corpse to be laid in the ground,
Heat like the mouth of a hell,
      or a deluge of cataract skies,
Stench of old offal decaying and
      infinite torture of flies,
Thoughts of the breezes of May
      blowing over an English field,
Cholera, scurvy, and fever,
      the wound that *would* not be healed.

TENNYSON   *The Defence of Lucknow*

TAPLINGER
PUBLISHING COMPANY
NEW YORK

First published in the United States in 1973 by
TAPLINGER PUBLISHING CO., INC.
New York, New York

Copyright © 1973 by Michael Edwardes
All rights reserved
Printed in Great Britain

Library of Congress Catalog Card Number: 72-11088

ISBN 0-8008-7015-8

CONTENTS

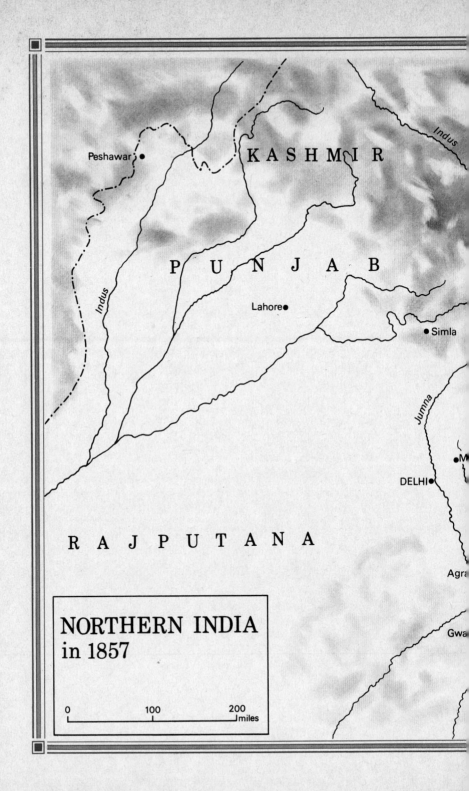

KASHMIR

Indus

Peshawar ●

PUNJAB

Lahore ●

● Simla

Indus

Jumna

DELHI ●

● M

RAJPUTANA

Agra

Gwa

NORTHERN INDIA
in 1857

0   100   200
                    miles

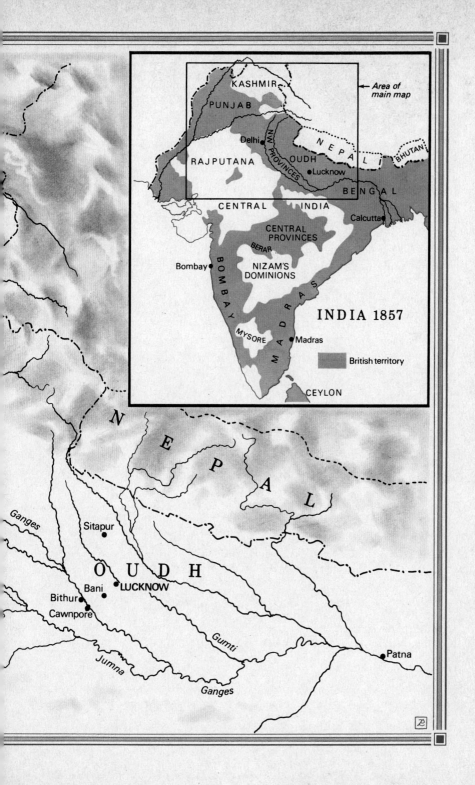

KASHMIR

PUNJAB

NW PROVINCES

Delhi

RAJPUTANA

OUDH

Lucknow

NEPAL

BHUTAN

BENGAL

CENTRAL   INDIA

CENTRAL
PROVINCES

Calcutta

BERAR

NIZAM'S
DOMINIONS

Bombay

B O M B A Y

M A D R A S

MYSORE

Madras

British territory

INDIA 1857

CEYLON

Area of
main map

N   E

P   A   L

Ganges

Sitapur

O U D H

Bani   LUCKNOW

Bithur

Cawnpore

Gumti

Patna

Jumna

Ganges

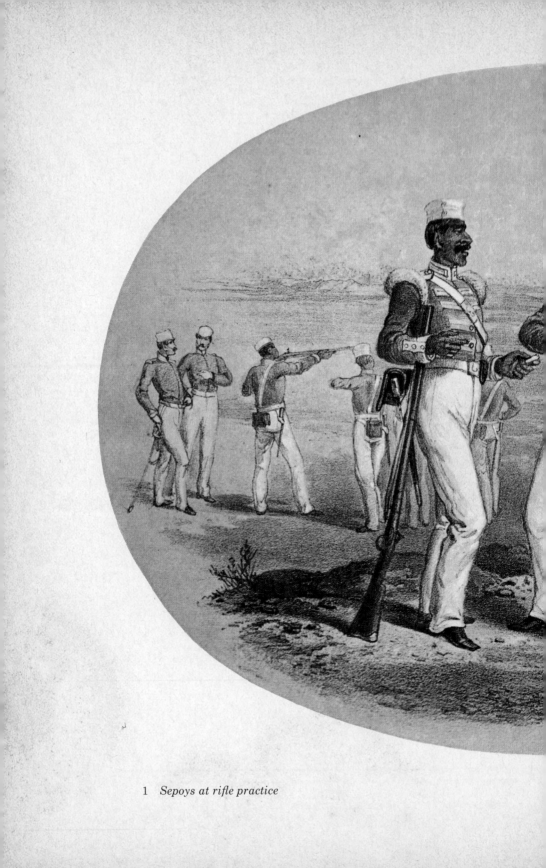

1 *Sepoys at rifle practice*

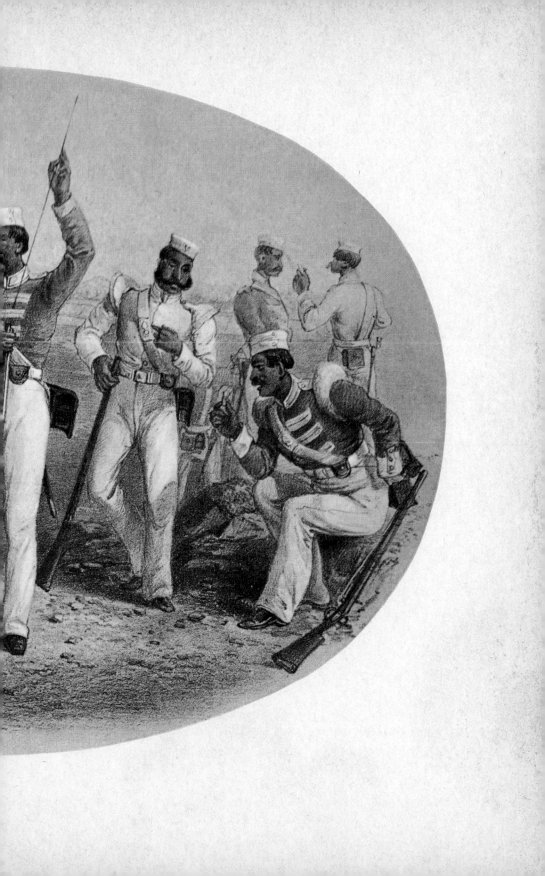

PREFACE

WHAT FOLLOWS is the story—the inside story, from the defenders' side—of a siege which took place in mid-nineteenth-century India. Altogether, the siege lasted for 140 days; though, on the eighty-seventh, reinforcements broke into the besieged area, they were not strong enough to break out again.

This is not the story of a simple military operation—of a small, gallant force of professional soldiers holding out in a strong fortress against overwhelming odds. For one thing, there was no fortress. As one of the survivors put it: 'We were in no fort at all: we occupied a few houses in a large garden with a low wall on one side and only an earthen parapet on the other, in the middle of a large city . . . swarming with thousands of . . . foes.'[1]

Inside this area were nearly 600 European and Eurasian women and children. Of the 1,700 fighting men at the start of the siege, 153 were civilian volunteers. Just over 700 of the fighting men were Indian soldiers, many of them belonging to the same regiments as were besieging them. For this was a military rebellion —the Indian Mutiny of 1857.

The defence of the Residency at Lucknow was one of the epics of the nineteenth century. Celebrated in much bad verse by such poets as Lord Tennyson and John Greenleaf Whittier, it captured the imagination of the Victorian public, not only in Britain but in Europe and the United States.

The story here is told from the letters, diaries and reminiscences of the time. The point of view is always that of the besieged, cut off from the outside world. Events taking place there are seen only in the light of such information as reached the besieged from the reports of spies and the rumours deliberately spread by the enemy. Except in the Introduction and the Epilogue, nothing has been added. What is presented is only what was known or believed, suffered or enjoyed, at the time.*

From the following pages, the story emerges of a few great and many small heroisms, of military incompetence on one side, matched almost equally on the other. Inside the besieged area there were many avoidable privations and much unavoidable

---

*For what was, in fact, happening outside Lucknow, see Appendix 2, p. 311.

disease. Fundamentally, the record is one of ordinary human beings, with all their arrogance, bloody-mindedness, pettiness, and capacity for genuine sacrifice. In spite of its exotic imperial background, this is not so much a British—or even British-Indian —story as a universal and timeless one of average people responding to extreme danger and stress, in what one survivor remembered as 'a season in hell'.

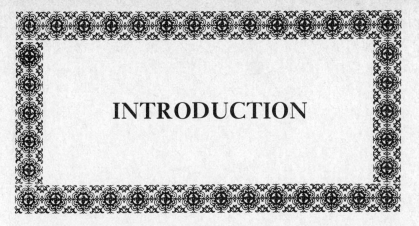

INTRODUCTION

By the end of 1856, northern India was trembling with unease. The foreigners who ruled—agents of the English East India Company which had first begun the conquest of India with Robert Clive's victory at Plassey in 1757—had, through ill-judged political, social, and legal reforms, antagonised most levels of Indian society. The heirs of rulers, or former rulers, for example, had been deprived of their inheritance—in some cases of territory, in others of substantial pensions—on what seemed to most Indians the most specious of excuses. In exile in Calcutta, the king of Oudh—deposed a year earlier, his state annexed—still hoped to regain his kingdom, as did many of his family. In Delhi, where the last of a line of kings who had once ruled all India lived as a pensioner of the British, there were men who dreamed of reviving an empire.

But there was no chance of successful rebellion while the British still retained the allegiance of their army. That army, which had conquered India for the British, was an army of Indians —a mercenary army which would remain true, it was thought, to its British officers and the government that paid it. By the end of 1856, however, the army's loyalty had worn very thin, though the British did not seem to have noticed it.

The Company's army in northern India, known as the Bengal Army, was mainly recruited in Oudh, and many of the soldiers believed they had suffered from the annexation of their homeland. There was also a growing belief that the British were planning to force the Hindu and Muslim sepoys (soldiers) to become Christians like themselves. Agents of the disaffected seized their opportunity. If only the sepoys could be convinced, absolutely, that the British intended to attack their religion, they would be

15

the spearhead of revolt. The British collaborated in this plan.

Both Hindus and Muslims believed that contact with certain animal substances was so polluting that it would cut them off from their faith, their gods, and the certainties of salvation. Among these substances were cow fat—the cow is a sacred animal to Hindus—and the fat of the pig, which is abhorrent to Muslims. In 1857 the British decided to introduce into their army, as a replacement for the old smooth-bore musket, the new Enfield rifle. To load this, it was necessary to bite or tear a greased cartridge. The rumour, not altogether unfounded, flew around that the grease was made of cow or pork fat. It seemed to be the long-expected attempt to break the sepoys' faith. Slowly at first, but with increasing momentum as *agents provocateurs* got to work, the sepoys began to refuse the new cartridges. Be prepared, they were told. Have no fear. British rule will end on the anniversary of Plassey. Refusal to accept the cartridges began at Berhampur in Bengal in February. By April it had spread to the Punjab. On May 3, a mutiny was just averted in Lucknow, capital of the annexed state of Oudh. On May 10, at the military station of Meerut, the sepoys broke into open rebellion, killed their officers, and departed for Delhi, some forty miles away, without any attempt being made to stop them.

The news reached Lucknow a few days later, and an already uneasy situation hardened into menace.

Part 1

❧

PRELUDE

1
MUTINY
AT MARIAON

THE SOUND of the evening gun was to be the signal. So the informer had said. At 9 p.m. on Saturday, May 30, 1857, the men of the 71st Native Infantry would set fire to their huts and bungalows and murder their officers.

In a climate stifling with rumours and alarms, it was no more than another rumour. But some precautions were taken. Men of Her Majesty's 32nd, white soldiers—safe soldiers—were put on standby. There were guns on the edge of the infantry lines, covering the road from the military cantonment at Mariaon to the city. Sir Henry Lawrence and his staff were also in the military lines, partly as a gesture. See, the British, nonchalant and unworried, taking dinner at the very hour of mutiny! Partly, also, as a threat, for Lawrence's presence meant the presence of British troops and British guns, however few they might be. But wholly, taking a terrible risk.

Sir Henry was just sitting down to dinner when the evening gun sounded. For a moment there was silence. 'Your friends are not punctual,' remarked Sir Henry to one of his staff, but the words were scarcely out of his mouth when the answer was heard, a ragged stutter of musket fire, the soft surge of shouting, quickly followed by the crackle of flames catching the dry thatch of huts and bungalows. The display of nonchalance had failed, the threat gone unheeded. The risk remained. The death of Lawrence and all his staff would make a crushing triumph for the rebels.

Dinner forgotten and horses called for, the men wait impatiently on the verandah of the house. The night, though velvet dark, is reddened by the fires of burning bungalows. Opposite, a house goes up in flames, and the glare harshly outlines the men of Lawrence's guard—an Indian guard, soldiers of the 13th Native

19

Infantry under an Indian officer. Thirty men with muskets thirty yards away, and in the background the sounds of a mutiny whose underlying cause is racial fear. The Indian officer comes forward and salutes: 'Am I to load?' And Lawrence replies: 'Oh yes, let them load.' The leaden bullet slides down the barrel, the soft thud of the ramrod can be clearly heard. Then the capping. For this, the gun has to be brought up and levelled. As the barrels come up, Lawrence cries out to the guards: 'I am going to drive those scoundrels out of the cantonment; take care while I am away that you all remain at your posts and allow no one to do any damage here, or enter my house, else when I return I will hang you!'

The drill movement continues. To everyone's relief, the guard shoulders arms. Either these soldiers are loyal, or Sir Henry's threat has meaning. He and his staff ride off, and his is the only house in the cantonment that night which is neither pillaged nor burnt.[1]

Back at Lawrence's headquarters in Lucknow city, where it seems no one has been told that a mutiny among the 71st was even suspected, the noise from the cantonment comes as a frightening surprise. Martin Gubbins, next to Lawrence the senior civilian in Lucknow, has gone up on the roof of his house after dinner and is just about to go back down to bed when he hears firing from the direction of the cantonment. Hurrying below, Gubbins rouses the men, women and children living in the house and sends them up to the roof, where arms, ammunition, water and food have been stored. Soon the glare of burning huts and bungalows can be seen distinctly. It is not until early in the morning that reliable news of what has been happening reaches Gubbins.

The anxiety of Mrs Inglis, wife of the colonel of the 32nd, is relieved rather earlier by a note from her husband which reaches her about midnight. But for most, it has been a night of worry and tension, especially for those who live outside the headquarters (Residency) area or the cantonment.

Along the road between the cantonment and the town, a French merchant, M. Deprat, has a country house, part of which he has fortified at his own expense, with encouragement from Lawrence, who has given him command of a detachment of a hundred native policemen. Deprat, who was once a soldier and served with the French army in Algiers, intends to hold his house as a strong-point and, from there, to delay the progress of the mutineers should they try to reach the city.

Staying with Deprat is a Calcutta merchant, a Mr Rees, who is tranquilly asleep in bed when his host's servant wakes him with

20

the news that the regiments in the cantonments have mutinied. Deprat himself calls out: *'Le jeu a commencé. Dépêchez-vous!'* Not waiting to dress, Rees grabs his clothes and a double-barrelled rifle and makes for the fortified magazine opposite the dwelling-house. The windows and doors have been filled in, and access to the roof is by a movable ladder. On the flat terrace there are a couple of beds, a kind of tent, supplies of powder, ball, and cartridges, and two small three-pounder guns. There is also food and water.

Like Gubbins at the Residency, the two men can see clearly the fires in the cantonment and hear the sound of musketry and then of heavy guns. There is a lot of activity along the road, horsemen galloping up and down, but none is allowed to pass without challenge. To one horseman riding furiously towards the town, Rees shouts: 'Halt!' The rider holds his horse. 'Who are you?' demands Rees. 'A friend,' comes the reply. 'I carry a message to the Residency.'

'What news, then?'

'Good news.'

'Well, *what* good news?'

'The bungalows are being burnt and the Europeans are everywhere shot down!'

Rees fires his pistol—and, in the darkness, misses. But the news is enough to send Deprat off with some of his men to the cantonment to see what he can do to help.[2]

In the cantonment, the noise of firing and the stench of burning thatch are intense. So, too, is the confusion. Sir Henry and his small party, after leaving his house, at first join up with a party of 300 men of the 32nd whose function, with four guns, is to hold the road to the town and prevent the mutineers from crossing the river at the iron bridge. Meanwhile, the officers of the native regiments have hurried into the lines to reason with their men. At the officers' mess of the 71st there is little but a smouldering ruin, though the officers themselves have escaped. Someone has ordered the guns to fire on the men of the 71st, and flurries of grapeshot whirr through the air. In their flight, the mutineers have murdered one of their officers, dragging him from under a bed where some of his own men have tried to conceal him.

In another part, Brigadier Handscomb, the commander of the Oudh Brigade, has come up with a detachment of the 32nd against a body of the mutineers. The order to fix bayonets is given, but then Handscomb hesitates. In the dark, who can tell friend from foe, loyal sepoy from mutineer? Handscomb insists on going forward to talk to the men—and is shot dead. When the detachment rushes forward, the lines are empty, and there is nothing for them to do but return to the artillery ground where Sir Henry has set up a temporary headquarters.

There are many fortunate escapes. Lieutenant Chambers of the 13th Native Infantry has two. First he is shot in the leg but, in falling to the ground, misses being riddled by a burst of musket fire. Managing to reach his own house, he has his wound dressed by his servants, then mounts his horse and makes for that part of the cantonment which he knows is held by European soldiers. On the way, he meets up with a party of fifty mutineers. Galloping straight at them he finds that surprise carries him right through without a scratch; the darkness cuts off pursuit.

The darkness, too, has added to the confusion. With musket shot whistling about indiscriminately, and grape sheeting a wide area, it is difficult to muster the loyal sepoys. Colonel Palmer of the 48th Native Infantry has assembled his men on their parade ground, but though they are not joining the mutiny they will not move against the mutineers. Men are slipping away in the darkness, and Palmer calls on the remainder to follow him to the Residency. By the time his party reaches the iron bridge, there are only fifty-seven men around the colours.

Fire and shot, and an invitation to plunder. Lieutenant Hardinge, with a small force of cavalry, is trying to prevent the looting of officers' houses and the shops in the regimental bazaars. But there is too much, it is too widespread, and Lieutenant Hardinge gets a bayonet thrust through the arm.

Mrs Bruere, wife of an officer in the 13th, has paid for her foolishness in returning to the cantonment against orders. With her five little children she has had to remain in her house protected by one loyal Sikh soldier while the mutineers plunder and burn everything they can around her. With the soldier's aid, she and the children slip out into the open countryside and spend the night, miserable and afraid, in the dry bed of a stream.

None of this, of course, is known to the watchers in the Residency. At about 2 a.m., however, Captain Germon of the 13th arrives with a note from Sir Henry. The general impression is that the mutiny had been suppressed, at some cost in British lives. Captain Germon frightens his wife with his appearance. His trousers are soaked with blood—but it is only the blood of his horse. The news he has brought unwinds some of the tension in the Residency. Ever since nine o'clock on the previous evening the men have been standing by, revolvers and rifles loaded and

22

ready, while the women—fully dressed, each equipped with a little bundle of linen and other necessaries—have been waiting in case they have to move to safer quarters in the old fort. Only the children have slept.

But the mutiny is not, in fact, over. Mr Gubbins, going down to the military cantonment at first light on the 31st, hears the sound of firing and learns that Sir Henry is out with the artillery in pursuit of mutineers. The scene in the lines is one of devastation and death. Most of the officers' houses have been burnt to the ground. Bodies are scattered around, some of them showing the dreadful open holes and flayed skin of grapeshot wounds. Grain merchants and other tradesmen are bustling about complaining that their stocks have been looted. Everywhere lie broken sacks, pots, rags of clothing, even the occasional coin that someone has missed.

The cantonment is yesterday's theatre. The action has moved to the open plain away to the north. Gubbins attaches himself to a group of cavalry and joins in the chase, thinking himself reasonably insured against the risk of being shot by his own men by promising them a hundred rupees for each mutineer killed or captured.

He finds the going slow. The orders are that the cavalry should keep in line with the guns. Though the main body of mutineers is still ahead, the plain seems full of men and women, all carrying bundles on their head. It takes Gubbins a moment to realise that these are villagers and camp followers who have taken advantage of the mutiny to join in the plunder and are now making off with their loot. But among them is an occasional soldier, slower than the others to get away. Some surrender—and Gubbins, who has no sword, takes the opportunity to arm himself with one from a captive—others manage to make off faster than the pursuit can follow. Gubbins is not a very good shot, and even with steady aim misses every target. Fortunately, the mutineers are little better, and, caught in an ambush, he is still able to ride away unscathed despite the shots buzzing round his head. When he returns to the cantonment at 11 a.m., he finds that the main force has returned an hour earlier. Having followed the mutineers for about ten miles, they have brought back sixty prisoners.

'We are now positively better off than we were,' wrote Sir Henry to the governor-general, Lord Canning, in Calcutta. 'We now know our friends and our enemies. The latter have no stomach for a fight though they are capital incendiaries.'[3]

Better off, perhaps. The British certainly knew their enemies.

23

What was more, they had permitted most of them to escape with their arms and ammunition. The pursuit had never caught up with the main body of the mutineers, and the prisoners consisted only of a few stragglers. The rest were loose in the countryside fanning the flames of revolt.

And in the city, rumours and alarms filled the streets. There were reports of mobs assembling at strategic places. Some 5,000 men were said to have crossed the river at a ford and to be making for the military cantonments where Sir Henry still had his headquarters. Others were moving on the Residency area. At noon, word came that the expected rising had taken place and could not be contained by the armed police in the city. Most of the wives of senior military and civil officers were at lunch at Sir Henry's house in the Residency enclosure when the alarm was raised. No one quite knew what to do. Should they stay where they were, or return to the various houses in which they were lodged? Their anxiety was not lessened when they were told that the Residency building was not very strongly constructed and that the floors might not bear the weight of a large number of people moving about. Some returned to their houses. Mrs Inglis chose to stay, with her three children, and moved into a small room on the top floor which was already occupied by Mrs Case, wife of a senior officer of the 32nd, and her sister, Caroline Dickson.

Naturally, everyone was still worried about what was happening in the city. There was the almost continuous sound of firing and the murmur of crowds. In the streets, men were seen here and there carrying dolls dressed up as English children. For the entertainment of the mob, they solemnly chopped off the dolls' heads with a sword. There were reports that the landowners of the districts surrounding Lucknow were marching on the city with the intention of killing every Christian they could lay hands on. Mrs Inglis was more than glad, as darkness fell, to see the men of the 32nd, with Sir Henry Lawrence and her husband, John, at their head, marching over the iron bridge.

When the troops reached the Residency, Sir Henry made a speech which was loudly cheered. In fact, one soldier shouted 'Long life to Sir Henry!' with such vigour that he broke a blood vessel. Lawrence had decided to concentrate most of his forces, and make their headquarters in the Residency area. The cantonment was too exposed, communications were too easily interrupted. A small force of the 32nd, commanded by Colonel Case and supported by four guns, was left in the military lines. Another small detachment was sent up river to the old fort of the Machchi

Bhawan to reinforce the troops already guarding the vast quantity of shot, ball ammunition and gunpowder that had been collected there. There was little else Lawrence could do with the small forces at his disposal and doubts about the loyalty of some of the native troops who had so far stuck by the British. He had no intention of abandoning Lucknow—even if that had been possible. He saw the city as a symbol, and retreat from it would, he believed, have the worst possible effect on a situation already serious enough. Preparations to resist attack had to continue until the last possible minute, behind a barrier of warlike postures and threatening gestures.

One of these was the public hanging of the prisoners taken during the futile pursuit of the mutineers.

In the first days of June, courts martial worked rapidly to condemn the mutineers. All were found guilty, but the sentences varied. Thirty-six were condemned to be hanged, but not all the death sentences were confirmed by Sir Henry Lawrence. The executions were carried out in front of the Machchi Bhawan; eight or nine men were hanged in the morning, four or five in the evening. A number of gallows had been erected in an open space, leaving as much room as possible for spectators. In case of trouble, the area was fully covered by the guns of the fort, from artillery on the roof platforms to muskets and rifles at loopholes along the wall. One large gun, an eighteen-pounder primed with canister and grapeshot, the portfire alight, stood outside the fort as an open reminder of the weapons within.

One day, with a crowd of a few thousand waiting, there was a movement towards the gate of the fort which almost surrounded the British soldiers guarding the prisoners about to be executed. The sentry at the gate, fearing an attack, called the garrison to arms. But the sight of the artillerymen about to apply the fire to the eighteen-pounder stopped the crowd and it moved slowly back. The prisoners were marched up the steps of the gallows, the nooses were adjusted, and the drops pulled.

Other days found the crowd silent, too silent for some of the condemned. On one occasion an officer heard a prisoner, the noose already around his neck, demand from the crowd whether there was no one who would save him from these cursed Christians? No one replied. Was it fear, or indifference? It was hard to tell. The city was calmer now than it had been for some weeks. British officers and others still went about freely, and though they were greeted with scowls, there was no abuse, and no violence. Mr Rees, the Calcutta merchant, taking his regular evening ride

25

2   *The Residency, before the siege*

between the Residency area and the fort, once dropped his pistol, and was surprised—and relieved—to have it politely handed up to him by a passerby.

An order had been issued banning the carrying of arms by natives, but this was difficult to enforce. There could be no doubt that there were trained soldiers in the city. Not infrequently, men would be seen with a matchlock and spear, or a musket and a belt stuck with pistols, whose bearing was obviously military. On these occasions, British officers usually looked the other way.

There was an air of waiting. The British still hoped for reinforcements from Calcutta, the inhabitants of Lucknow for some sure proof that British rule was really at an end. It was certainly disappearing from the province of Oudh. On June 12, Lawrence was forced to write to the lieutenant-governor of the North West Provinces at Agra: 'Every outpost, I fear, has fallen, and we daily expect to be besieged by the confederated mutineers and their allies.'[4]

2
ESCAPE
TO LUCKNOW

THE LUCKNOW mutiny of May 30 had been the signal for risings throughout the province. News of burning and looting, of the massacre of British officers and their wives and children, trickled into the Residency. Yet there were survivors. Some owed their lives to loyal sepoys, others to landowners not yet sure which side it was safer to join. Some made the long, difficult and dangerous journey to Lucknow.

In the city one day there was a call for volunteers to go out into the countryside and escort a number of English fugitives back to safety. Hearing of this, Captain Anderson, a young officer of the 25th Native Infantry, rode over to the cantonment to offer his services to Captain Forbes, who with a party of Sikhs and a number of elephants was about to depart. Captain Forbes, it seems, had not been expecting volunteers, but he suggested that Anderson should take charge of the elephants. This was too much to ask. 'I declined the honour,' Anderson later wrote in his journal, 'stating that I had come to form part of an escort for the . . . refugees, and not for elephants.' Fortunately, Captain Forbes 'politely permitted me to join his party, or else I should most certainly have returned to Lucknow, as I had no idea of being made an elephant driver, although I was fully prepared to assist in escorting the unfortunates we were expecting.'[1]

Protocol satisfied, Anderson rode out with the party in the direction of the village of Mudkipur, a few miles away from the cantonment and formerly the barracks of a regiment of irregular cavalry. Just past the village, the party came across some men in a clump of trees, armed and ready to fire. It was the refugees who, seeing the Indian soldiers, had taken them for mutineers. With the men were a number of women and children looking,

29

Anderson thought, 'tired and careworn'. It was not surprising. All of them had travelled a considerable distance in constant fear of attack, not only by mutineers, but by villagers. The sight was perhaps something new for Anderson, but not for Captain Forbes. This was the second time he had gone out to bring in refugees from out-stations.

Forbes was an officer in the 1st regiment of Oudh Cavalry, usually known—after its commander—as 'Daly's Horse'. The regiment was stationed at Sikrora, a place about fifty miles north-east of Lucknow, but Forbes himself had been in Lucknow when mutiny broke out in the cantonment. His first thought was for his wife and children, and for the wives and children of his fellow officers at Sikrora, where there were only native troops and no fort to protect the British. Convinced that there would be mutiny at Sikrora, Forbes set out from Lucknow early in June, with some Sikh and volunteer cavalry, to bring the women and children back to the comparative safety of the Residency.

He and his men arrived at Sikrora on June 7. Despite an obviously tense situation, no attempt had been made to concentrate the women and children from other out-stations at Sikrora, so that it was only after Forbes's arrival that messages were sent out calling them to join the convoy. One messenger reached the little town of Gonda, sixteen miles to the east of Sikrora, at four in the afternoon. The letter he carried stated that the convoy would leave Sikrora at eight that evening. Gonda was a very small station and there were only two English women there. One was Katherine Mary Bartrum.

Katherine was twenty-three, a shy dark-haired girl, daughter of a silversmith in Bath. She had spent eight months at Gonda—until the end of May, a peaceful, retired life. In so small a station, where there were only ten Europeans and one other woman, there was little to do. Katherine found that it was only letters from home which marked the passage of time. Until May 22, that was, when news reached Gonda of the massacres at Meerut and Delhi. Just over a week later, it became known that the bloodshed had spread to Lucknow. The men decided to build a wall round one of the Gonda bungalows so that there would be at least some protection if the native troops stationed at Gonda broke into rebellion.

There was talk of sending the women—Katherine and her fifteen-month-old son, Bobbie, and Mrs Clark and her child—down to Calcutta, but both women refused to go, thinking it would be better to die with their husbands than to leave them

alone. At least there were no signs—no obvious signs, that is—
that the sepoys were planning mutiny. Yet all the time the news
from outside was of massacre. Katherine, 'never very brave', she
claimed, could 'neither sleep, eat or do anything', and used to 'sit
and cry over my baby, thinking it might soon be snatched from my
arms and murdered before my very eyes'.[2] At night she and her
husband Robert, who was the station doctor, slept with a sword
under Katherine's pillow and a loaded pistol next to Robert's
hand. She did not think they would have much chance of escape
if they were attacked, but consoled herself with her husband's
promise that 'should things come to the worst he would destroy
me with his own hand rather than let me fall into the power of
those brutal sepoys'.[3]

When the messenger arrived from Sikrora, Katherine did not
want to leave. She had 'often contemplated death with her husband, but not separation from him'.[4] She pleaded with him to let
her stay but Robert was immovable. She must think of Bobbie.
For his sake she must go to Lucknow. Convinced, but still reluctant to go—'God alone knows how bitter was the struggle to feel
that it was my duty to leave him'[5]—Katherine gathered together
a few things and 'took one last look round the house which had
been to me such a happy home, that the thought of sorrow reaching me there had seldom crossed my mind'.[6]

At six that evening, the little party set out for Sikrora—
Katherine and her husband, Mrs Clark and hers—mounted on
elephants. It was thought unsafe to take the direct road in case
they might meet up with mutineers. They had a native guide, and
Katherine was greatly afraid that he would lead them into a trap.
He did not, but the circuitous route he chose delayed their arrival
at Sikrora until 11 p.m. They found that Captain Forbes had left
with the women and children two hours earlier. The only thing to
do was to try and catch up with them.

After half an hour's rest and some tea, with milk for the children, Katherine and Mrs Clark were ready to go on. But who was
to escort them? Neither Mr Clark nor Robert Bartrum was prepared to leave his post; they would not go further, though their
wives begged them to. They would have to trust their wives and
children to an escort of sepoys, for there was no one else. Were
they loyal? Would they wait only until Sikrora was out of sight
and then murder their helpless charges? The risk had to be taken.
A more comfortable seat was made on the elephant by padding a
large wrapper into a saddle. Katherine took her baby in her arms
and gave her husband a last, tearful look. 'Goodbye dear Kate,'

said Robert. 'Keep up your spirits, we shall soon meet again and take care of my little darling.'[7]

For the two women it was a nightmare journey. The escort would sometimes stop and make the elephant stand, while they sat down and joked among themselves. At one halt, Katherine saw the sepoys loading their muskets, and asked what they were doing. 'Oh, there are so many bad people about, we are going to fight for you,' was the reply.[8] But at least when they were asked for water for the baby, they would always fetch it.

At eight o'clock in the morning they at last reached the river Gogra and saw the party that had left Sikrora before them on the other side. The women and children went over in a boat, while the elephants crossed at a ford. When they joined Captain Forbes's party they stopped at the house of a friendly native official to bath the children and eat some breakfast.

Captain Forbes's party now consisted of seven women, twelve children, and four officers. The weather was extremely hot, with the harsh, dry, dust-laden heat of northern India before the coming of the rains. All were suffering, the children in particular. It was sensible to rest in the shade and wait for the cool of the evening before going on. It was also safer to travel by night, especially as large bodies of mutineers were known to be operating around the approaches to Lucknow.

The dark did not give complete protection, however. As the little party made its way across a countryside littered with the shells of burned-out buildings, it was constantly approached by small bodies of men—who fortunately made no attempt to attack. But the terror of that night remained, for Katherine Bartrum, both indescribable and indelible. Their safe arrival at Lucknow seemed 'little short of a miracle'.[9] As they sighted the iron bridge, the party hurried on, leaving part of the escort from Sikrora behind. 'Weary and exhausted with hot winds, dust and scorching sun, and worn out with fatigue in addition to the anxiety we felt as to the fate of those dearest to us, whom we had left behind', they entered the Residency—and found it a 'scene of the utmost confusion'.[10]

3
CONFLICTS AND PREPARATIONS

THE CONFUSION inside the Residency which so struck Katherine Bartrum was genuine enough. It was due, in part, to panic, for in spite of all the warnings the mutiny of May 30 had taken many by surprise. But it was also due to a lack of detailed planning. Sir Henry Lawrence had done his best to prepare for the worst, but he could do no more than outline and embody the larger strategy. Tactics had to be left to lesser people, and many were found wanting.

Lawrence was fifty-one years of age and looked seventy. Even his immense energy could not conceal that he was an old man— and everyone spoke of him as one. Tall and very thin, he wore a long, straggly beard. Only his eyes betrayed the man behind, for they were never still. There was a general impression, especially among his friends, that he was not long for this world. One who visited him in Lucknow in early April wrote that 'grief had made him grey and worn, but it became him like the scars of battle . . . He had done with the world except for working for it while his strength lasted, and he had come to that calm, peaceful estimate of time and eternity, of himself and judgement, which could have only come of wanting and finding Christ'.[1] On the surface, odd qualifications for the chief commissionership of Oudh.

Lawrence's service in India had been marked by the trauma of great achievement never actually fulfilled. He had made enemies in places so high that they had frustrated most of his ambitions. When the governor-general had offered him the chief commissionership, he had welcomed it as a belated recognition of his qualities, even though his doctors had advised him to leave India for the sake of his health. To his sister, Charlotte, he wrote: 'I stay simply because it is my duty, and that I can do good.'[2]

For years Lawrence had been warning his superiors of the possibility of a revolt in the native army. No one had taken any notice. The first months of 1857 had only confirmed his fears. Throughout the army, rumours and suspicions that the British were determined to convert every soldier to Christianity were causing anxiety and hysteria. As for Oudh, when Lawrence arrived there it had been annexed for barely a year, and all the tensions of an occupied state were added to the general feeling of unease.

The first commissioner had been Sir James Outram, but he had been followed by a bureaucrat who had soon rubbed through the thin skin of the people's acceptance. Lawrence's initial task was to apply a soothing ointment. This he did with a mixture of firmness and sympathy which might have worked with the people of Oudh if it had not been for the fears of the soldiers on whom British power depended. When at the beginning of May, sepoys of the 7th Oudh Irregular Infantry had refused to accept cartrides for the new Enfield rifle, order had been restored, but the news of the outbreak at Meerut and the loss of Delhi completely undermined British authority. The mutiny of May 30 had been the natural consequence.

During May Lawrence had made discreet preparations to meet a possible rising. One of his first acts was to ask the governor-general to invest him with military as well as civil command, so that he could rearrange the disposition of troops in and around Lucknow. For it was Lucknow that really had to be defended and held. In a profound sense, Lucknow *was* Oudh. It was also a great and beautiful city. When William Howard Russell, the famous war correspondent of the London *Times*, saw it he was astounded by its magnificence. 'A vision of palaces,' he wrote, 'domes azure and golden, cupolas, colonnades, long facades of fair perspective in pillar and column, terraced roofs—all rising up amid a calm still ocean of the brightest verdure. Look for miles and miles away, and still the ocean spreads, and the towers of the fairy-tale city gleam in its midst. Spires of gold glitter in the sun. Turrets and gilded spheres shine like constellations. There is nothing mean or squalid to be seen. There is a city more vast than Paris, as it seems, and more brilliant.'[3]

Lucknow was certainly one of the largest cities in India, covering some twelve square miles and inhabited by between 600,000 and 700,000 people. As the capital of what had once been an independent kingdom, it was full of public buildings, palaces and mosques. On the right of the river Gumti, running approximately from the north-west, there was a line of palaces and public buildings, the central ones of the Chuttur Munzil (or Old Palace) being near the river bank, while the Kaisarbagh—a much larger and more modern structure—was set back from it. To the south-east, surrounded by a park filled with deer and antelope, tigers and peacocks, was another palace, the Dilkusha, or Heart's Delight. Nearby was La Martinière, once the residence of a French adventurer, but now for many years a school for European and Eurasian boys.

The Residency lay to the north on a raised plateau; with the fort of Machchi Bhawan, it occupied the only commanding position in the city. To the south and west lay the city proper, bounded to the south, south-east, and south-west by a canal. Across the river to the north-east, there were other buildings forming a kind of suburb. This bank was connected with the other by a stone bridge near the Machchi Bhawan, an iron bridge a little up stream from the Residency, and a bridge of boats beyond the Chuttur Munzil. The buildings of the city pressed very close upon the Residency.

The term 'Residency' was used to describe not only the building itself but the whole of the area in which it stood. The Residency building was classical in design, with lofty rooms and wide verandahs supported by Doric columns. Above, there was a tower and a flagstaff; below, that splendid invention of northern India, a *taikhana*, an underground room whose thick walls acted as insulation against the great heat of the hot season. There was also a large underground swimming pool. Except for the underground rooms, the Residency was not well suited for defence. The windows were very large, reaching almost to the floor, and the construction was of light brick and stucco.

Surrounding the Residency were a number of other buildings— a church, offices, private houses—each with its own gardens and its own well. Around these the chief engineer, Major Anderson, and his second-in-command, Captain Fulton, were instructed to prepare a line of defences. There had not been much time, for the serious work of erecting fortifications and laying in supplies only began after the news of the outbreak at Meerut reached Lucknow on May 17. The decision was then made that, should there be a close siege, the Residency area would be the most easily held; as a second point of defence, however, it was decided that the Machchi Bhawan should be put into some state of repair and stocked up with arms and ammunition. A few heavy guns were moved in to the fort, as well as a large number of mainly ceremonial weapons

—most of them useless—taken from the various palaces and erected on the walls of the fort to give an impression of great strength.

The engineers, not knowing when an attack might come, drew the outer defences of the Residency area as a line, joining up existing walls wherever possible with trenches and palisades. Outside this rampart, steadily built up as the days passed, a field of obstacles was sown. Great iron spikes, some of them with four points, were set in the earth. Pits were dug and lined with sharpened stakes. All this was designed to hinder a storming party before it reached the main defence. The whole area was roughly diamond-shaped, with each of the faces about a quarter of a mile in length.

As the work continued, Lawrence received a number of deputations from the citizens of Lucknow, all, it seemed, intent on dissuading him from fortifying the Residency. One day a respectable-looking Hindu claiming to be a wellwisher of the British asked to see Sir Henry. On being invited to state his business, he suggested that a number of monkeys should be brought into the Residency and looked after by high-caste Hindus. This, he insisted, would not only propitiate the Hindu gods but tend to make British rule popular once again. Sir Henry, putting on his hat, remarked: 'Your advice, my friend, is good. Come with me and I will show you my monkeys.' Slowly, he led the Hindu to a newly-completed battery in which an eighteen-pounder gun had been mounted. Laying his hand on the barrel, he said: 'See, here is one of my monkeys; *that*,' indicating a pile of cannonballs, 'is his food; and this,' pointing to a sentry of the 32nd, 'is the man who feeds him. There, go and tell your friends of *my* monkeys.'[4]

But, in fact, progress was slow. For one thing, the garrison itself could spare little time from its necessary patrols in the city and the environs to help in the construction of defences. This work was carried out by gangs of natives who worked reluctantly and had to be watched carefully or they would disappear into the narrow lanes of the city, never to be seen again. Furthermore, Sir Henry showed a certain lack of realism. The works were not to be hurried, he said, in case it should be seen as a sign of panic. Yet it was plain for all to see that the British were preparing the Residency for a siege. Even before the mutiny of May 30, the streets leading to the Residency were frequently lined with long convoys of carts filled with grain and munitions. Lawrence also refused to allow the houses overlooking the Residency area to be blown up before a register had been made and all of them valued—

36

so that compensation could be paid to their owners at some time in the unforseeable future.

Yet it was not for this reason that Martin Gubbins wrote to the governor-general: 'Sir Henry Lawrence is no longer, I think, firm, nor his mental vision clear.' Gubbins, a brave and energetic man whose reactions occasionally betrayed something of the psychotic personality that underlay his forceful character, had been constantly pressing for radical measures, especially against those sepoys who remained apparently loyal to the British. But Lawrence was determined to keep as many as possible, for without them he was sure that the Residency could not be held; otherwise, he had only 700 or so men of the 32nd. Sir Henry was therefore conciliatory, making rewards in cash and promotion for conspicuous service, and generally raising the standard of pay. Gubbins prophesied doom. Lawrence remained adamant. He would not dismiss the sepoys.

But on June 9, the day Katherine Bartrum reached the Residency, Gubbins was given his chance. Sir Henry was suddenly taken ill and Dr Fayrer, the senior doctor in the Residency, insisted that he should have a complete rest. To take over his responsibilities, Lawrence appointed a Council of Five, consisting of Major Banks—whom he had already recommended to the governor-general as the best man to succeed him if he should be killed—Colonel Inglis, Major Anderson, Mr Ommanney (a senior civilian), and Martin Gubbins.

No sooner had Lawrence retired to his bed than Gubbins insisted that the native troops be sent on leave—without their arms. The majority of the council was opposed, but this did not deter Gubbins. Without consulting the other members, he instructed the officers of the sepoy units to prepare to dismiss their men. On June 11, in fact, a large number of the men were already on their way. It was too much for Lawrence. The next day he resumed command, dissolved the council, and sent messengers after the sepoys to recall them. He had the satisfaction, according to his military secretary, Captain Wilson, 'of seeing numbers return to their post, with tokens of delight'.[5]

One effect of Gubbins's ill-judged activities was that the police battalion in the city—which he had himself considerably increased in numbers, on the assumption of their 'superior fidelity' —broke into revolt, and had to be chased away by a party of British soldiers, cavalry, and two guns. The pursuit went on until nightfall. About forty of the mutineers were killed, for the loss of two Sikhs and one British soldier who died of heatstroke. 'The

37

effect,' wrote Sir Henry, 'will I hope be good on the town.'[6]

But it made no difference to Gubbins, who continued to badger Lawrence with his demands for action. 'Mr Gubbins would be continually sending fifty men on elephants, forty, fifty, and more miles off. He is perfectly insane on what he considers energetic manly measures. His language has been so extravagant that, were he not really useful, I should be obliged to take severe measures against him. He is the one malcontent in the garrison.'[7]

Ignoring Gubbins's repeated warning that there was every reason not to trust the sepoys, Lawrence began to recall pensioners to the colours. It was a sensible move, for these veterans had a most powerful incentive for supporting the British—the continuance of their pensions. Something like 500 made their way to Lucknow. Many were obviously incapable of active service. Some were on crutches, maimed by old wounds, others were blind. But Lawrence received them all, thanked them for their loyalty to their old masters, and selected 170 of the more able-bodied. This brought the number of loyal native troops to about 800.

There was no doubt that, with only a few hundred British troops to add to the sepoys who might, or might not, remain loyal to the end, the possibility of defending the Residency against a long siege seemed more and more remote. Lawrence still hoped for reinforcements that would prevent him from being besieged at all. But if the worst came to the worst, he thought he could hold out for a month. Even then, he knew that he would need every man who could load and fire a gun. Early in June, Lawrence decided that all civilians—British and Eurasian—in government employ, should be enrolled as 'volunteers', given arms and ammunition, and taught how to use them. Those who could ride well were taken into the cavalry; the remainder were to be drilled as infantry.

When these men were first brought together to drill under the eye of the sergeants of the 32nd, it seemed a totally hopeless task. 'There were men of all ages, sizes, and figures. Here stood a tall athletic Englishman—there came a fat and heavy Eurasian with more width across the waist than about his chest. Next to the Eurasian came another of the same class who looked like a porter barrel . . . and the belt round his waist very closely resembling a hoop! Not far off you observed an old, bent-double man, who seemed too weak to support the weight of his musket and pouch.'[8] Some rather objected to military discipline but soon learned to respect military punishment. Their drill, to the intense disgust of the sergeants of the 32nd, remained appalling, but they learned how to shoot, which was what really mattered.

As June progressed, the weather got hotter and the news from outside more threatening and tragic. Work continued inside the Residency. Treasure was brought in and buried. There was tremendous activity—and the pretences were being abandoned. Everywhere there were 'soldiers, sepoys, prisoners in irons, men, women and children, hundreds of servants, respectable natives in their carriages, coolies carrying weights, heavy cannons, field pieces, carts, elephants, camels, bullocks, horses, all moving hither and thither, and continual bustle and noise was kept up from morning to night'.[9] The lawns in front of the Residency buildings were being levelled and cleared. Beautiful old trees were ruthlessly cut down and undergrowth cleared away. Even the church was turned into a store for grain. It seemed as if everyone had suddenly become conscious that time was running out.

The news that the sepoys had risen at Cawnpore, the military station forty-eight miles from Lucknow on the river Ganges, reached Lawrence early in June. Throughout the month, there were reports that about 200 men with nearly 400 women and children were being besieged and could not hold out indefinitely. Lawrence would have liked to send reinforcements, but this he could not do even when General Wheeler, an old friend and the commander at Cawnpore, wrote: 'Surely we are not to die like rats in a cage?'[10] When Lawrence consulted his officers, he was informed that even if the men could be spared it would be impossible to get them across the river Ganges to the besieged on the other side, as the bridges had been destroyed and all boats were in possession of the rebels. If this did not seem a very satisfactory excuse to Lawrence, the smallness of the garrison at Lucknow did. Lawrence could only advise Wheeler that reinforcements were supposed to be on their way, and recommended him to 'husband your resources, and not accept any terms from the enemy, as I much fear treachery. You cannot rely on his promises. *Il a tué beaucoup de prisonniers'.*[11]

Lawrence's fears proved to be justified. On June 26 Wheeler surrendered on the promise of safe conduct to Allahabad. The day after, most of the garrison was massacred at the river side and the few survivors were taken prisoner. The news reached Lucknow on the evening of the 28th, reinforcing a report that there was a serious concentration of mutineers at Nawabganj, about twenty miles north-east of Lucknow. There was now no doubt in Lawrence's mind that Lucknow itself would be besieged within two or three days.

Preparations in the Residency were speeded up. But there was some difference of opinion about the Machchi Bhawan. Should it be defended? Lawrence had put the question several times to his principal military advisers. All had stood out for two strongpoints. Lawrence could not make up his mind. On one occasion he ordered that supplies and ammunition should be moved out of the fort and into the Residency. While the operation was in progress, he ordered the supplies back into the fort. But now, with the threat of attack imminent, he instructed the civilians who had been lodged in the fort to move their belongings and themselves into the Residency.

Mr Rees and his friend Deprat had been living in the fort for some time. Rees thought the place looked formidable enough but that 'its old walls would have crumbled to dust by the reverberations of our own cannon'.[12] He and Deprat had been ordered into the Residency and then sent back on more than one occasion already. Deprat had moved his goods into the fort—and then had been 'prohibited from taking them away, Government, Sir Henry said, holding themselves responsible for any loss he might sustain'.[13] The two men decided that the best thing they could do would be to use up as much of Deprat's stock of food and wine as possible, and had been living almost exclusively on tinned salmon and Cambridge sausages and other delicacies, washed down with bottles of good burgundy. 'We seemed,' wrote Rees, 'to have a presentiment of what privations we had afterwards to undergo, for we enjoyed ourselves as much as good living could effect.'[14]

The civilians from the fort were not the only ones to be concentrated at the Residency. The outlying detachment of the 32nd which had been left at the military cantonment under Colonel Case came in to join the rest of the regiment. Most people had tried to save as many of their possessions as they could. The refugees from the outstations had, of course, little more than the clothes they had fled in and a few personal possessions in a bundle. But those already living in Lucknow had moved their furniture, their plate, and—in one case—a substantial library of books and manuscripts into the Residency. They were to come in very useful as barricades when the siege began in earnest. At the last moment, it was decided that the crown jewels of the deposed ruler of Oudh, now living in exile in Calcutta, should not be left in the Kaisarbagh palace at the mercy of any plundering sepoy.

'It did not seem right,' wrote Captain Birch, who was sent out to fetch them, 'to leave the palace of the king of Oudh to be plundered by the enemy.' If the king were loyal, he went on with a combination of fair-play and cupidity, 'he was entitled to our protection, if on the other hand he had joined in the machinations against us, the crown jewels . . . would make a pleasant addition to the army prize-money.' They were certainly very impressive. There were 'some very fine pearls and emeralds, some of the latter being as large as eggs'. There was also a bonus in the form of a large brass cannon and a quantity of small arms, so many in fact that it took all day to load them on to carts and take them to the Residency.[15]

About 10.30 a.m. on June 29, Gubbins, who was in charge of the Intelligence department, reported that his spies had seen the advance guard of the mutineers, now reinforced by those from Cawnpore, begin to advance on Lucknow from Nawabganj. A party of 500 infantry and fifty cavalry, with one small gun, had moved as far as Chinhat, about eight miles from Lucknow, and were collecting supplies for the main mutineer force. Gubbins called on Sir Henry to take action, and when he hesitated, ex-claimed hysterically: 'Well, Sir Henry, we shall all be branded at the bar of history as cowards!'[16]

Unfortunately, there were others who agreed with him, and all seemed determined to force an action. Lawrence had his own sources of information and had, like Gubbins, been receiving reports throughout the day; from these it was clear that Gubbins could no longer be trusted. About Gubbins's own report, he wrote: 'The evidence shows that the force now (4 p.m.) *almost certainly* greatly exceed 500 foot and 50 horse.' Lawrence felt sure 'that there are 2 or 3 thousand men at Chinhat, and that in the morning there will be many more'.[17] But his sound judgement did not sur-vive the pressure of the militants. It is possible that Lawrence, exhausted both by the responsibilities of his position and the constant demand for action, convinced himself that if a decisive victory could be won it would demoralise the enemy and inspire his own men with confidence and hope.

Whatever Lawrence's real intentions, whatever arguments he had privately considered, he seems to have been dangerously vague with his senior officers. At an informal council of war called late in the evening of June 29, he gave the impression that he had decided upon no more than a reconnaissance expedition in force. He would lead it himself and would go no further down the road to Chinhat than the bridge over the Kukrail river, about six miles from Lucknow. 'If he met the enemy he would oppose them at *that* point, or if they were coming on that day he would wait for them there, and if they were not coming on he would return—as he said that even in the latter case the demonstration among the city people, of our being quite prepared to meet the

41

3   *The Iron Bridge from the left bank of the Gumti*

mutineers would have a good effect.'[18]

Preparations for the expedition went on throughout the night. It was decided that the force would consist of 300 British soldiers, nearly half the total, accompanied by 230 native infantry, 36 of the volunteer cavalry, and between 80 and 120 Sikh horsemen. The first plan was to take only four light guns and an eight-inch howitzer, with British crews. But at about 3 a.m. Lawrence issued an order first to add two more, and then a further four, manned by native artillerymen. When an officer suggested that there seemed to be too many guns, Lawrence replied: 'Good Heavens, do I not know that? But I believe it safer to take them than leave them here.'[19] It was only one of many errors of judgement which were to lead to disaster.

4
DISASTER
AT CHINHAT

THE FIRST mistake was to delay the departure of the force from daybreak until after the sun was up. It was very hot, and the line of march was into the sun. Further, the British soldiers, already fatigued from constant work and guard duties, were suffering from the excesses of the previous night. Though the fact was obvious, no one thought of issuing a ration of rum 'to prevent a reaction of the system, and to invigorate them for the fatigues of the journey'. Nor was any food prepared for them. With empty stomachs and throbbing heads, the men of the 32nd marched out. Before them was an advance guard of Sikh and volunteer horse, a detachment of mixed British and native infantry, and five guns. With them marched the main body of native infantry. In the rear, apparently intended as a reserve, were four guns and fifty or sixty native infantry.

The road to the bridge over the Kukrail was at least metalled and, despite the heat, the force made the journey without incident. It is obvious that nothing much was expected of the exercise, for no preparations had been made to cover a possible retreat. Sir Henry had ordered his carriage to wait halfway, but that had been merely to save him some of the discomfort of riding a horse. At the Kukrail, the force halted. Though rum, coffee and biscuits had been carried, for some reason unknown they were not served out to the men. All the soldiers of the 32nd could get was water. There had been no sign of the enemy at all, and everyone expected to be ordered back to Lucknow.

In fact, after a short personal reconnaissance on the other side of the bridge, where there was no metalled road and the path was broken and muddy from rain, Lawrence did order a return. But while his aide, Captain Wilson, was carrying these instructions to the officers and men across the river, Lawrence changed his mind. Some 'native travellers', it seemed, had told him that the village of Chinhat was *not* occupied by mutineers, and in another moment of weakness he gave in to the appeals of one or two of the more militant of his officers that they should go forward. The orders were therefore changed and the force crossed the bridge. From there onwards, everything went wrong.

The British troops, their stomachs empty and the full force of the sun beating down on them, began to drop out. The native water-carriers disappeared quietly into the countryside, knowing better than their masters what dangers lay ahead. The native gunners were showing signs of insubordination, and even the senior officers seem to have lost interest. They did not take the most elementary of precautions to prevent the force from walking into a trap. No scouting parties appear to have been sent out ahead, for, without warning, a 'turn in the road showed us the enemy drawn up with their centre on the road and their left resting on a lake'.[1] And the enemy force was a very large one. About 5,000 infantry, 800 horse, and twelve or more good pieces of artillery. The Lucknow defenders did not have a chance.

The British deployed as rapidly as they could, bringing up the guns and opening fire on the centre of the mutineers' line. For a while it seemed that the mutineers were in retreat, but in fact they were spreading out in order to surround the British. A party of the 32nd was sent to take Ismaelganj, a small village nearby. Weak with hunger and thirst and suffering severely from the effects of the sun, the men of the 32nd were further demoralised when Colonel Case, who was leading them, fell with a bullet in his chest. The men lay down on the grass and kept up musket fire— but they would move no further forward.

The situation was obviously serious. The commander of the mutineers was a better tactician than those who opposed him. The plain between Ismaelganj and Chinhat was 'one moving mass of men: regiment after regiment of the insurgents poured steadily towards us, the flanks covered with a foam of skirmishers, the light puffs of smoke from their muskets floating from every ravine and bunch of grass in our front'.[2]

There was nothing the British could do but retreat. The native gunners and some of the cavalry had deserted. The elephant pulling the howitzer had been driven off. The mutineers continued to advance, standards waving. 'A field day on parade could not have been better; and what was to hinder the enemy from doing just as they pleased?'[3] The retreat was about to become a rout.

A few British gunners, the volunteer cavalry, the remainder of the 32nd, and some of the native infantry stood fast—for a moment. But the mutineers pressed more closely, unlimbering their guns and sweeping the British with canister and grapeshot. The mutineer infantry kept up a 'deadly *mitraille* of musketry . . . one leaden shower'.[4] The line broke. Men of the 32nd were mixed up with the guns and cavalry. Some of the wounded were given a stirrup to hang on to by the cavalry, or carried on the limbers of the guns. But many had to be left behind at the mercy of the enemy's cavalry. The native infantry who had accompanied the force covered the retreat, and were seen carrying the European wounded 'to the gun carriages, abandoning their own wounded comrades on the ground'—perhaps hoping by this means to assure their officers of their loyalty.

The aim of both sides was to reach the bridge over the Kukrail first. The river at this point was in a deep ravine, and if the mutineers could take the bridge the British would be completely cut off. The enemy cavalry had already gained the road near the bridge. To one present, it appeared that they were commanded by a European, 'a handsome-looking man, well-built, fair, about twenty-five years of age, with light mustachios, and wearing the undress uniform of a European cavalry officer, with a blue and gold-laced cap on his head'.[5] Was he a Russian? It had been rumoured that one such had been arrested, but later released just before the outbreak at Lucknow. It hardly mattered. Whoever he was, he and his men must not be allowed to block the bridge.

During the retreat, Lawrence was to be seen constantly rallying the men. At the bridge itself he ordered an artilleryman to light the portfire of a gun even though there was no powder or shot, in the hope that it would deter the enemy infantry. For a moment it caused a diversion. But there was still the enemy horse, which could be seen riding up with two nine-pounder guns. It was time for the volunteer cavalry to show what it could do. When it had ridden out that morning, there had been only thirty-six horsemen and few of them had been in action before. In command was Captain Radcliffe.

In the distance the red and blue pennants of the enemy cavalry grew thicker on the ground. The voice of Captain Radcliffe is heard. 'Three's right! Trot!'[6] The little band of horsemen sweeps out of the trees in which it has been sheltering and makes for the enemy. Within a quarter of a mile, the enemy's guns begin to fire and the shot whistles overhead. Above the din a trumpet sounds and Radcliffe screams out the order to charge. Sabres flashing,

47

thirty-six men ride forward. Miraculously—or so it seems—the enemy cavalry turns and gallops away. The bridge, at least, is saved. Lawrence appears to be trying to get the men to make a stand at the bridge. But it is too late and he knows it. 'My God, my God,' he is overheard to exclaim, 'and I brought them to this.'[7]

Some of the British soldiers retreated in good order, still firing steadily on the pursuing enemy, but most were too worn out to do more than make for the Residency as fast as they could. Lawrence, not before time, handed over his command to Colonel Inglis and, with Captain Wilson and other members of his staff, made off as fast as he could to organise some kind of support for the retreating troops. Halfway back, they came across Sir Henry's carriage, mounted the horses and left the carriage standing where it was.

As soon as he reached the Residency, Lawrence ordered out fifty men of the 32nd to hold the iron bridge, and two heavy guns on a battery overlooking the bridge were readied for action. As the men came in, the guns in the Residency effectively kept the pursuers from crossing the bridge.

It was a sad sight for the watchers in the Residency. Mrs Inglis, herself ill with smallpox, saw from her window the men coming in, 'a melancholy spectacle indeed—no order, one after the other; some riding; some wounded; some supported by their comrades; some on guns; some fell down and died of exhaustion not half a mile away from our position'.[8] The last of the survivors came in about midday, and a few hours later Lawrence sat down to write a letter to General Havelock, who was believed to be marching in the direction of Cawnpore and Lucknow.

'My dear Havelock,' he wrote. 'This morning we went out to . . . Chinhat to meet the enemy, and we were defeated and lost five guns through the misconduct chiefly of our Native Artillery, many of whom deserted. The enemy have followed us up, and we have now been besieged for four hours, and shall probably tonight be surrounded. The enemy are very bold and our Europeans are very low. I look on our position now as ten times as bad as it was yesterday; indeed it is very critical. We shall be obliged to concentrate *if we are able*. We shall have to abandon much supplies, and to blow up much powder. Unless we are relieved quickly, say in ten or fifteen days, we shall hardly be able to maintain our position . . .'[9]

Ten or fifteen days. No one in the Residency, surrounded by the panic and the confusion, could have believed that before Havelock could come to their aid eighty-seven long, terrifying, and bitter days would have to pass.

48

Part 2

❧

THE FIRST SIEGE

1
RETREAT TO
THE RESIDENCY

THE SCENE inside the Residency after the return of the defeated force was one of almost indescribable confusion. That morning when the force had left, work had begun on the fortifications as usual. Hundreds of coolies and prisoners from the jail were erecting stands for artillery, digging trenches, and throwing up mounds of earth, and palisades. The whole area was crowded with soldiers, British and Indian, guns and carts, horses, camels, bullocks, and the great hulking shapes of elephants. Then, without warning, the workmen and their overseers had made off. A few moments later, a horrified Martin Gubbins was being told of the defeat at Chinhat. Not long afterwards, the first survivors had begun to come in.

Once again, there seems to have been no preparation for an emergency. Women and children rushed to places that seemed to offer the best protection against shot and shell. Men ran to their posts, while others put up barricades. Gun crews were still dragging their cannon into position, and many of the walls had still not been loopholed. The wounded were brought in on litters, and the hospital filled up with shattered men. As the surgeons performed amputations, women moved around trying to bring some comfort from the heat with fans and ice water. For most of them, it was the first introduction to the horrors of war.

There were many new widows that day. While Mrs Inglis had been watching the sad sight of the returning force, Mrs Case had joined her and said: 'Oh, Mrs Inglis, go to bed; I have just heard from one of the grooms that Colonel Inglis and William [Case] are both safe.' Mrs Inglis replied: 'Why, I did not know Colonel Case was out!' A few minutes later, Colonel Inglis arrived. His eyes were full of tears. He kissed his wife, and then turned to Mrs Case.

51

'Poor Case,' he said. Mrs Case gave a cry of agony, and the junior chaplain's wife, Mrs Polehampton, led her away to her own room and tried to comfort her[1].

The city had gone strangely quiet. At first the anxious watchers could see people hurriedly leaving the houses round the Residency. Riderless horses galloped about in terror. Bullocks, camels and elephants were hurried away by their drivers. The boatmen on the river worked their boats as far away from the Residency and the iron bridge as they could go. Soon, the whole area seemed deserted. But not for long. From the lookouts on the roofs came reports of movement. Lower down the river, the enemy was making his way across a ford. Both the iron bridge and a stone bridge by the Machchi Bhawan were covered by British guns, but this was not going to deter the mutineers. They could be seen collecting boats to build a bridge further down stream.

On the town side, mutineers were taking possession of the houses around the entrenchment and cutting the walls for loopholes. On the opposite side of the river, a battery opened up, one of the guns being the eight-inch howitzer abandoned that very morning by the British. Shot and shell soon drove the defenders in to shelter. Mr Capper, one of the volunteers, made an unfortunate choice of refuge. A roundshot hit one of the pillars of the verandah under which he was standing and brought three or four feet of masonry down on top of him. Those who came running could hear a faint voice calling: 'I'm alive! Get me out! Give me air, for God's sake!' Fortunately for Mr Capper, one of the beams had come down at such an angle that it supported the weight of the debris. But to the would-be rescuers it seemed hopeless. 'Someone remarked, "It's impossible to save him", upon which Mr Capper's voice was heard to proceed, as if from a vault, saying: "It *is* possible, if you try."'[2]

Try they did, moving huge pieces of masonry, and in doing so blocking up Capper's supply of air with dust and rubble. The rescuers had only some six inches of brick wall to protect them against the fire of the mutineers, and they were forced to lie on their stomachs and work with their hands. After about three quarters of an hour, they got Capper's body free and began to work on his legs. Everyone expected to find him with all his bones broken. But on the contrary—'he had merely a few bruises and felt faint'![3]

While all this was going on, Sir Henry was to be seen making the rounds of the posts and batteries, however exposed the position, however hot the fire. Some of the defenders thought the marksmanship shown by the attackers—and especially the accuracy of the artillery fire—meant that the mutineers must be commanded by European officers, 'wretches for whom no punishment would be ignominious or severe enough'.[4] Mr Rees was convinced that a certain Captain Rotton, who had once commanded the king of Oudh's artillery and had 'adopted native habits, costumes and ideas and . . . always kept aloof from European society', was among them, as well as a certain Leblond—'as great a villain as ever breathed'. It was, of course, also well known that 'some Russian officers had entered the army of the insurgents'.[5] Whatever the reason, the enemy's fire was beginning to tell, and everyone was very grateful when nightfall came and the shooting broke off.

Most unhappy of all were the women, for they were confined to their quarters, some of them underground, without light, and with no news of how the battle was going. To their inexperienced ears, the noise of musket fire and artillery sounded terrifying. Mrs Inglis, still suffering from smallpox, thought the place would be taken, and 'tremblingly listened to every sound'. Mrs Case, who, with her sister, had stayed with Mrs Inglis, 'proposed reading the Litany and came with her sister and knelt down' by her friend's bedside. 'The soothing effect of prayer was marvellous.' It made them feel 'different beings, and though still much alarmed'[6] they found they could talk calmly of their danger, knowing that they were in God's hands, and that without His will not all the fury of the enemy could hurt them.

That fury started up again as soon as it was light. The muskets and cannon opened a heavy fire while an attempt was made to rush the main gate of the Residency. With some difficulty, the attackers were driven back, but there was no let-up in the shelling. The Residency building itself seemed to be the main target. The eight-inch howitzer concentrated its fire, particularly upon the upper storeys. It is possible that spies had told the mutineers that Sir Henry was still occuping a room on the top floor. Perhaps it was merely that the tower and its flag were seen as a symbol that had to be destroyed. On the afternoon of July 1, a shell from the howitzer burst in the room between Sir Henry and his secretary, Mr Couper. Neither was injured. When Lawrence's staff pressed him to move, at least to a lower storey, he replied jokingly that he did not believe the enemy had an artilleryman good enough to put another shell into that small room. But he did agree, after further shots had hit the upper storey, to move down the following day.

In the meantime, he believed, there were more urgent matters to attend to. The most important was the plight of the garrison in the Machchi Bhawan. The troops there had been cut off from direct communication with the Residency on the afternoon of June 30. The mutineers had occupied the space between the two points and had moved some guns there. Attempts to send letters to Colonel Palmer, commanding at the fort, had failed. The native runners had deserted, and no one else seemed to know the long way round through the city. Palmer, however, did manage to get a message through, saying that though he had plenty of gunpowder and small-arms ammunition, he was short of both shell and food. Lawrence had intended to evacuate the fort and concentrate on the defence of the Residency. It was now essential to move the garrison from the fort before it was too late.

On Lawrence's instructions, a semaphore had been erected on the roof of the Residency tower. It was, however, an extremely odd machine, and one that was both difficult to work and to understand. It consisted of a single post with a crossbar, from which hung a row of black bags each attached to a separate pulley. Captain Fulton, who appears to have devised this strange machine, tried for some time to attract the attention of the garrison in the fort, and finally succeeded in doing so—only to find that he had caught the attention of the mutineers as well. A hail of musket fire descended on the tower and the operators, who consisted of Captain Fulton himself, George Lawrence (Sir Henry's nephew), and another officer.

Some of the cords broke, or were cut by musket balls. The pulleys jammed, and on two occasions the contraption had to be lowered and re-assembled. It was three hours at the hottest part of the day before the semaphore could be made to convey a comprehensible message to the fort and receive an acknowledgement. The message was short and simple enough. 'Blow up and retire at twelve tonight. Bring prisoners guns and treasure.'

It was thought better not to tell Colonel Palmer that his daughter had been gravely wounded until the operation was over. Miss Palmer, eighteen years old and 'an accomplished young lady',[7] had come out to India to join her father the previous December. Despite warnings, she and some other women had decided not to move from their rooms on the second storey of the Residency, though they had begun to transfer their possessions to a safer place. While Miss Palmer was carrying some china from a cabinet, there was a terrible crash, and she was seen to fall, hit in the leg by a cannonball. When help reached her, she at first

54

seemed stunned, and then cried out: 'My leg is shot off; I know I shall die!'[8] The surgeon who arrived quickly bound up the wound and had her moved to a safer room. There she was conscious enough to see that the doctors intended to amputate her leg. In fact, the shot had almost completely severed it. She begged them to leave her alone and let her die in peace, but chloroform was given and the leg cut off. The doctors, optimistic—against all the evidence of their experience—thought she might recover.

Meanwhile, unknowing, her father was making his dispositions for the evacuation of the fort. His orders were carefully written down and handed to the officers concerned, so that there could be no possibility of misunderstanding—a wise precaution. The guns that could be removed without difficulty were to be removed. The remainder were to be spiked, but not until the very last moment. The women and children and the sick and wounded were to be placed in waggons drawn by bullocks. A number of important prisoners who had been detained partly on suspicion of conspiracy and partly as valuable hostages were also to be carried, bound, gagged, and blindfolded; if there was any attempt to rescue them, they were to be shot. As it was quite impossible to remove the large quantity of munitions stored in the fort—240 barrels of gunpowder, and nearly a million rounds of ball and gun ammunition—it had to be detonated. Lieutenant Thomas, the Deputy Commissary of Ordnance, was personally to fire a twenty-minute fuse as the rearguard left the fort. Everyone was 'to be in readiness to move out at midnight, from the eastern gate', and, added Palmer, 'in perfect silence, under penalty of death'.

At 10 p.m. the troops stood by and the guns were limbered for the move. As midnight approached, everyone except the lookouts was paraded quietly in the open space in the centre of the fort. The column was formed—infantry first, then the artillery, then the carts with the women and children, the sick, the wounded, the prisoners and the servants, and infantry bringing up the rear. At midnight precisely, the sentries were withdrawn from the ramparts, the last of the barricades removed from the eastern gate, and the column moved slowly out.

All went well until one of the guns caught a wheel in the narrow opening. The horses were fractious, and their drivers not too experienced at handling them; most of the Indian drivers had deserted. But some of the British officers took their places and managed to get the gun moving. After that there was no trouble. The word was passed to Lieutenant Thomas—'light the fuse'.

Outside the fort it was quiet except for a battery in the Residency, firing grapeshot in order to distract any potential attack from the city. But none came, for the mutineers had chosen that night to loot houses and bazaars. The column made the journey between the fort and the water-gate of the Residency in fifteen minutes, without a shot being fired. But the danger was not yet over. The column had arrived before it was expected. The gate was locked and, in the dark, the man with the key could not be found. A shout from someone in the column to 'open the gate' was almost mistaken by the Residency defenders for an order to 'open with grape', and they were just about to fire when an officer stopped them. The gate was opened at last, and the column passed through.

As the last of the rearguard went through the gate, the fort blew up with a tremendous crash. The shock broke windows inside the Residency and shook the walls. Mrs Inglis, who had not been told what was to happen, thought the Residency itself had been hit by a shell. Mrs Bartrum, down in her underground room, sprang from her bed, firmly convinced that the mutineers had blown up the defences and forced their way in. The room was so thick with dust that, even after the candles had been lit, the occupants could barely see one another. Pieces of brick and mortar had fallen from the ceiling, and the children were screaming with terror. Bobbie Bartrum was standing up in bed, 'shouting for mamma, who was as much frightened as he was'.[9] Fortunately, an officer from the fort rushed in and reassured everybody, especially his wife, who 'was almost overpowered with joy at seeing her husband come in safely'.[10]

Not all were so fortunate. Some wives had hoped that their husbands, who had been engaged at Chinhat, might have escaped to the fort. For most, there was only sad news. For Colonel Palmer, there was his daughter, dying, yet calm, concerned only that there should be someone to care for him after her death.

The evacuation and demolition of the fort could be counted a great success. Everyone had been transferred to the Residency; there had been not a single casualty. But, in fact, not quite everyone *had* been evacuated. An Irish soldier of the 32nd, lying in a drunken stupor in some corner of the fort, could not be found when the roll-call was taken. When the fort blew up, he was thrown into the air. His clothes were ripped off, but he was uninjured—and merely resumed his sleep. When he awoke the following morning, he discovered himself alone in a heap of ruins. Walking over to the Residency, and acquiring a couple of stray bullocks along the way, he stood outside the water-gate and shouted up: 'Arrah, by Jasus, open your gates!'

Roaring with laughter, the men let him in, and asked if he had not met any mutineers. 'Sure,' he replied, 'I didn't see e'er a man in the place.'[11]

4   *The Baillie Guard Battery and Hospital*

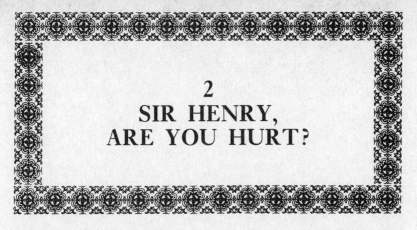

2
SIR HENRY,
ARE YOU HURT?

THE LIGHT relief supplied by the Irish soldier was soon to be engulfed by a sense of gloom shared by the whole garrison. At about eight o'clock that morning, July 2, Sir Henry Lawrence had returned with his nephew George to the Residency building, after making an inspection of the posts and batteries. The sun was already beating down, and both men were very hot and tired. The room was fitted with a punkah, a long piece of cloth fixed to the ceiling and pulled backwards and forwards with a cord, to create a draught. A coolie squatted in a corner, pulling the punkah steadily. At least the room was cooler than outside. Lawrence lay down on his bed without removing his clothes, and George lay down on another bed a few feet away.

Lawrence asked Captain Wilson, who was also in the room, to draw up a memorandum on how the rations should be issued, and Wilson left, reminding Lawrence of his promise to move to a safer room downstairs. Lawrence replied that he was very tired and would rest for a couple of hours before having his things transferred. Half an hour later, with the memorandum drafted, Wilson returned and, standing between the two beds, with his knee resting on the one occupied by Sir Henry, read out his notes. He had just finished reading and Lawrence was about to make his comments when there was a sheet of flame and a terrific explosion, followed by darkness.

Wilson, thrown to the ground by the force of the explosion, was stunned for a moment, and when he recovered found that his shirt had been torn off and that he was wounded in the back. But what of Lawrence? Wilson could see nothing through the smoke and dust. 'Sir Henry,' he called out. 'Sir Henry, are you hurt?' There was no reply. 'Sir Henry,' he called again. 'Are you hurt?' There was still no answer. But at the third time of asking, Wilson heard Lawrence's voice, very quiet, reply: 'I am killed.'

As the dust cleared away, Wilson could see that the sheet on Lawrence's bed was crimson with blood. George Lawrence, though covered with bricks and plaster, seemed otherwise unhurt. The punkah coolie had had a foot blown off.

Some soldiers of the 32nd rushed in and lifted Lawrence into a chair, carrying him gently downstairs into one of the lower rooms and there placing him on a table. George had meanwhile run over to the house of Dr Fayrer in search of assistance.

Fayrer came immediately. Lawrence was conscious, and his first question to Fayrer was: 'How long have I got to live?' Fayrer replied: 'For some time, I hope.' But when he had cut away the torn clothing and examined Sir Henry, it was clear that his wound was fatal. Again Lawrence asked the question. 'I want a distinct answer. How long? I have a deal to do.' The doctor's answer was distinct enough—forty-eight hours at the maximum. The upper part of Lawrence's thigh had been severely lacerated by the shot, and splinters had caused extensive injury to the bones. Lawrence seemed satisfied with this and asked for Colonel Inglis and Major Banks to be sent for.[1]

It did not seem wise to leave Lawrence in the Residency building, as it was under constant bombardment, so his staff decided to bear him to Dr Fayrer's house, which had a well-built verandah facing away from the direction of fire. They carried Lawrence through a hail of bullets and placed his bed in the most sheltered spot, but somehow the news must have been conveyed to the mutineers for, shortly after, heavy firing was opened on the verandah. It was only by sheltering behind the pillars and the jutting-out walls of the adjoining rooms that Lawrence's staff were able to remain with him. When Inglis and Banks arrived, the senior chaplain, Mr Harris, said the Anglican communion service and administered the bread and the wine to Lawrence and the rest of those present. Afterwards, Lawrence was moved to another part of the house.

Having himself been prepared for his Maker, Lawrence was anxious to prepare further for the defence of the Residency and all those inside. He had already made arrangements about his successors. Inglis was to take over the military command, and Banks the civil. Now, in the presence of witnesses, this was confirmed, and a Military Council was formed consisting of these two men and Major Anderson, the chief engineer.

Lawrence than dictated his final orders and personal requests.

Banks noted them down in his diary, haphazardly and baldly.

'I Reserve fire, check all wall firing.

II Carefully register ammunition for guns and small arms in store. Carefully register daily expenditure as far as possible.

III Spare the precious health of Europeans in every possible way, from shot and sun.

IV Organise working parties for night labour.

V Entrench—entrench—entrench—erect traverses, cut off enemy's fire.

VI Turn every horse out of the entrenchment, except enough for four guns. Keep Sir Henry Lawrence's horse *Ludakee*—it is a gift to his nephew George Lawrence.

VII Use the state prisoners as a means of getting in supplies, by gentle means if possible, or by threats.

VIII Enrol every servant as bildar or carrier of earth. Pay liberally, double, quadruple.

IX Turn out every native who will not work (save menials who have more than abundant labour).

X Write daily to Allahabad or Agra.

XI Sir Henry Lawrence's servants to receive one year's pay; they are to work for any other gentlemen who want them, or they may leave if they prefer to do so.

XII Put on my tomb only this— "Here lies Henry Lawrence who tried to do his duty. May God have mercy on him".

XIII Take an immediate inventory of all natives, so as to know who can be used as *bildars*, etc.

XIV Take an immediate inventory of all supplies and food, etc. Take a daily average of expenditure.'[2]

There was little more that could be done for Lawrence other than to make his last hours as comfortable as possible. A more thorough medical examination under anaesthesia had revealed that the pelvis was fractured, and that even if he could have withstood the effects of amputation, it would not have saved his life. Lawrence was in considerable pain, especially when the tourniquet had to be tightened to reduce the bleeding. He was given doses of laudanum and, when the pain became particularly severe, chloroform. Under their influence his mind wandered, sometimes perfectly clear, at others clouded. He talked of his dead wife, and repeated some of her favourite texts with tears in his eyes. He constantly told his officers that there should be no surrender, no thought of doing anything but ensure the continued safety of the women and children. The disaster at Chinhat was obviously much on his mind, for he mentioned it several times, asking those around him to see that he was not condemned for an error of judgement.

Throughout July 3, as the bombardment continued, he spoke very little, though he joined in the prayers and psalms that Mr Harris read to him. The following day, it was clear that he could not last much longer. All he could swallow was a little cooked arrowroot and some champagne. At eight o'clock in the morning of July 4 he died, so quietly that his nephew George, who had been wounded in the shoulder a little earlier, did not notice until one of the doctors told him.

It was impossible to keep the body lying about in the great heat inside the house, so it was wrapped in a sheet and taken outside by a party of four men of the 32nd who were on duty with the guns outside Fayrer's house.

The burial had to wait until dark, as the mutineers' fire showed no signs of slackening during the day. But that night, too, shots continued to pour into the Residency. The burial party was small: a few of Sir Henry's staff, Mr Harris, the chaplain, and the pall-bearers. Lawrence had asked for no fuss, so the ceremony was short. Mr Harris read the burial service, shot whirling around him. The body was lowered into a trench already occupied by the bodies of several gunners who had been killed during the day.

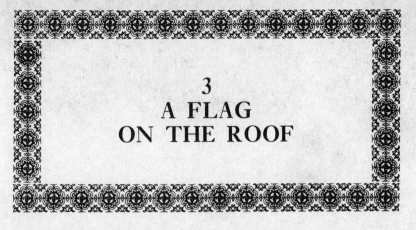

3
A FLAG
ON THE ROOF

THE Military Council would have preferred to conceal the fact of Lawrence's death for as long as possible. They feared that, when the garrison heard the news, it would be demoralised by the loss of one who had seemed to inspire confidence in everyone. But the news soon swept through the Residency, filling all the defenders with grief and many with alarm. For the latter emotion there was justification, even if Sir Henry had not died. The siege was being pressed with vigour, and the defences, though much had been done, did not inspire confidence.

The chief engineer, Major Anderson, and his assistant, Captain Fulton, had hurried on with the construction of walls, batteries, trenches and other defences throughout the threatening days of June, but much still remained to be done when the disastrous affair at Chinhat precipitated the retreat on the Residency and its investment by the mutineers. Within the rough outer defences, a number of strongpoints had been constructed. The most important of these was the Redan battery, which jutted out from the main line of defences facing the river. In front was the only space on which an assaulting force could assemble for a mass attack. Two eighteen-pounder guns and one nine-pounder were placed in the battery itself, and along the walls nearby were seven guns of smaller calibre. To the rear of the Redan lay the Residency building itself, and there a detachment of fifty Europeans was stationed as a reserve.

To the east of the Redan stood the old banqueting hall, now converted into a hospital and dispensary. Between the two points was the water-gate—blocked up after the arrival of the men from the Machchi Bhawan—and three guns. At the hospital itself there was a battery of three mortars. In the right wing of the hospital a workshop for the making of fuses and cartridges had been established. Almost a continuation of the hospital was the Baillie Guard, which was made up of the former Treasury building and what had once been the ceremonial entrance to the Residency. It was named after Colonel Baillie, a former Resident, and was rather a grand structure. The gateway itself was blocked with earth behind which, to cover any attackers who might break through, were three more guns.

The eastern face of the defences was particularly vulnerable to the mutineers' fire. It was skirted by the road to Cawnpore, and the buildings and walled gardens which lined the other side of the road had not been destroyed, in accordance with Lawrence's instructions to 'spare the holy places, and private property too, as much as possible'. (Where not possible, a thorough valuation of the property was to be made before demolition.) The buildings along the Cawnpore road were, in many cases, barely twenty-five yards from the Residency fortifications. They had been quickly occupied by the rebels, who had loopholed the walls for muskets and used the houses as bases for mining operations against the Residency positions. The only advantage to the defenders was that the road was too narrow for an attacking force to muster in any large number without great danger to itself. The defence on this side of the Residency was a solidly built perimeter wall reinforced by a number of houses with loopholes in the walls and flat roofs surrounded by parapets. Near the wall itself and just below the Baillie Guard stood the office of the Financial Commissioner, known simply as the Financial Garrison. It had been strongly barricaded with furniture and files, but the surrounding outhouses and the gateway, though blocked up, were not thought to be very secure. Nor was Mrs Sago's house, which had once been a school. Next in line came the building which housed the office of the Judicial Commissioner, a large two-storeyed house defended by a sizeable bank of earth and palisades. These points were among the most dangerous spots in the defensive line. They were reinforced and supported from the house of Dr Fayrer and the Post Office. There were two guns by Fayrer's house and four at the Post Office. As both these buildings were on higher ground than the outer defences, the guns could cover a large area between the Baillie Guard and the Judicial Garrison in case of a break-through at these points.

Almost at the south-east angle of the Residency wall stood the post commanded by Captain Anderson and named after him. There Mr Capper had had his unfortunate experience under the collapsed verandah. The house, two-storeyed with a flat roof, had been barricaded. In front were a deep trench and a palisade. In the angle itself stood the Cawnpore Battery. Two nine-pounders and an eighteen-pounder, set in an entrenchment of earth, commanded the road and were designed to prevent reinforcements moving up from the south. Linked with the battery by a trench and a hole in the wall was a house belonging to Mr Rees's merchant friend, Deprat. The house was a substantial structure with deep cellars, now full of furniture and stores.

Along this side of the defences, the houses on the other side of the street were even closer than on the Cawnpore road side, some being barely forty feet away. Most of the houses still stood untouched or had had only the top storey destroyed by the Residency defenders, in the belief that the lower parts might give some additional protection. But one house, that of a Mr Johannes, an Armenian merchant, still retained a turret which dominated the neighbouring outposts. At one time it had been hoped to incorporate the house in the defensive line. Failing that, it was supposed to have been blown up. But the task had been left until too late.

Next to Deprat's house and joined to it by a mud wall was a house formerly belonging to a Hindu banker but now occupied by fifty boys from the Martinière College, under the command of their principal, Mr. Schilling. By the side of the Martinière boys' post, a road had been blocked up by a bank of earth and a palisade, and on the other side was the former Brigade Mess, a high building with a high parapet to the roof, manned chiefly by officers of the native regiments which had mutinied. In command was Colonel Masters of the 7th Light Cavalry who, because it was his habit to mount to the topmost point of the roof and hail the men in the surrounding posts, was known as 'the admiral'.

Two open areas surrounded by low buildings which had been parapeted with boards and sandbags on a kind of scaffold were known as the Sikh Squares, for the very good reason that both were occupied by Sikh troopers. To the north of these, in another enclosed space, the artillery bullocks and the cavalry horses were stabled. A narrow lane commanded by a twenty-four-pounder separated the stables from Mr Gubbins's house. Gubbins had been fortifying his house since the month of May. The outhouses had been loopholed for muskets, and the groundwork for a battery had been laid. But the Engineers had never considered the position itself really defensible, and they had constructed a bridge into the next position so that the defenders could retire quickly if they found themselves under heavy attack.

67

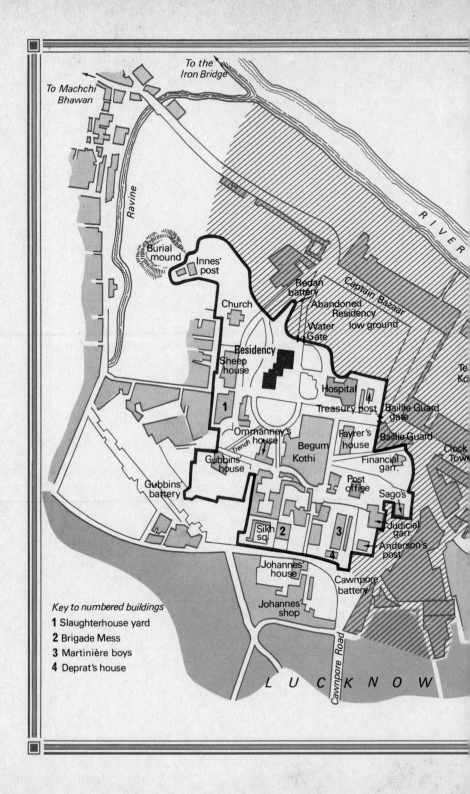

To the
Iron Bridge

To Machchi
Bhawan

Ravine

RIVER

Burial
mound

Innes'
post

Redan
battery

Captain Bazaar

Church

Abandoned
Residency
low ground

Water
Gate

Residency

Sheep
house

Hospital

Te
Ko

1

Treasury post

Baillie Guard
gate

Ommanney's
house

Trench house

Fayrer's
house

Baillie Guard

Clock
Tow

Begum
Kothi

Financial
garr.

Gubbins'
house

Gubbins'
battery

Post
office

Sikh
sq.

2

3

Sago's

Judicial
garr.

4

Anderson's
post

Johannes'
house

Cawnpore
battery

Johannes'
shop

Cawnpore Road

Key to numbered buildings
1 Slaughterhouse yard
2 Brigade Mess
3 Martinière boys
4 Deprat's house

L U C K N O W

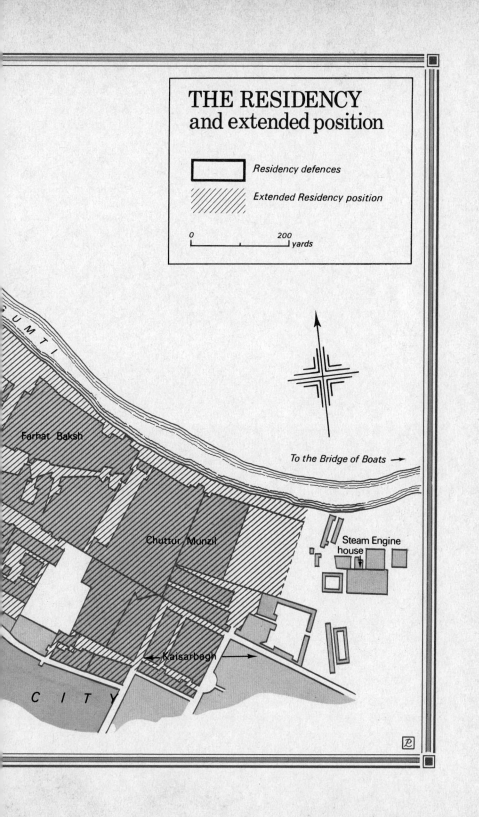

THE RESIDENCY
and extended position

Residency defences

Extended Residency position

0   200
                          yards

UMTI

Farhat Baksh

To the Bridge of Boats →

Chuttur Munzil

Steam Engine
house

←—Kaisarbagh——→

C I T Y

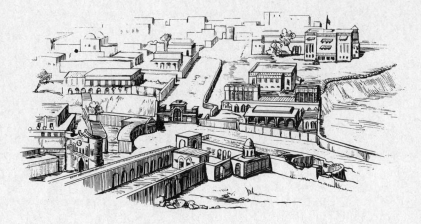

Hospital or East Angle

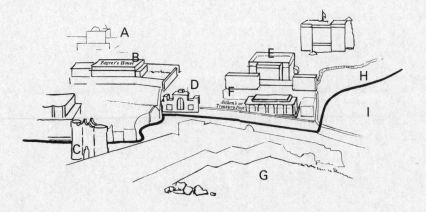

A   *Begum Kothi*   F   *Treasury Post*
B   *Fayrer's House*   G   *Tehri Koti*
C   *Clock Tower*   H   *Scarped Front*
D   *Baillie Guard Gate*   I   *Neutral Ground*
E   *Hospital*

With the sudden investment of the Residency by the mutineers, Gubbins had insisted that work should be speeded up on the site of the battery, for without the protection of artillery, the post at his house had no chance of being held. The main problem was that the half-finished site was actually outside the walls of Gubbins's garden, the parapet was too low to give much protection against sniper fire, and there was a large hole still left in it, facing outwards, through which the coolies had carried their baskets of earth. On the evening of June 30, Gubbins collected his servants and a number of men whom he armed as auxiliaries, and offered the substantial sum of two rupees a night to all who were prepared to work. Lieutenant Hutchinson of the Engineers agreed to supervise, and a number of British soldiers and civilians offered to help. As dusk fell, a window in one of the outhouses overlooking the site was carefully opened and the volunteers quietly let themselves down on ropes.

Fortunately, the enemy did not appear to notice what was going on. Some of the volunteers were even able to go outside the parapet to collect planks and other pieces of timber which had been left when the coolies deserted. No one fired on them, and work went on without interruption. Mrs Gubbins and one of her guests kept up supplies of hot tea and brandy-and-water throughout the night, and just before dawn everyone climbed back through the window and barricaded it up again. Gubbins paid the Indian workers as soon as they had finished—and there was no shortage of volunteers for the following night. The pay was high, sixteen times the normal rate for a whole day. In fact, it was so tempting that others of the garrison began to complain that their servants were deserting them. But the windfall did not last. On the fourth night the enemy discovered what was going on, occupied one of the adjacent houses, and opened up with muskets and abuse. Nevertheless, the work continued, though no one now ventured outside to collect wood, and the numbers of volunteers suddenly shrank.

To the north of Gubbins's house was a range of low buildings housing sheep and cattle awaiting slaughter. A racquet court with high walls had been filled with fodder for them. The church, already used as a grain store, stood on low ground soon to be transformed into a cemetery. The position was considered weak, as it had not been possible to construct batteries to cover the whole of the western side. Fortunately, the ground in front was rugged, sloping to a ravine which ran down to join the river Gumti.

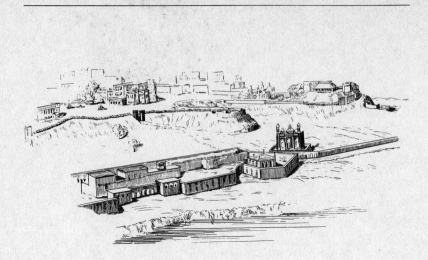

River or Redan Front

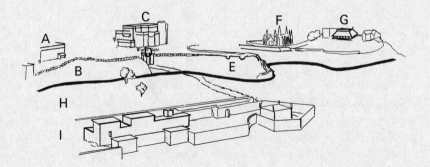

A	Hospital	F	Church
B	Scarped Face with Ditch at foot	G	Innes' Post
C	Residency	H	Neutral Ground
D	Water Gate	I	Captain Bazaar
E	Redan		

The most exposed position of all was the house commanded by Lieutenant McLeod Innes of the Engineers. The house itself was single-storeyed and sited on a spur of high ground projecting out of the main line of the entrenchment. Overlooking it was a Muhammadan cemetery, as well as a number of large houses which had not been demolished. But it was a valuable point of observation, and was protected by the heavy guns of the Redan as well as by those placed near the church.

There was certainly no shortage of guns or ammunition. As well as the guns fixed on their sites, there were eight eight-inch howitzers mounted on limber, which could be moved about to where they were most needed. Near the Redan were about two hundred guns of various sizes, most of them taken from the palaces or magazines of the king of Oudh. These were stored, unmounted, on the ground. The main problem was to find men to handle the guns, and the regular artillerymen had to be reinforced by volunteers who were given a quick course in gun drill.

In fact, how to use the available manpower to the best advantage was Inglis's principal headache. The losses at Chinhat had been high. 118 Europeans killed or missing, 54 wounded, many of them seriously. The loss of Indian troops had been even higher; 175 killed, though only 24 wounded. To man an awkward and ill-fortified perimeter just over a mile in length, Inglis could muster only 1,640 active men, and 80 at various stages of sickness. There were 103 British officers, including doctors, 671 British non-commissioned officers and men, 51 Christian drummers (mainly Eurasians), and 153 volunteers, all civilians but having at least some knowledge of weapons. 1,008 Christians bound together, if not all by race, at least by religion. 712 Indian troops, not quite trusted but most of them loyal, had remained with the garrison.

As for non-combatants, when the siege opened there were 510 women and children, and the fifty boys from the Martinière. The elder ones, though not officially combatant, were armed with muskets and helped their masters in the defence of their quarters; the younger boys helped with some of the domestic work when servants deserted, or carried messages and ammunition to the posts. 680 Indians—servants, coolies, and camp followers—were scattered about-the Residency area.

With so few men, Inglis could only man the posts and keep a few troops in reserve. Each post was regarded as a separate garrison, and its members rarely left their post except at night, to help bring supplies. There were no reliefs. Officers and men took their turn at guard duty without distinction of rank. Each little garrison

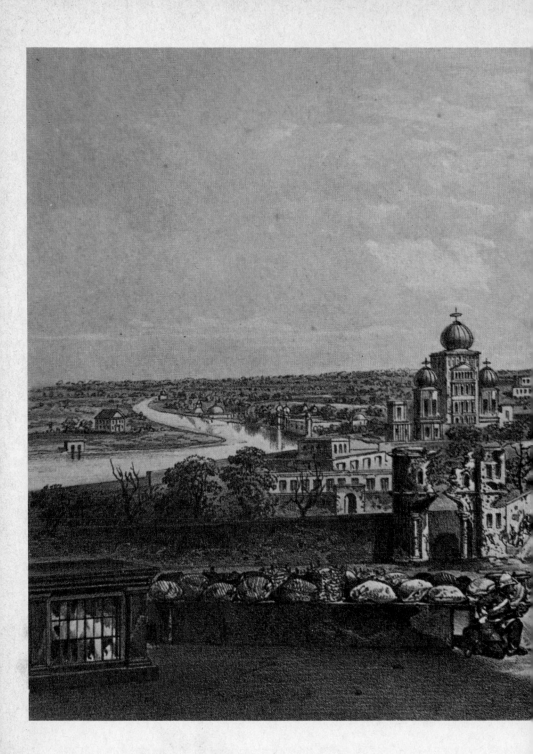

5   *The riverside palaces, from the Residency*

was expected to use its own initiative in repelling attack, to keep its defences in good repair—with the advice of the Engineers—and to make local sorties if they thought them necessary. Inglis, now with the local rank of brigadier, and his staff were the only people to visit all the posts. Inglis, at forty-two, was not renowned either for intellect or ability. He was a competent regimental officer and a crack shot. But he did have real qualifications, some of them rare in commanding officers of any nation or time. He was liked and trusted by his men, though not by all the officers of the garrison. He would also listen to advice, and was shrewd enough both to recognise when it was good and to take it when it was opportune. He was fortunate—as were those who depended upon him for their protection—that he was not faced with any great military talent on the enemy's side.

It was believed that the Residency was surrounded by between 8,000 and 10,000 mutineers. These were thought to comprise the 6,000 who had faced Lawrence at Chinhat, plus ex-soldiers of the king of Oudh's army and various hangers-on hoping for loot. The sepoy regiments were still in military formation; all they had lost was their British officers. Every morning, bugles sounded the Assembly and other regimental calls, while in the morning and in the evening their bands paraded in front of the Residency area playing favourite English tunes, such as 'The Girl I left behind me', or 'See the Conquering Hero comes'—to the general annoyance of the garrison. Worst of all, the evening's performance invariably ended with 'God save the Queen'.

Against this form of psychological warfare the garrison could do little. But on the tower of the Residency building they placed a large Union Jack as symbol of their defiance. It soon became a favourite target for the mutineers. Bullets from sharpshooters riddled the cloth and frequently cut the halyards and splintered the flagstaff. Even heavy-calibre shells were occasionally lobbed at it. Every night after dark the flag was brought down, the holes patched and new cords fitted, and in the morning as the sun came up the mutineers would find it flying again.

4
CHUPATTEES
AND SAUTERNE

IT TOOK some time for order to be imposed inside the entrenchment. The needs of immediate defence meant that important
decisions and actions were not taken. Then there was the simple
fact that the British, military and civilian alike, were so used to
having the basic—and unpleasant—things done for them by
servants and camp followers that, when the servants and followers
deserted, they did not quite know what to do. There was the case
of the commissariat bullocks, for example. With no one to look
after them, they wandered about the defences searching for food
and getting shot by the enemy. The artillery and cavalry horses,
neglected by their grooms, who had deserted or preferred to stay
under cover, became maddened by hunger and thirst, broke loose,
and were either killed by the enemy or had to be shot. Within a few
days, the stench from their decaying carcases was overpowering.
A violent downfall of rain on the 5th helped to clear the air a
little, but the only satisfactory solution was to bury the carcases.
At last the order was given.

Fatigue parties, usually volunteers and non-combatants, were
detailed to drag the carcases into shelter and then bury them. It
was neither a safe nor an easy job. Mr Couper, who had been
Lawrence's secretary, spent a whole tiring night disposing of one
camel. It was at night, too, that the garrison's own dead were
buried, and the sick and wounded moved from the posts to the
hospital. Guns and mortars were hauled to new positions, repairs
were made to old defences and new ones built. All ranks were
expected to help in this gruelling work, and most of them did,
though the Sikhs of the cavalry refused, and some of the men of
the 32nd—drowning their depression over the twin blows of
Chinhat and Lawrence's death—were too drunk to turn out.

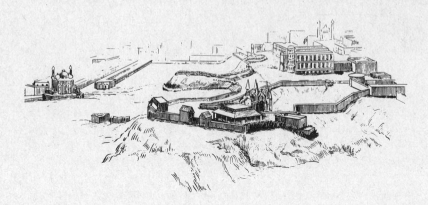

Church or North Angle

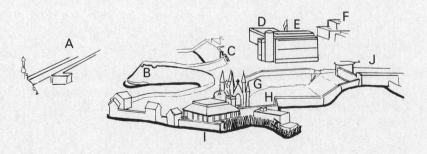

A Captain Bazaar   F Fayrer's House
B Redan   G Church
C Water Gate   H Cemetery
D Hospital   I Innes' Post
E Residency   J Sheep House

There was considerable drunkenness, especially among the British soldiers and the volunteers, and there were large quantities of rum and beer to help sustain it. When Lawrence had been laying in supplies, he had placed particular emphasis on getting stocks of alcohol. There was also plenty of grain. A substantial amount had been stored in a plunge bath underneath the Residency. Large stacks of firewood had been piled in various parts of the area, and mounds of lime and charcoal for sanitary purposes were scattered about the positions. Unfortunately, Lieutenant James, the officer responsible under Lawrence for the storing and registering of supplies, was severely injured at Chinhat. His native clerks fled, taking the records with them, and the men who took over from James were new to the work.

The first stores to be opened were in exposed positions and could only be approached at great risk. It was not until a number of servants collecting supplies had been wounded and killed that the stores were moved to less dangerous positions. It was, too, only after this move that a scale of rations was actually worked out, with appropriate amounts for combatants and non-combatants, Christians, Muslims, and Hindus, carefully fixed. It was the responsibility of each post commander to make a return of those requiring rations every morning, to collect the supplies, and to make his own cooking and eating arrangements.

The women and children were housed in the less exposed outposts and in buildings away from the perimeter. The Residency itself gave shelter to a number of officers' families, and the wives of soldiers of the 32nd were accommodated in one of the underground rooms. The Lucknow residents were, on the whole, more comfortable than the refugees from the outstations. Mrs Inglis, for example, had managed to keep several of her servants, but the people who had succeeded in making their way to the Residency from a distance had come mostly without either servants or baggage. Some found it very difficult to adapt themselves to a life without servants. They had to clean their own rooms, draw their own water, cook their own food, and wash their own clothes. On top of this, they had to attend to their own children.

But not all found the new life lacking in compensations. Mrs Bartrum, who had been quartered in the Begum Kothi, a building which had once been the house of the European wife of one of the kings of Oudh, found it 'almost a blessing to have no servants, because it gave us so much occupation that we had less time to dwell upon our troubles and anxieties concerning those absent from us'.[1] There were troubles enough. Even before the siege

West Front

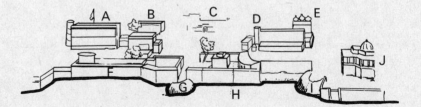

A *Residency*   F *Sheep House*
B *Hospital*   G *Sheep House Battery*
C *Baillie Guard Gate*   H *Slaughter House*
D *Ommanneys' House*   I *Slaughter House Battery*
E *Begum Kothi*   J *Gubbins' House*

had begun, one of the women with whom she shared a room had died of cholera—the first time Katherine Bartrum had 'ever seen death in any shape'. The threat of death lay particularly heavy upon the children confined to the crowded, stifling room, so full of flies and mosquitoes that when food was put on the table it was impossible to tell what it was, 'for it looks like a black and living mass'.[2]

The rations consisted of meat, flour, attah (a coarse-ground wheat flour), dal (a kind of lentil), and salt. Mrs Bartrum thought the rations adequate and the quality quite good, but unfortunately the latter was ruined by the cooking. It was impossible to cook inside the crowded room, so the occupants were dependent on native cooks. These insisted that all the rations should be put together with ship's biscuit and water to make a stew. Under normal circumstances the result would hardly have been very palatable. But when it was cooked in a large copper saucepan, from which the tin lining had disappeared, the result was green in colour and nauseous in taste. Only hunger made it eatable. There was no bread, for the bakers had deserted and none of the women knew how to make it, even if yeast had been available. With the stew, therefore, they ate chupattees, flat cakes of flour and water cooked on a griddle. Neither the stew not the chupattees tempted the children, already sickly from the heat. Milk was almost impossible to obtain, though Mrs Inglis had her own supply from some goats which she kept in a little enclosure near her quarters. Ice, which might have made things a little easier both for the children and the wounded in hospital, was no longer available, as the ice-pits in which it was stored lay outside the perimeter of the defences.

Some of the more farsighted of the Lucknow residents had made their own preparations. Others had, with considerable generosity, distributed stores to all who asked for them. M. Deprat—though a merchant who may have had an eye to future business goodwill —annoyed his friend Rees by giving away *saucissons aux truffes*, hermetically sealed provisions, cigars and wine, and brandy without payment, and in such quantities that he left none for himself. Mr Gubbins, too, was generous, but with more discretion. He also had laid in stocks of wheat and rice and clarified butter, soft sugar and tobacco, charcoal, wood, and some tinned foods. Bottled beer, considered something of a luxury, was reserved for the sick and the ladies who nursed them, but at lunch Mr Gubbins served the people quartered in his house with one glass of Sauterne, and in the evening the gentlemen were allowed a ration

6 *Mr Gubbins's house*

Gubbins' Angle

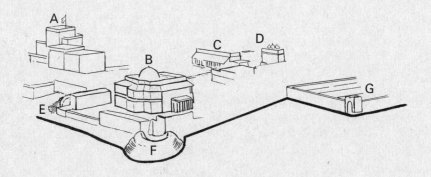

A   *Residency*   E   *Slaughter House Battery*
B   *Gubbins' House*   F   *Gubbins' Battery*
C   *Ommanneys' House*   G   *Sikh Square*
D   *Begum Kothi*

of one glass of sherry and two of champagne or claret, the ladies rather less. But there was tea three times a day, with sugar *and* milk, as one of the guests had thoughtfully come provided with two cows.

On the whole, those staying at Mr Gubbins's house lived rather well, and there was a certain amount of envy among the less fortunate. Gubbins did, on occasion, invite members of the garrison to dinner, when there might be a rice pudding, or even a plum or a jam pudding which Mrs. Gubbins would serve out with such generosity that she left none for herself.

The non-combatants spent their day in a variety of ways. Katherine Bartrum, in her underground room, had taken on the job of keeping things neat and clean, for most of her companions were either physically or mentally ill and did not seem to care what state the room was in. Katherine, however, was troubled by the mess. As long as God gave her health, she would do her best to add to the comfort of the others, even though they sometimes called her a 'servant-of-all-work'. The routine of the day began when a light could be seen through the small window at the top of the wall. Unlike Katherine's first quarters, this room was whitewashed. There were seven native bedsteads—wooden frames crossed with ropes—one long table, three chairs, and some boxes and bundles to hold the few possessions the refugees had brought with them.

The first task was to wash and dress the children and tidy up the beds. Breakfast was served when the cooks chose to bring it. The rest of the day was spent in trying to keep cool, for the temperature often reached 110°F. When the children were safely in bed at night, the others would gather round their dining table, drinking tea (rather weak and dusty-tasting) by the light of a candle stuck in a bottle. There would be talk of pleasant bygone days, of happy homes in distant England, 'bringing from memory's stores tales to cheer the passing hour'. There was much thought of loved ones far away, 'of the father that knew not as yet that his child was a captive in a foreign land; of the bright band of sisters and brothers who formed the family circle: but most of all of the husband fleeing perhaps for his life, whose heart was with his wife and child in their captivity, and who might even then be coming to their rescue—and many were the prayers sent up to heaven that such might be the case'.[3]

At Dr Fayrer's house, all the servants had fled on the first day of the siege and the cleaning and cooking were shared by the women and two Martinière boys. Mrs Fayrer's health was not

Brigade Mess Front

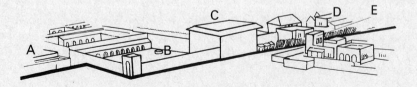

A *Gubbins' House*   D *Martinière boys*
B *Sikh Square*   E *Johannes' House*
C *Brigade Mess*

good, and the supervision of the household was left to the senior chaplain's wife, Mrs Harris. There, too, the women and children were housed in the taikhana. There were eleven women, seven children, and no beds. The mattresses had to be laid on the floor. But there was a punkah, and Dr Fayrer had found a coolie to pull it. During the day the mattresses were rolled up and piled against the wall. What few chairs there were, were reserved for the sick, and the others took their meals sitting on the floor. Even during the day the room was very dark and candles had to be lit at meal-times, adding to the heat. Sometimes, after the sun had gone down and the enemy were preparing their evening meal, the musket and cannon fire would slacken off enough for the women to be allowed up for a breath of air.

Others took the air in the morning. There was, in effect, little to choose between the times, except that in daylight it was difficult to avoid seeing unpleasant sights. Mrs Bartrum was standing with Bobbie one morning at a door looking into a courtyard. A little girl, probably one of the soldiers' children was playing with a cannonball when she was struck in the head and killed instantly. It gave Katherine such a shock that she fainted and could never afterwards 'think of that poor child without a shudder'.[4]

Casualties were high until everyone learned to keep their heads down and take care. The spaces between the posts were often raked with fire, and the only way of crossing them was to make a run for it. At the beginning of the siege, many officers refused to do anything so undignified—and were wounded or killed for their arrogance. During the first week there were between fifteen and twenty deaths a day. Burial was, of course, after dark, and the two chaplains, Harris and Polehampton, took the service. The bodies were wrapped in sheets and laid in a common grave, usually under fire, which made it difficult to get labour. On one occasion, Polehampton had to threaten the coolies with a pistol before he could bury a little boy who had died of cholera, and then one of the party was wounded in the arm.

Cholera and smallpox had broken out early among the garrison, but fortunately did not seem to be spreading. Mrs Inglis had not infected Mrs Case and her sister with smallpox, and had recovered remarkably quickly. People suffering from these two diseases were not allowed into the hospital for fear of general infection. At least there were plenty of doctors. Some, though competent, were a trifle eccentric. The chief medical officer, Dr Scott, would lose his temper with patients who winced under his knife, but to those who did not he made the the gift of a cheroot. The real

Cawnpore Battery or South Angle

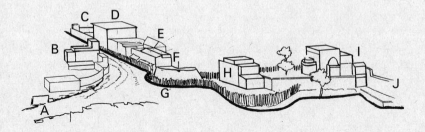

A   *Cawnpore Road*   F   *Deprat's*
B   *Johannes' House*   G   *Cawnpore Battery*
C   *Sikh Square*   H   *Anderson's Post*
D   *Brigade Mess*   I   *Judicial Garrison*
E   *Martinière boys*   J   *Sago's House*

problem was nursing. There were no female nurses in British military hospitals in India—it was only three years since Florence Nightingale had introduced them into hospitals in the Crimea, and it was to be nearly forty years before they reached India. Mrs Polehampton was the Florence Nightingale of the Residency and, with two newly widowed ladies, offered her services. They moved into a small room on the south side of the hospital building where they were later joined by Mr Polehampton.

The nurses' room was in the line of fire, and musket balls were constantly flying through the windows. As a precaution, all the glass was removed from the two windows, and the four inhabitants slept in the space between them, waking every morning to find a number of spent bullets on the floor. An attempt had been made to gain some kind of immunity for the hospital by moving into it a number of state prisoners—a brother of one of the kings of Oudh, a potential claimant to the throne, and two princes of the imperial house of Delhi. It was assumed that the enemy did have spies inside the Residency and that the news would soon reach them, as it had done when Sir Henry Lawrence had been moved to Dr Fayrer's house. The firing did slacken after a few days, but it did not stop altogether. A visitor, a soldier of the 32nd bringing some present for a comrade, was shot and killed. One poor invalid, well on his way to recovery from a serious wound, was shot dead in his bed as he lay there smoking his pipe.

Generally, the chances of recovery were not high. Major surgery was often followed by death, especially if a limb had to be amputated. Any open wound was in danger of immediate infection, for the hospital could not be kept clean, and linen could not be washed properly as there was a shortage of soap. There was also a shortage of bandages and of cloth to make them. Men would lie on their beds covered with blood. The air was foetid and heavy, as all the windows except those facing the Residency and the Baillie Guard had been barricaded. Though there were frequent attempts at fumigation by burning camphor, the effect was only momentary.

Yet patients did survive, even private soldiers who did not receive quite the same attention as their 'betters'. The 'poorer class of sufferers'[5] had, however, one friend in Mr Higgins, the head apothecary. 'This good and humble-minded man never let an opportunity pass by to do a charitable action, not the less acceptable because it was done in silence and without ostentation. The lower the rank of the patient, the more did Mr Higgins consider him entitled to his good offices.'[6]

Mr Polehampton, whose simple, reassuring presence was wel-

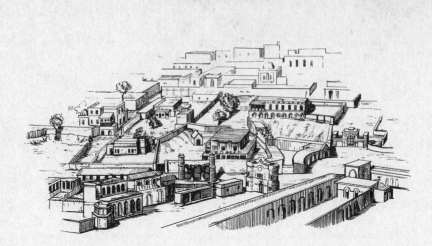

Baillie Guard Front

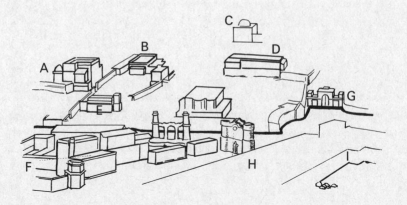

A	*Financial Garrison*	F	*Jail Buildings*
B	*Post Office*	G	*Baillie Guard Gate*
C	*Begum Kothi*	H	*Clock Tower*
D	*Fayrer's House*	I	*Tehri Koti*
E	*Sago's House*		

comed by everyone, was a constant visitor to the wards. One morning he received a message from Miss Ommanney to tell him that her father, who had been the Judicial Commissioner before the siege, had died from the injuries he had received a few days before. Polehampton immediately went over to the Ommanneys' house to comfort the widow. There he washed the body and laid it out ready for burial that night. Returning to his own room in the hospital, he shaved, and then stooped down to roll up his mattress. He felt a searing pain in his side. For a moment he thought he had been hit by a spent ball, but then discovered a hole in his side. Fortunately, the bullet had passed right through. Polehampton insisted on walking to the hospital's receiving room but fainted away before he reached it. After his wound had been dressed, he joined the other wounded in the front ward.

With Polehampton in hospital, Mr Harris found his work doubled, and Mrs Harris waited every evening for his return from the cemetery with great anxiety. At least she no longer had to worry about their dog, Bustle, who had been a constant companion ever since a dying soldier had given it to Mrs Harris some three years earlier, with a request that she should never part with it except through sheer necessity. In June, it had been ordered that all dogs found wandering inside the Residency would be destroyed, and rather than confine Bustle to Dr Fayrer's garden, Mrs Harris had sent him out to the Martinière college. There he so obviously pined for his mistress that Mr Schilling took him back to the Residency. After the siege began, Bustle's presence was not approved of by the inhabitants of Dr Fayrer's house, and Mr Harris took the dog out on a chain one morning to an outpost manned by some men of the 32nd.

Harris asked if one of the soldiers would kill the dog. There was not enough food to spare for pets. One of the men said he would shoot the animal as he wanted to empty his musket in order to clean it. But another soldier of the 32nd, Private Henry Metcalfe, was sitting on the verandah and overheard this conversation. He asked Mr Harris whether he could have the dog to keep. Mr Harris objected that Metcalfe, surely, had little enough food for himself, but Metcalfe insisted, and Bustle's life was spared on the understanding, said Harris, that if Metcalfe, Mrs Harris and himself all survived the siege then he would give the dog back to Mrs Harris. Metcalfe promised.

From then onwards, the two were inseparable. Mr Harris, touched by Metcalfe's care for the dog, asked one day whether there was anything he could do for him. Metcalfe thought for a

7　*The Church*

moment, then asked for a pipe, as his own had just been stolen. Harris had expected something rather different.

'Metcalfe, you have almost stunned me,' he said, for he had been thinking more in terms of Metcalfe's promotion in the regiment. 'But I must see if I can get you one. I don't smoke myself or I might have no difficulty.'[7]

No pipe was to be had, but Metcalfe proved more than content with the gift of a box of good cigars.

5
WAITING
FOR ATTACK

DURING THE second week of July the garrison suddenly seemed to settle down into an understanding of what they were doing. It was not just that the professional soldiers were recovering their nerve, or that the civilian volunteers were becoming more soldierly. It was as if every day without a serious assault by the enemy increased the defenders' belief in survival. The possibility of a major attack of course remained. One small civilian volunteer was worried enough to enquire of Captain Anderson: 'What are we to do, sir, if we are charged by elephants?'[1] After laughing at the absurdity of the idea. Anderson had the sense to treat the question seriously. At least it showed that the volunteers were genuinely concerned. But all he could answer was that he did not know, and relied on every man to do his best.

Captain Anderson, in fact, seems to have had more than his fair share of characters under his command. Perhaps the most flamboyant was Signor Barsatelli, a merchant who had come to Lucknow to dispose of a consignment of Florentine alabaster. The Signor went on guard with a double-barrelled sporting rifle in one hand and a musket in the other. At his side hung an immensely long sabre which seemed always to be getting between his legs. Across his chest, a large cartridge pouch—filled with sixty rounds of ball and looking very much like a hurdygurdy—impeded most of his movements until it was suggested that he might wear it on his back instead.

Barsatelli particularly disliked being awakened by visits from the staff. One night, after being shaken from a sound sleep by such a visit, he exclaimed: 'I think these grand round officers do this for their own amusement.' On another occasion, when one of the volunteers was audibly worrying about presenting arms,

Barsatelli consoled him by saying: 'Never mind, sir. Make a leetle noise. Who's to see in the dark?'[2]

Anderson's post, among others, was suffering during the day-light hours from the activities of a sniper. The enemy had left Johannes' house unoccupied for the first few days, under the impression, perhaps, that the building had been mined. But they soon overcame their fears and a number of expert marksmen took possession, taking it in turn to pick off men in the Residency. From the tower of Johannes' house the snipers had a clear view of the Cawnpore battery, Anderson's post, and even as far as the Begum Kothi and the hospital. All these were in range. One of the snipers was known as Jim the Rifle, or Bob the Nailer, because he nailed every man he fired at with his double-barrelled rifle. This man was a large negro, said to be one of the ex-king of Oudh's harem eunuchs. He was certainly a magnificent shot, and the casualties he caused were growing.

On July 7 it was decided that something had to be done. A party of fifty men of the 32nd and twenty Sikhs assembled at the Martini-ère post at noon, just after the men had had their dinner. With them and their officers were Captain Fulton and another Engineer. Brigadier Inglis said a few words and the party filed quietly through a hole in the wall. At the same time, a brisk fire was opened by the artillery on the adjacent posts, while officers on the roof of the Brigade Mess kept Bob the Nailer occupied with their rifles. Johannes' house was soon occupied. Some of the enemy were found asleep and were quickly bayoneted. Bob, distracted by the fire from the Brigade Mess, was taken by surprise and shot. The Engineer officers were preparing charges with which to blow up the house when the Brigadier ordered their return. Lookouts had observed the approach of a large party of the enemy.

They reached the defences without any fatalities and only three wounded. One of these, Private Cuney—a bandsman of the 32nd— had been out on a sortie only a day or two before and had silenced a nine-pounder which the enemy had brought up near the iron bridge. The Brigadier sat him down on the verandah and gave him a drink of brandy, praising him for his bravery. One of the officers had had his trousers blown off, but was otherwise unhurt. Fifteen or twenty of the enemy had been killed. Everyone was delighted with the success of the expedition. It was inspiring to see the defenders taking the initiative for a change. But Johannes' house still stood, and no one could stop the enemy from occupying it again.

There was still no direct assault, though there were plenty of false alarms, especially at night, when the men ought to have been resting or working on essential fatigue duties. One night, a wall of the racquet court collapsed, letting the fodder that was stored in it flow out. Every available man had to help collect it up and cover it with tarpaulins. Though the animals were now properly looked after, there were still carcases to be buried, stores to be carried to the posts, and repairs to be attended to. Even without extra alarms, most of the defenders were on duty from thirteen to twenty hours a day. Now that the distribution of rations was under control efforts were being made to organise supplies so that they would last as long as possible. Every third day the ration for officers was cut, though the men's remained the same. They suffered most from a shortage of tobacco, which despite Lawrence's foresight, soon became scarce. There were times when the European soldiers refused to go on duty, too tired and depressed to care what punishment might be given them. But most rallied when there was an alarm.

About four o'clock in the morning of July 8, there was the sound of bugles calling the Advance. The Baillie Guard proved to be the main target, but a few rounds of grapeshot soon dispersed the enemy force of about 300 men, and they did not return to the attack. There was also a rather half-hearted attack on the Cawnpore Battery, but that was easily repelled—fortunately, as most of the men were in a drunken stupor. Despite every precaution, they had managed to make a tunnel into the cellar of M. Deprat's house, where he had stored his last remaining bottles of brandy, champagne, and other wines, as well as some boxes of valuables. Some of the valuables had been stolen, as well as most of the brandy and champagne. The claret and Sauterne had found few takers.

That day the enemy's fire increased, despite the fact that they were short of ammunition. Nails and ramrods had been fired at the garrison, and numbers of the enemy had been seen out in the open picking up stray bullets. Mr Rees shot one of the collectors, but regretted it deeply when the body began to rot. The hail of fire continued, however, and so did the casualties, filling the already overcrowded hospital with more and more of the wounded.

There did not seem to be much hope of a relieving force, though there was a good deal of talk going the rounds. Several attempts had been made to send out messages, but the enemy was searching anyone found in the streets near the Residency area. On one occasion, one of the sepoys volunteered to leave the entrenchment in full uniform with a message concealed beneath the metal plate on the stock of his musket. He proposed to pretend that he was a deserter. But he was never heard of again Neither was an old woman who promised to deliver a letter to a friend in the city. But information was getting *in* to the Residency. Most of this came through the Sikhs, who were allowed to maintain contact with comrades who had deserted. There was also a brisk trade in opium by this route. Perhaps some of the 'news' stemmed from an opium dream, or was deliberately set about by the enemy in order to raise and than dash the hopes of the defenders.

On July 10, Major Banks sent out another messenger in the hope that he might reach Allahabad. 'The enemy has not done much harm to our defences,' he wrote, 'though many men have been killed and wounded. We think we have food for fully six weeks, nevertheless we look for relief when possible. Today we hear that Cawnpore is in the hands of our troops. I am writing thither. The enemy's fire is slackening, and his attacks are diminishing, why we cannot tell . . .'[3] The enemy was in fact saving his ammunition for a fresh assault.

The story that the British had retaken Cawnpore was not believed by all the defenders. Mr Rees was among the sceptics. 'They say troops are coming; but when and where from? . . . I fear there can be nothing in the many reports they confidently give out as true, that we are to be soon relieved. Talk of reinforcements. Where from? Maybe the Cham of Tartary and the Grand Lama of Tibet, at the head of an army of Cashmere goats!'[4]

There was no attack on the 11th, though the garrison had been standing to since one o'clock in the morning. During the 12th, the enemy could be seen preparing gun emplacements near the south-east angle of the defences. As it was Sunday, the ladies living at Dr Fayrer's had gathered that evening on the verandah to sing hymns. Just as they finished the first verse of the evening hymn, the garrison was called to arms. A party of the enemy advanced against the Baillie Guard gate and was driven off. Later, an attack was mounted on Gubbins's post. The bugles could be heard blowing the Advance, but soon after midnight the enemy withdrew, contenting itself with firing into the Cawnpore Battery for the rest of the night.

On the following day, the snipers returned to Johannes' house and again made life uncomfortable for the men in the posts it faced. Every attempt to dislodge the enemy with musket and artillery fire failed. There was an order from the Brigadier that cannon should not be fired without direct instructions from a member of his staff. Every cannonball fired was soon returned in the direction of the Residency, as was any shell that failed to explode. The enemy gunners would pick up the roundshot and fire it back. Unexploded shells were immediately fitted with new fuses and returned. It was felt that this way of replenishing the enemy's stocks of ammunition should be discouraged as far as possible.

There were constant rumours that the enemy was undermining the entrenchment. From the houses near the defences, it would have been comparatively easy to sink a shaft and then excavate a gallery outwards, filling the end with explosives and blowing a breach in the walls without any danger to the attackers. But the sentries could hear no digging, nor could one of the Engineers, who crept out in the dark to listen for sounds of mining near the Redan.

While all this was going on, the monsoon rains continued to fall. One moment the garrison was being scorched by the sun, the next drenched by a downpour. Long periods of rain meant that clothes could not be dried, and as few of the defenders had more than they stood up in, fighting and working had to be done in wet clothing. The only good thing that could be said for the rain was that it would often drive the snipers down from the roofs. Furthermore, as the Residency was on high ground, the water drained away from it into the enemy's trenches. But though it helped to wash away some of the dirt, it could not lay the smells of decaying flesh and ordure. Though latrines had been dug before the siege began, they were soon full, and as most of the sweepers—the Indian servants who were responsible for the removal of what was elegantly described as 'night soil'—had deserted, it was quite impossible to maintain reasonably sanitary conditions. Mr Rees was, perhaps, somewhat unfair to Dr Ogilvie when he wrote in his journal: 'Before the siege commenced, there was a very smart sanitary commissioner appointed. The uncompromising zeal that he had displayed in having the chance deposit of a cock-sparrow cleaned up was then something magnificent to behold. Pity that it afterwards flagged!'[5] As well as cholera and smallpox, many of the British began to suffer from painful boils on the face and scalp.

With the houses overlooking the defences occupied by the mutineers, watch could not be relaxed at any time. It was difficult for the men on the posts to be always vigilant. A few of the enemy could keep all the men awake for most of the night. Private Metcalfe found the dog, Bustle, invaluable. He would accompany Metcalfe on watch, and at any sign of drowsiness took his master's trousers in his teeth and shook them vigorously. But what if the enemy mounted a really determined attack? There was less than one man to each yard of the defences, and the whole line could not be patrolled, even though the parapets had been raised, trenches deepened, and screens and palisades erected along the inner pathways.

Should the enemy attack in force, it was to be each post for itself. There were virtually no reserves. And if one post fell there would be little hope for the rest. Sir Henry Lawrence had said: 'Never surrender!' and everyone was determined, if necessary, to die at his post. It was the women and children on whom concern was focussed. An officer took Mr Gubbins aside one day and told him that his wife had begged him to shoot her, should the enemy break in. The officer wanted Gubbins to agree that, if one of them were killed, the other would shoot both their wives. Gubbins refused—he could never bring himself to do it. Others had thought of poison, but Dr Fayrer, for one, was not prepared to supply it. The only firm suggestion was that the woman and children should be blown up with the magazine. Mrs Inglis described this scheme as 'impracticable', but the problem remained. Some of the women found other doctors more cooperative than Dr Fayrer and obtained a supply of prussic acid, but others, like Mrs Case, believed they should just prepare themselves for death and 'leave the rest in the hands of Him who knows what is best for us'.[6]

From about the middle of the month, there was considerable enemy activity. The snipers on the roofs kept up a steady fire. New batteries were being constructed and trenches dug, and the enemy gunners had apparently received fresh supplies of ammunition, for the cannonade increased in both weight and duration. Brigadier Inglis had continued to sleep in the Residency building, going across every day to breakfast and dine with his wife and children. The building had been reasonably free from artillery fire for some time, but after a roundshot had wounded Inglis's soldier servant on a verandah that had been thought safe, and another had penetrated Inglis's own room while he was out, he became convinced that the enemy knew where he was sleeping. That day he moved his quarters.

It was also the fourth birthday of Inglis's son, Johnny. One of the merchants inside the entrenchment had managed to keep a small quantity of toys and sold some of them to the Brigadier, so at least there were presents. Mrs Inglis found the day sad. When the regiment had been stationed at Cawnpore it had been her usual practice to give a party to the children of the station on her son's birthday. Now she could not stop herself from brooding about what was happening to them all.

There was some news from outside that day, though not about

the captives at Cawnpore. A column *had* made its way up from Allahabad but was too weak to attack the enemy in the town and had halted to await reinforcement. Was it true? Major Banks believed it, but others thought that when relief actually came it would come from Delhi. The reports also said that the besiegers were short of food, and that the Sikh deserters wanted to return to the entrenchment. None of this news was confirmed from any absolutely reliable source. Confirmation could only come from a messenger from General Havelock or some other commander of a relieving force.

On the morning of July 18 a dead body was seen lying outside the Baillie Guard gate. For some reason it was thought that this might be a messenger who had been caught as he tried to enter the defences. After dark, Inglis himself led out a party to bring in the corpse, which turned out to be that of a woman. There were neither letters nor papers of any kind upon the body.

One thing now seemed certain. The enemy *was* preparing an assault. Some of the defenders became a little jittery. The Martinière boys, fifteen of whom had been armed with muskets, would blaze away at everything in sight, even at the delicious-looking pumpkins ripening in the garden of Johannes' house. There was also a great deal of noise in the city. Mobs were constantly seen marching about the streets shrieking, beating drums, and blowing horns. They also did this in the middle of the night, which irritated the garrison considerably.

'I say, Bill,' a soldier of the 32nd was heard to remark. 'I'm blowed if these here badmashes don't yell like so many cats.'

'Yes, they do,' was Bill's reply, 'and I only wishes I was behind them with a tin pot of biling water as they opens their damned mouths.'

There was then a terrifying blast from the horns outside, and another soldier said:

'I only wish I had a hold of the black rascal that plays that; I'd not kill the vagabond, I'd only break that infernal instrument over the bridge of his nose.'[7]

Casualties mounted even though there was no major assault. Rees estimated that ten of the Europeans died every day. He did not know or care how many of the Indian defenders were killed. The native casualties were not even counted. 'We feel their loss is nothing very great; but it pains us all to hear of a poor European being knocked over.'[8] Rees did not think much of the doctors, either. 'Brown shot—leg amputated,' he noted in his journal. 'Now he will die; he *shall* die; for it is a law of medical science, as

101

practised by the garrison surgeons, that death follows amputation as sure as night follows day.'[9]

Even an apparent recovery was often a sad illusion. Mr Polehampton, despite conditions in the hospital, had recovered rapidly from his wound. But on July 19 he was struck down with cholera. He was in terrible pain, and there was no doubt that he would die. But to visitors he tried to smile. 'I am not in the least frightened,' he would assure them, 'and I know exactly how I am.'[10] As Mrs Polehampton sat by his side, she was convinced that she was watching her husband enter into the joy of his Lord, and that she was able to share in the joy. Polehampton died on the morning of the 20th, in the middle of the long expected assault. His wife was determined that he should be buried in a coffin, and not in the usual sheet. While the defenders held out against the attacks of the enemy, Polehampton's fellow chaplain, Harris, searched and found one under a staircase. That evening he read the funeral service alone with the young widow, before the body of her husband was carried away to join the others who had died that day.

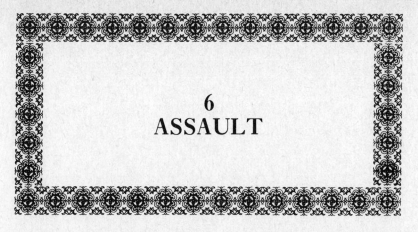

6
ASSAULT

ON THE morning of July 20, Rees was cleaning his musket and whistling a gay tune when the cry of 'To arms', and the sound of men going past his room at the double, brought him to his feet. The enemy had been sighted assembling in great numbers across the river and at other points near to the defences. It was half past eight and everything was ominously quiet. No sound of guns, no musket fire, only the call of the enemy's bugles. Lookouts on the Residency tower and the Post Office reported no move from the enemy, and some of the garrison stood down for breakfast. Inglis joined his family, leaving word that he was to be informed of the enemy's movements.

At a quarter past ten, there was a terrific explosion which shook the ground. Rees thought that one of the magazines had been hit by a shell. Inglis knew better. As he ran from the breakfast table, he called to his wife that the enemy had at last set off a mine. He was right. The mine had been intended to blow up the Redan Battery, but it was short by a hundred feet and also out of direction. The result was a large crater and a great deal of dust, but no breach in the defences.

The attackers did not learn of their failure, however, until, they arrived at the Redan, for the dust and smoke of their own explosion was increased by shells from the guns in the battery. A storming party rushed towards the sloping bank in front of the Redan, expecting a breach in the walls. But they were held up by the obstacles outside and then mown down by grapeshot and musketry fire from the defenders. Their leader could be seen, his cap on the end of his sword, trying to rally his men, but as they moved forward he was shot and they fell back again. Again they rallied, but the grapeshot tore into them and the covering fire from the houses nearby seemed to have no effect on the defenders.

By now, the whole of the defences were under attack. Rees was convinced that this was the end, said a prayer, committed himself to God's care, and began firing. Making his way to the water-gate under a shower of musket balls, he saw the enemy advancing, but not quite, he thought, as boldly as before. He picked off a few of them and felt a strange sensation of joy come over him. Forgetting his fear, he thought only of the number he could kill. The men on the posts had been joined by everyone who could carry a weapon. Even the wounded from the hospital had dragged themselves from their beds, found a musket, and made for the defences. Pale and trembling with weakness, some had their wounds re-opened by their efforts. The feeblest acted as loaders; a soldier with only one arm attempted to fire his musket despite the handicap.

While at the water-gate, Rees caught sight of Brigadier Inglis a little distance away on the Redan, shouting encouragement to the defenders. Above the noise of the attack, Inglis and his staff could be heard shouting 'Bravo! Bravo!' in the direction of Innes's post. There the commander, Lieutenant Loughman of the 13th Native Infantry, was trying to hold the most exposed position in the defences. All the support he had was twenty-four men of the 32nd, twelve volunteers, and about twenty-five sepoys of his own regiment. His orders had been clear. If he thought that he could not hold the post he was to retire immediately. Loughman had no intention of retiring, and neither had the volunteers.

When the attackers appeared in great strength, Loughman cried out: 'Give me a shout, boys, a loud one and a strong one.'[1] Everyone began to cheer, from one side of the post and then another, and so loudly that the attackers thought the defence was concentrated in considerable strength. There was a pause, but not for long, and the enemy came on again. Soon, despite heavy fire from some of the volunteers on the roof of the house, they had reached the shelter of the overhang and could be heard calling for scaling ladders. A rapid discharge from a number of additional muskets, already loaded and waiting to be picked up with no delay between one shot and the next, gave the impression that the post was defended by a much larger force than the attackers had thought. In the absence of grenades, two of the volunteers began hurling down bricks and mortar 'and other missiles of a very impure nature'.[2] These drove the enemy away to a position where they could be shot at.

While one of the volunteers was firing at the enemy, he was surprised to hear a shot whine past his ear which could only have

104

come from behind. Turning round he saw the terror-stricken face of a 'loyal' sepoy. Suspecting treachery, he turned quickly and was about to bayonet the man when Lieutenant Loughman called out: 'Never mind, don't bayonet him yet, there's lots of time afterwards.'[3] When the attack slackened the sepoy was able to convince the volunteer that the shot had been accidental.

One corner of the defences was held by two sepoys and a Eurasian called Bailey. Bailey spoke Hindustani well, so well, in fact, that the enemy, when they heard him shouting abuse at them, took him for one of themselves and called on him to join them.

'Come on,' they cried. 'Come over to us and leave those cursed Europeans. Come over to us. What have you to do with them? Will you be made a Christian too? Or have you already lost your caste?'

'Take that,' Bailey shouted back, firing his musket in the general direction of the voice. 'Do you think that I have eaten pig's flesh like yourselves? Do you think I shall disgrace myself by proving unfaithful to my salt? Take that, thou son of a dog. Thou whose grandfather's grave I have dishonoured.'

Highly coloured abuse and musket fire passed between the two sides.

'Wait, you offspring of a dishonoured mother,' shouted one of the enemy. 'We are coming. My sword is sharp.'

'Is it?' cried Bailey. 'Come along then. We are all prepared, and as for you, I shall catch you on the point of my bayonet.'[4]

Bailey's enthusiasm outran his supply of ammunition, and he was soon in need of replenishments. He could not leave the post himself, as he thought his two sepoys might desert if he did. He could not attract the attention of the main party because of the noise of the firing. During a lull he at last managed to communicate with Loughman, who sent out a volunteer with ammunition, but not before one of the sepoys had been wounded and Bailey himself hit in the jaw by a bullet which passed right through his neck.

The pressure on other parts of the line was just as heavy. At the Financial Garrison and Sago's, one of the attackers came forward carrying a green flag, the symbol of the prophet Muhammad, and shouting: 'The Faith! The Faith! Kill the Europeans!' A shot brought him down, and the flag caught on one of the spikes of the outer defences. One of the enemy rushed forward to retrieve it, and succeeded, although he was hit in the right arm.

Captain Sanders, commanding the Financial Garrison, had a clear view for about two hundred yards down the road outside

105

the defences. When the mine had exploded at the Redan, the road had been empty. But a moment later, a bale of cotton, followed by others, rolled towards the defences. There was still no sign of anyone in the road. Then a head appeared over the top of one of the bales. Sanders took a quick shot, and hit the man. After that the bales stayed where they were.

At Anderson's post, Mr Capper—still suffering a little from having been buried alive—was in charge of the volunteers. One of them, hearing a shout of 'Come on, brothers, there's nobody here' from an enemy leader, bellowed back 'There are plenty of us here, you rascal!' and shot the man dead.[5] Major Banks, who was present during the attack, spent his time bringing up ammunition even under the hottest fire. A short man, he would not stoop low even when the breastwork was lower than his head, and it was astonishing that he was not hit.

At Gubbins's post, the main attack was upon a bastion that still remained uncompleted. Lieutenant Grant was leaning over the rampart throwing hand grenades, when one exploded and blew off his hand. Another officer next to him was severely wounded. Nevertheless, the attack was beaten off and, despite continuous firing, beating of drums, and blowing of bugles, at about three o'clock in the afternoon it became obvious to the defenders that the tempo was slackening. An hour later, the enemy could be seen in retreat carrying some of their wounded with them. A little later, there was a request for a truce, so that the rest of the dead and wounded could be taken away. The defenders agreed, for sanitary reasons, and cartloads of the attackers were seen being driven away. It was clear that the enemy's casualties had been numerous. The defenders had lost only four Europeans dead and twelve wounded, and perhaps ten sepoys.

Everyone was exhausted. The heat had been intense, and for some unknown reason the day had been free of rain. Mr Rees, grateful to be alive, ate his chupattees and drank a glass of brandy and water thoughtfully brought to him by his friend, Deprat, 'with a relish that is inexpressible in words. I was filthy and black with gunpowder; and a wash, a little repose, my poor dinner, and a cigar after it put me in the most enviable frame of mind. I had not been so happy for a long time—not even before I had been imprisoned by these cursed insurgents'.[6]

In fact, everyone was rather pleased with the way they had behaved and their success in beating off the first major assault. Brigadier Inglis issued an order congratulating all on the way they had fought. Only Major Banks received a reproof. Inglis wrote him a strong letter reminding him how valuable his life was, and what a loss it would be to the garrison if he were killed. He ended by begging him not to expose himself to the enemy's fire.

The night was quiet, but on the following morning the usual firing opened up again. Then an attack was suddenly mounted at Gubbins's house. Large numbers of the enemy appeared and occupied the houses opposite, and then some low buildings which had walled yards abutting on to a narrow lane. Once they had broken through the wall into the lane, the only obstacle before them was a low mound of earth surmounted by a canvas screen. Gubbins himself was on duty on top of an outhouse which had a loophole commanding the lane. Hearing a shout from one of the lookouts, Gubbins went to the loophole with a pair of double-barrelled shotguns and opened fire on the intruders, driving them back to the protection of the wall. Gubbins's position was by no means safe, as there was another large loophole by his side through which the enemy could reach him. Before this could happen, however, he was joined by a private of the 32nd carrying some boards; together, they barricaded the dangerous loophole.

The enemy now began to throw over the wall picks and shovels with which they obviously intended making a hole in the defences of the unfinished bastion. At that moment, Gubbins heard a European voice behind him and, without turning, asked the speaker to have loopholes made in the wall of the Sikh Square which projected to the rear of the enemy, so that it would be possible to fire on anybody attempting to break into the bastion. Just then he heard the sound of a fall. Turning, he found Major Banks—dead, shot cleanly through the head. Only that morning, hearing the groans of a man wounded in the spine, Banks had said to Dr Fayrer: 'I hope when my time comes, I shall not suffer like that.'[7] He had his wish.

With the attack at its height, there was nothing Gubbins could do. The private of the 32nd had been replaced by an Indian orderly, who acted as loader for Gubbins. It was not until a mortar was brought up and opened fire on the enemy in the yards, driving them out, that he could relax. Major Banks's body had to lie there until it could be taken away in the late afternoon. He was buried that same night, in a common grave, sewn up in a sheet like the others.

8   *Sinking a shaft*

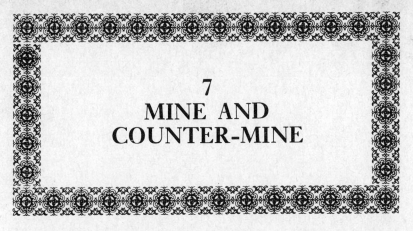

7
MINE AND
COUNTER-MINE

THE BEHAVIOUR of the enemy during the assault had proved to most people's satisfaction that they were lacking in overall, experienced leadership. The attacks had certainly been strongly pushed, but there had been no proper coordination between the attacking parties and the artillery. If all the enemy artillery had been carefully concentrated on specific weak points in the defences, the wall could have been breached by gunfire alone. Instead, the guns were fired at random targets, usually at individual defenders who had shown themselves to the gunners. Because of faulty elevation, the gunners often fired right over the Residency and into their own trenches on the other side.

But they were very good at digging positions for themselves and their guns. A gun would be sited at the bottom of a ramp and, when ready to fire, run quickly to the top; the recoil carried it down to the bottom again. Some guns were sited behind walls, run out, fired, and dragged back again before the defenders could reply.

After the assault of July 20, the garrison began once again to fear that they would be undermined. The mine tunnel at the Redan might not have been long enough, or even in the right place, but it proved that the enemy had recognised the importance of blowing up the defenders from underground. The best place for mining operations was the south face; the houses outside the defences were so close that there was little likelihood of getting the direction wrong.

The best way to counter a mine was to tunnel another one to meet it. The trouble was that the defenders could spare few men for digging, while the enemy, on the other hand, had a constant supply of labour. There was also a shortage of tools, as the coolies who had been working on the fortifications before the siege had taken theirs with them when they deserted. Among the soldiers of the 32nd, however, there were a number of men who had had experience in the mines of Cornwall and Derbyshire, and these were organised by Captain Fulton of the Engineers into a squad of instructors. One instructor was attached to each post, to teach men to listen for the sounds of enemy mining and to dig and shore up counter-mines.

By accident, a volunteer overhead Lieutenant Innes deploring the shortage of picks and shovels, and told him that there was a large stock of miscellaneous tools on the roof of M. Deprat's shop. Innes would not even wait for a ladder to be brought so that he could reach the roof from a safe side, but made his way up an open outside staircase in full view of Johannes' house. He found plenty of useful stuff and, ordering a mound of straw to be placed on the ground, threw down picks and shovels and tarpaulins, before descending again himself—without the enemy seeing him.

With the new tools, counter-mining could really get under way. Essentially the technique was simple. A shaft would be driven, preferably inside a house or behind a wall, vertically into the ground, and then a tunnel or gallery was excavated horizontally towards the region in which it was thought the enemy were digging *their* galleries. Shafts were usually about four feet in diameter, and were dug to a depth of between twelve and twenty feet. Ten men made up a mining party, five men to work and five to relieve them. The heat was trying enough above ground; below it was almost unbearable, and the men could only spend short periods down the shaft or inside the gallery. The five men worked as a team. Number One was the miner. With a pick or crowbar he would loosen the earth to a depth which would allow him to squat down while still leaving a few inches above his head. The earth was collected in a packing case by Number Two. When the case was filled with earth, Number Two would pull a string and Number Three, stationed at the bottom of the vertical shaft, would drag the case towards him. Numbers Four and Five at the top of the shaft were responsible for pulling up the case, emptying the earth, and sending the box down the shaft again.

The work was very fatiguing, but at least the ground was so firm that it did not need to be lined, and in most places the roof did not even have to be supported with pit props. Everyone helped in the construction, regardless of rank—officers and men, senior civilians and Eurasian clerks. The Sikhs turned out to be very skilful miners, and there was usually either an officer of the

112

Engineers or one of the former miners among the men of the 32nd to advise and help the diggers.

When the mine was finished, a man would be sent at regular intervals to the end to listen for the sounds of the enemy at work on their mine. Along the corridors there were no lights, as it was impossible to ventilate the mine, and the observer would make his way in extreme discomfort, banging his head on the roof, forgetting that there was a turning, and perhaps having to slither some way on his stomach. The galleries always seemed to be full of mosquitoes, and their constant buzzing made it difficult to hear the more secretive sounds. There were many false alarms when an inexperienced listener mistook some innocent noise—perhaps a member of the garrison chopping wood overhead—for the enemy.

Many of the officers would insist on listening for longer than the others, an offer which was rarely refused. Captain Fulton would listen for hours at the end of the mine to the sound of the enemy pickaxes, trying to decide which point they were making for. When the sound was really close, he would draw his pistol, cock it, and wait patiently for the enemy miner to appear. If Captain Fulton were needed in the Residency, it became almost a matter of course to assume that he was down some mine, 'like a terrier in a rat hole, and not likely to leave it, either, all day'[1]—as a sergeant of the 32nd put it.

Enemy mining activity on the south face of the defence kept everybody there on the alert. A lady in her bath, hearing strange noises, would immediately assume that the mine had reached a point beneath her bathroom. Officers, without warning, would fling themselves down and place an ear to the ground. A dried pea placed on a drum was said to move if there was mining underneath. At night, an officer would make his way outside the defences to listen. On the south face, the counter-mines soon formed an extensive underground warren. At the Cawnpore Battery, after the discovery that the enemy was digging near it, new galleries were added to the existing mine and charges of gunpowder were placed at the ends.

Near Gubbins's post, the buildings that had been used to shelter the enemy at the time of the attack which had led to the death of Major Banks were now believed to be sheltering enemy mining parties. At sunset, the area was shelled so heavily that the enemy could be seen moving out. A group of men from the 32nd, led by Brigadier Inglis himself, made a sortie through a hole cut in the defences at Gubbins's house. The party reached the buildings without opposition, and could find no evidence of mining. Setting the roofs of the buildings alight, and waiting only to see that the fire had taken a good hold, the party retired the way it had come. But a private of the 32nd, straying too far from the main party, was mistaken for one of the enemy and shot by one of the defenders from the roof of the Brigade Mess.

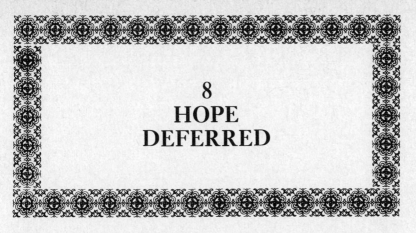

8
HOPE
DEFERRED

THE MORALE of the garrison, raised by success in repelling the assault of July 20, was to be raised even higher by the news that, this time, reinforcements really were on the way. Martin Gubbins, still in charge of the Intelligence department, had gone to bed early on July 22, as he was not feeling very well. Soon after midnight, he was awakened with the information that a messenger had come in. It turned out to be Angad Tewari, a sepoy pensioner who had been among those called in for service by Sir Henry Lawrence. Angad had been sent out on June 29 to find out what had happened to the mutineers who were allegedly on their way from Cawnpore to Lucknow. He had not reappeared, and the garrison had discovered the mutineers for themselves, at Chinhat.

Angad told Gubbins that he had been kept virtually a prisoner by the mutineers for thirteen days but had finally made his way to Cawnpore, which he had left again only two days earlier. His other news was so much what the defenders in the Residency had been wanting to hear that Gubbins doubted its truth, especially as Angad carried no written messages. According to Angad, a relieving force, commanded by Brigadier-General Havelock and consisting of only a few hundred men with twelve guns, had defeated the rebel leader at Cawnpore, retaken the city, and was at that very moment preparing to cross the Ganges and make for Lucknow. Gubbins cross-examined Angad again and again, and was finally convinced that he was telling the truth. Gubbins then sent him across to Inglis's headquarters with a note of what he had said, and another asking the Brigadier whether he wished the messenger to return to Havelock with a letter from him. Inglis sent Angad back with a note saying that he himself did not propose to write.

As Angad was willing to return to Cawnpore, Gubbins prepared a letter for Havelock to forward to the governor-general. In it he gave an account of the siege to date, the number of the garrison, and the estimated strength of the besiegers. The despatch was almost ready when Inglis's aide-de-camp brought a message to the effect that, as the Brigadier was finding it difficult to sleep, he had changed his mind and would write a letter after all. Angad should not, therefore, be allowed to leave. Gubbins promised to detain him until the Brigadier's letter was ready.

As they waited, it began to rain very heavily. Angad was anxious to get away. Rain, he said, was the only cover that made it possible for him to bypass the enemy sentries. When Gubbins tried to keep him until Inglis's letter arrived, Angad insisted that, if he were not allowed to leave at once, he would refuse to go at all that night. Finally, Gubbins gave Angad his own despatch and let him go, sending an officer of his post over to the Brigadier to tell him what had happened. On the way, the officer met the Brigadier's aide-de-camp with the letter.

Not unnaturally, Inglis was angry, though there was very little else Gubbins could have done. But the Brigadier was already irritated by the fact that Gubbins had written him a letter announcing that, as the senior civilian official in the Residency after the death of Major Banks, he had assumed the office of Chief Commissioner. These pretensions Inglis immediately crushed.

Lucknow, July 23, 1857

'Sir,
    I am directed to acknowledge the receipt of your letter No. 1 of this date, in which you report that you have assumed charge of the office of Chief Commissioner for the affairs of Oudh and in reply to state that Sir Henry Lawrence superseded you in the post by the late lamented Major Banks, and he also expressed his opinion to Lord Canning and to more than one living member of this garrison that you should on no account be permitted to hold the office of Chief Commissioner. Under the above circumstances, the Brigadier, with the entire concurrence of Major Anderson, thinks it his duty to inform you and to publish in this day's orders, for general information, the the office of Chief Commissioner is for the present vacant, and that Martial Law, and the highest Military Authority will be paramount in Oudh, until a successor to Sir Henry Lawrence shall be duly appointed by the Governor General in Council.
    The Brigadier therefore requests that you will for the future abstain from sending any message to the relieving force, or perform-

ing any act whatever connected with the public service without previously communicating what you propose to do for his information.

As your messenger was despatched without waiting for the Brigadier's letter to the officer commanding the Relieving Force he requests you will furnish him with a copy of your communication.

T. F. Wilson, Capt.
Offg. A.A. Genl.

To: *M. Gubbins, Esq., C.S.*
Lucknow.[1]

The news Angad had brought was soon going the rounds of the defenders. There was a certain amount of scepticism. It had been heard too often before. But the next day there were fewer of the enemy in sight than usual, and the more hopeful among the garrison concluded that they had gone to oppose Havelock's advance. The rain came down, almost continuously. Rees, like everyone else, found it very unpleasant, for 'though one shower cools the air after a hot day, when it lasts too long the heat, instead of being dry, is moist like a vapour bath and suffocating to a degree. And to stand sentinel at night when it is as cold as the day is hot, and to shiver in the wet, is also far from agreeable'.[2] The heavy rain also washed away some of the palisades and earthworks, but the lull in the firing gave the garrison a chance to carry out repairs.

Work could go on only slowly, for the men were weakened by the constant calls to arms, the coarse food, and attacks of diarrhoea or dysentery. Cholera and smallpox were still taking their toll. Mrs Case's sister, Caroline, had caught smallpox and Mrs Inglis was afraid that the infection would spread. Fortunately, Caroline's attack turned out to be mild, but others were not so fortunate. Mrs Inglis tried to relieve some of the gloom by reading to the patients, but found it was impossible for any of them to think about anything outside the entrenchments, and gave up. In Dr Fayrer's house, the ladies living in the underground rooms took turns to watch through the night. Why, they found it difficult to say. But they were sure that something terrible was about to happen, and could only sleep if they knew one of their number was on guard.

Just before midnight on July 25, Angad returned to the Residency. With him he brought a letter from Lieutenant-Colonel Fraser Tytler, serving with General Havelock's force. At least there could now be no doubt about Angad's honesty. The contents

117

of the letter were even more inspiring than this proof of integrity and loyalty.

'My dear Sir,
Your letter of the 22 has reached us. We have two-thirds of our force across the river, and eight guns in position already. The rest will follow immediately. I send over more news to-night or to-morrow. We have ample force to destroy all who oppose us. Send us a sketch of your position in the city, and any directions for entering it or turning it that may strike you. In five or six days we shall meet. You must threaten the rear of the enemy if they come out, and we will smash them.

Yours truly,
B. Fraser Tytler'[3]

Naturally, this tremendous news was passed to the defenders at the posts and to the women. Even the children were told that soon, very soon, help would come and the nightmare would be over. At Rees's post the defenders were having a sing-song in celebration, and were just about ready to encore 'Cheer, boys, cheer' when a sentry reported men moving about. Everyone set off to confront the enemy with joy and hope in their hearts, because they were certain of success and speedy deliverance. But it was only another false alarm.

Some of the garrison were so sure that relief was on the way that they decided it was time to make some provision for the future. They broke into a locked room in the Residency building and stole a large quantity of the jewels of the former kings of Oudh, which had been put there for safe keeping. It had, in fact, been intended to bury these with the rest of the treasure, but Inglis had been unable to spare men for the task.

Angad had brought other news with him, not so welcome to the besieged garrison. As he spoke in the room in Gubbins's house, the screens up and only a single candle flickering, he told of the massacre of the women and children at Cawnpore just before Havelock's arrival there. This time, everybody hoped that Angad lied. He told them also that one of the mutineer generals had been killed by a shot from the Residency, and that a young son of the ex-king of Oudh had been declared king by the mutineers, with his mother as regent.

Angad was allowed a day's rest and was then asked to go out again, carring a large packet of plans and advice for the relieving force. With it was a letter from Inglis.

118

'My dear Sir,

At Bashiratganj there are about 1,000 matchlock men, and about as many more at Nawabganj. It is said that the 3rd Oudh Irregular Infantry left this to oppose you on the night of the 24th, and was followed yesterday by the 22nd Native Infantry. The bridge at Bani is believed to be entire, but being a good defensible position, it is likely that the enemy will oppose you there. There is another bridge, however, at Mohan, about eight miles further up, though the road is indifferent. The bearer, though, will give you later information of the state of the road, and the force on it. I send you a plan of the town and our position, and a memo by the engineer. The distance from the entrance to the city to our position is about a mile and a half. We can assist you by shelling your flanks for the last 1,500 yards or more. In the event, however, of the enemy disputing your entrance, you might endeavour to work round his left flank by diverging to the right towards the Dilkusha Park, and making your entrance by the European barracks. The road, however, will be very difficult and heavy for guns, and likewise lined with houses. I would suggest the direct route. If you have rockets with you, send up two or three at 8 p.m. on the night before you intend entering the city, by way of warning to us, at which signal we will begin shelling the houses on both sides of the road. Ignorant of the strength of your force and of its formation, I can only offer these suggestions with the assurance that the utmost that our weak and harassed garrison is capable of shall be done to cause a diversion in your favour as soon as you are sufficiently near. Should the bridge at the entrance of the town be broken down, there is another on the side of the Dilkusha Park. It is a good mile and a half from the first-mentioned bridge to our position.

J. Inglis, Brigadier

To officer commanding relief force.[4]

Altogether, the despatches Angad was expected to carry made a rather bulky package. On previous occasions, the messages had been written on the smallest piece of paper possible, and rolled up in a quill which could be quickly concealed. Angad had not before asked for payment for his work, but this time he was offered the immense sum of five thousand rupees if he delivered the package safely.

Life went on as before, with alarms and constant firing by day and night. On the morning of the 27th, observers on the south face of the defences noticed that two planks had been placed across the road from Johannes' house, which had not been there when darkness fell the night before. An officer, watching with a tele-

119

scope, saw a man's hand appear round the edge, and soon after some of the earth at the side fell into what was obviously a mine, barely six feet from the palisade.

Work on a counter-mine that had already been begun was pressed along as fast as possible, while fire was concentrated from the Brigade Mess on the planking in the road. Captain Fulton, however, determined to take out a party and blow up the mine. He took a pillowcase to the commander of the Cawnpore Battery and asked for it to be filled up with gunpowder. But he was persuaded to wait and see what gunfire could do before endangering his own life and that of his party. An eight-inch mortar was prepared for action, and after a number of ranging shots succeeded in sending a shell right into the gallery of the enemy mine.

The mutineers gave up working on this particular mine, but continued on others. A listener in a counter-mine running out of the Sikh Square heard the sound of a pick. By about five o'clock in the afternoon of the 28th it appeared to be drawing close to the head of the counter-mine. When the enemy miners were only a few inches away, Captain Fulton broke down the remaining earth with a flourish. The enemy took off as fast as they could, pursued by Fulton and a sergeant of the 32nd. Finding the gallery quite deserted, however, Fulton returned to the counter-mine and ordered an officer to remain there with his pistol at the ready while he himself brought down a barrel of gunpowder. Fulton manoeuvred the barrel into the enemy's mine, packed stones and earth around it, and set it off.

The following day, there were rumours that some of the mutineers were leaving the city. Estimates varied, but the general tenor of opinion was that they had gone off to meet Havelock's force. From the Residency, it was impossible to tell whether the number of besiegers had diminished or not. They kept to the houses when they were not actually attacking, and there had been no sign of any concentrations of men since the assault of the 20th. During the afternoon, there were sounds of heavy firing in the Cawnpore direction, and at 6 p.m. there was another outburst which was thought to be nearer Lucknow than the earlier one. Inglis, with his wife and Mrs Case, had just sat down to dinner when they heard the sound of cheering. Everyone seemed to be rushing frantically around, crying that the relief had arrived. Mrs Case had the impression that the relieving force was actually at the gates.

Inglis went off to find out what was happening, and while he was away an officer came to Mrs Inglis, clasped her hand, and

congratulated her on her deliverance. Some of the ladies had made
for the flat roofs in order to see better. Even the sick and wounded
in the hospital had dragged themselves out. Just as Mrs Inglis had
picked up her baby and was about to go out and convey the news
to a sick friend, her husband returned, furiously angry, saying:
'It's the most absurd thing I ever heard.'[5] He ordered the ladies
back to their dinner. An officer on lookout had mistaken what,
it was later learned, had been a salute to the youthful new king
of Oudh for the arrival of Havelock's force.

Naturally, when the truth became clear, everyone was extremely
depressed. It was also feared that the morale of the Indian soldiers,
which had remained remarkably high so far, might suffer. The
enemy certainly hoped so, for they began to taunt the Indian
soldiers of the garrison. 'So you think your reinforcements have
come, do you? . . . Why, we have beaten them long ago.'[6] Instructions were given that the sepoys were to be carefully watched for
any sign that they might be considering going over to the enemy.

For many of the women, the excitement was soon submerged
again in the terrible routine of sickness and death. Mrs Clark,
who had been Katherine Bartrum's companion in the escape from
Gonda, had given birth to a child on the day of the assault. There
were now nine human beings in the tiny room. It was soon clear
to everyone, however, that Mrs Clark and her baby were dying.
The poor woman's mind was wandering, and she took no notice
either of her baby or of her elder child, who was also ill. At night
she would wake and shout out: 'Lighten my darkness, I beseech
Thee, O Lord!'[7]

On July 30, however, she seemed better. She sat up, and asked
Mrs Bartrum to bring her boxes and pack them, as she was going
on a long journey and must have everything ready. Katherine did
as she asked, sorting out her few possessions and putting them
into the boxes. 'Thank you,' said Mrs Clark. 'Now I am quite
ready. The litter is here, but the bearers have not come.'[8] Katherine
brought her a little food, but she never spoke again. That evening
she seemed so near to death that the chaplain came, and prayed,
and baptised the child. As it was a girl, they named it after her
mother. Mrs Clark's husband was still outside the Residency,
perhaps dead. Mrs Clark herself died a little after midnight. The
baby survived for another three days, the elder child, a boy, for a
couple of weeks. In that time Mrs Bartrum herself went through
the horror of seeing Bobbie stricken with cholera, and the joy of
seeing him recover.

Though, for some inexplicable reason, Colonel Fraser Tytler's letter had not been dated, it was assumed that he had written it on the 24th. By that reckoning, the relieving force should have been at least in sight by the end of the month. But the aching eyes of the lookouts on the roofs could see nothing. At night there was no sign of a signal rocket. Inglis began to think that perhaps Gubbins, in his letter to Havelock, had given a false impression of the size of the opposition he might have to face. Gubbins had not taken time to make a copy of his letter, and even after Inglis had written to him asking specifically whether he had given Havelock a probable estimate of the 'force likely to oppose him en route to this place', and whether he had mentioned 'the strong position at the Bani bridge', Gubbins's reply was far from reassuring. Inglis felt that there was no alternative but to send out another messenger.

'Lucknow, August 2, 1857

My dear Sir,

I wrote to you on the 22nd, 25th, 27th, and 30th ultimo, and sent 2 plans of our position and a memo by the Engineers, but have received no reply, and indeed only one letter, that of Colonel Tytler's from Cawnpore received on the 25th and addressed to Mr Gubbins. Unfortunately Mr Gubbins wrote without consulting the military authorities, and having kept no copy of his letter, we know not what he wrote you and we can only conjecture the strength of the Force gone against you. We suppose they have broken down the bridge at "Bani" and thus succeeded in arresting your progress here. Few of the enemy are in sight here, but they keep so much under cover it is difficult to form an estimate. We are still well off for provisions (say 20 days) both for Europeans and Natives, but our force is fast diminishing and we can no longer man all our guns. Our hopes have been very great, and we look for your arrival with great anxiety, fearing if it is much further delayed, the natives, hitherto faithful to us, will desert.

Yours truly,
J. Inglis, Brigadier

The Officer Commanding the Relieving Force.'[9]

Inglis and his staff tried to keep up an appearance of optimism, but as the days passed some of the defenders gave themselves up to a sullen, obstinate, silent despair. 'Thus hopeless of life and hoping only to kill before being killed, their existence became almost a burden to them, and many a one cast envious glances at the poor fellows carried to their grave every evening.'[10] Even Rees, who noted with sorrow this growing pessimism and tried not to give in to it himself, wrote in his journal that at no time had he ever felt so strongly the truth of the proverb: 'Hope deferred maketh the heart sick.'

9 *Cawnpore Battery*

9
ASSAULT
RENEWED

LACK OF faith in the possibility of relief, coupled with the general exhaustion felt by most of the garrison, led to both carelessness and a decline in vigilance. There was far less drunkenness, for the simple reason that most of the liquor had either been consumed or impounded by the authorities. The daily ration of rum and beer was not enough to drown even the smallest sorrow. Despite continued warnings, men would stick their heads out through a loop-hole just after they had fired, in order to see whether they had hit anything. They were usually killed by an enemy sniper who had seen the smoke of the discharge. As for vigilance, it became necessary for an officer to pay frequent visits to the sentry posts in case the guard had fallen asleep.

One night Captain Anderson saw one of the sentries apparently asleep. His head was bent on his chest and he did not challenge when the captain approached. In other circumstances, there would have been only one thing for Anderson to do—call the sergeant of the guard and have the sentry put under arrest, courtmartialled, and, inevitably, shot. But these were not ordinary times. Anderson understood what pressure the men were under.

'Sentry,' he called out softly.

The man gave a start, saw the officer, and was soon alert. Then he said, quite calmly, 'I was just thinking, sir, how sad it is that half the world does not know how much the other half suffers.'

Anderson was so surprised at this that he gave the man the benefit of the doubt. Perhaps he had not been sleeping at all, but in a 'state of deep thought'. Anderson stayed for a while and learned that the man had once been thought of by his comrades as of 'pleasant temper', but that after the death of his wife and child he had become surly and morose.

'I used to love that child, sir,' he said, 'and when it died, I became a wretched man and cared for nothing.'

Anderson went off feeling sorry for all the overworked men of the 32nd. Some of them, though sick, refused to stay in hospital and went on duty even though they could hardly stand. Anderson would try to send them back to hospital, and received the reply: 'Well, sir, in these times every man must do his best.'[1]

All things considered, what surprised many people was not the number of the casualties but the fact that they were not higher. The Residency was a very small area and there was no really solid protection for the defenders. Shells would smash into the rooms, filling the place with dust and blowing bedding and boxes around. But some were still able to make a joke of it. One day after a shell burst, Signor Barsatelli found that his trunk had disappeared completely. He still had a servant, a boy from Madras, and he shouted to him, 'Where is my trunk?'

The boy went to the corner where it was usually kept, and came back with a look of consternation on his face.

'Trunk not got, sir,' he told his master. Barsatelli pretended to be angry.

'Not got trunk, you rascal, where is it?'

Only when the boy was shown some pieces of wood which were all that remained of his master's trunk did he realise what had happened.

'Before trunk got, sir—*now*, not got—shell break him,' he exclaimed, in enlightenment.[2]

With shot whistling about, and even the possibilty of being hit by the defenders' own shells (as the targets were so near the defences), there were many hairbreadth escapes. Mrs Inglis, taking the air one evening with her child in her arms, heard a sharp sound near her cheek and saw a large splinter bury itself ten inches in the ground near her feet. Rees was saved by a soldier walking unexpectedly in front of him, who caught a bullet in his face. One day, a round shot from a new enemy battery sited not far from Innes' post broke the leg of a chair in which a lady was sitting in the Post Office. The shot caught in her dress as she fell, but rolled on across the floor.

Private Metcalfe, on guard duty with Bustle, had just fired through a loophole at a party of the enemy cutting trenches when a shell came right through the loophole and hit the wall behind, bringing it down in a shower of bricks and dust on top of Metcalfe. Bustle was barking furiously. An officer shouting: 'Is there anyone hurt?' received the reply: 'Yes, I think young Metcalfe is killed.' But Metcalfe, with the aid of Bustle, soon emerged, covered with white dust and looking, he said, more like a miller than a soldier.[3]

A friend of Metcalfe's came over one night to see whether he had any rum to spare. Metcalfe did not want his ration that night and, in any case, knew that he could ask for more from Mr Harris. He gave away his tot. His friend put it in a small bottle, remarking that it would be welcome when he was on sentry duty. At about ten o'clock that night Metcalfe saw an enemy shell flying over, and remarked that it looked as if it was heading directly for his friend's post. He was right. The shell hit the post where his friend was lying down, blew the pillow from under his head, shattered the bottle of rum, and hurled the man himself into a trench. After a moment of dust and silence, the man's voice was heard to enquire: 'Is my dram of grog all right?' An officer replied: 'I'm afaid not, my man. But never mind,' he added, 'I'll give you one, since that's all you care about!'[4]

Metcalfe's friend told him next morning that, now, he was sure he would never be killed. That same evening, however, a round shot shattered his leg and he died in terrible pain.

Most of the garrison was suffering from some disease or other. As well as malarial fever, cholera, smallpox and dysentery, there was also a kind of scurvy brought on by the absence of fruit and green vegetables from the diet. It was so widespread that it was christened 'Garrison Disease'. The symptoms were a high temperature, diarrhoea, skin eruptions, spongy gums and loose teeth.

Except for the shortage of fruit and vegetables, rations were still reasonably adequate. It was the Indian soldiers who suffered most. Being vegetarians they could not even eat the stringy bullock beef, and there were none of the spices they customarily used in their cooking.

The smell of death hung everywhere. The corpses of animals were buried whenever possible, but any that died outside the defences lay where they fell, and rotted. The butchers in the garrison threw the offal from the slaughterhouse over the wall, and there was no labour available to bury it. The number of flies seemed to be increasing every day, breeding on decaying flesh, blackening the windows and the tables, making it difficult either to eat or sleep.

The shortage of men to dig graves for the human dead was also causing trouble. The graves were now very shallow and the stench coming from them was so revolting that Mr Harris, the chaplain —advised by the doctors that it was dangerous to health—took to reading the burial service before the bodies were taken to the burial ground. He believed this to be a sensible solution, for as the only Protestant minister in the Residency, he owed as much to the living as to the dead. If he fell sick, there was no one to take his place.

Brigadier Inglis, however, did not agree. A letter from Captain Wilson informed Mr Harris that the Brigadier had personally inspected the burial ground and had failed 'to observe any smell sufficient to deter you from the performance of your legitimate duties as Chaplain to this Force'.[5] The terms of Harris's reply were not acceptable to the Brigadier, and produced another communication from Captain Wilson in which the chaplain was informed that if he did not intend to read the burial service at the graveside, the Brigadier would appoint an officer who would do so instead. Furthermore, he was warned that he was mistaken in thinking that he was not subject to military authority. 'Under present circumstances,' wrote Captain Wilson, 'Military Rule is supreme.'[6] At the same time, Inglis sent a rebuke to Father Bernard, one of the two Catholic priests in the Residency. He too had ceased holding the burial service at the graveside.

On Sundays, Harris would try to hold services at a number of places, so that as many of the garrison as could be spared might join in. One Sunday, before holding the service at Dr Fayrer's house, Harris went to the post where Private Metcalfe was stationed, and said: 'Well now, boys, I am about to have a little Divine Service, and any of you who wish to join me will be very welcome to come and attend, and those who don't care to come, I hope you will keep quiet and not disturb us.'[7] His hope was not to be realised.

For some time, the enemy had been firing a strange assortment of missiles at the garrison. There were shells of brass or stone, which gave off a kind of high shriek and were known by the defenders as 'Whistling Dicks'. These at least gave warning of their coming and an opportunity to take cover. There were also carcasses, incendiary shells filled with such inflammable materials as sulphur, tallow, turpentine, antimony, and saltpetre. These were very effective and caused a number of fires, including one in the Residency building itself. Some of the larger missiles were fired, not from guns, but from funnels set in the ground. On the Sunday of the service in Dr Fayrer's house, the enemy sent over a huge block of wood which whirred past to land near Metcalfe's post. A young Irish soldier was so impressed by this that he quite forgot what was going on, and rushed into the room where Mr

Harris was holding his service and shouted out: 'By Jabers, the devils are firing cook-houses at us!'[8] There was a commotion among the congregation, and a hasty retreat by the embarrassed soldier.

By August 6 there had been no further reliable news from outside the entrenchment. Inglis was gravely worried about the amount of food and the loyalty of the Indian sepoys. However, he concealed his fears from everyone but his own staff. He was showing the strain. His hair had gone grey, and he had suffered an attack of giddiness which might have been caused by the sun. He was also worried by the illness of his son, Johnny, who was thought to have contracted smallpox. But his main fears were about the relieving force. If it did not come soon, he believed the whole garrison was doomed.

About nine o'clock on the evening of the 6th a messenger arrived. Unfortunately, he carried no written message. It had, he said, been put in a quill which he had lost while covering the dangerous no-man's-land between the enemy trenches and the Residency. The man was a sepoy of the 1st Oudh Irregular Infantry, one Aodhan Singh, who had been sent out with letters a week before. He claimed that General Havelock had in fact crossed the Ganges and, in a battle with the mutineers at Unao—about eight miles along the road to Lucknow—had routed them; that he had moved to Bashiratganj, six miles further on, but had then fallen back on the village of Mangalwar about five miles from the river. There he had dug in to await reinforcements.

Aodhan Singh's story seemed truthful enough, especially as he named a number of officers known to members of the garrison. But his description of some of the British troops with Havelock puzzled the defenders—he said that one of the regiments had strange music played in front of it. This, however, was not of great importance. What really mattered was why Havelock had retired, and the explanation for that lay somewhere in the mud of the no-man's-land. There was nothing to do but wait. Inglis told his wife that it might be another eight days before Havelock could reach the city. Not all were so optimistic.

Though there had been a lull in the enemy's mining operations, the fear that the garrison might be blown up grew continually stronger. News from the city confirmed that the enemy expected to capture the Residency very soon. If another assault was contemplated, every one of the defenders would have to be especially alert. The enemy's heavy gun, which had been sited near Innes' post, was becoming a nuisance, and it was decided that an attempt must be made to knock it out. An eighteen-pound cannon was hauled up to Innes' post at night and earthworks, backed by bricks, were thrown up to give the gunners some protection. The enemy's gun was soon put out of action, and the eighteen-pounder was withdrawn the following night. Innes' post was so exposed that Inglis thought it foolish to leave the gun there.

In the first days of August the rains were particularly heavy. The trenches were flooded, and a large counter-mine at the Cawnpore Battery got so wet that a long fuse made of canvas hose stuffed with powder had to be carefully withdrawn and replaced. During the dry intervals, the enemy's guns were active as usual, and some of the buildings which had already suffered a severe pounding received direct and punishing hits. The Residency house, by now partly in ruins, had been completely evacuated except by a few people who remained in the underground rooms. The enemy obviously knew this, for they began to concentrate their fire on Gubbins's house, where many of those from the Residency were now quartered.

On August 9 at about 5 p.m., Private Metcalfe—who had been put on duty at the Baillie Guard—was chatting with a young lady, the daughter of Colonel Alford, who had arrived in Lucknow from England on the very day the native regiments had mutinied. Miss Alford was convinced that the enemy would break in before long. She even went so far as to prophesy an assault on the Baillie Guard gate that very night. Metcalfe told her that they would have to attack while he was on guard, because the moon would have risen by the time he was relieved and no attempt would be made in moonlight. He went on duty that evening accompanied as usual by the faithful Bustle.

Sitting down on an empty packing case with his musket between his knees, Metcalfe was thinking of his conversation with Miss Alford when Bustle, in his usual way, took hold of Metcalfe's trouser leg and pulled. His master peered through the loophole and saw one of the enemy approaching the gate carrying a large bundle of tarred wood. Metcalfe then noticed that another man had already laid a similar bundle against the gate. Quickly, he aimed and brought down one of the men. The other, however, made off before he could reload.

Next morning the lookouts reported a great deal of activity in the enemy lines. Guns and waggons could be seen moving along the roads, as well as troops of cavalry escorting what appeared to be important people riding on elephants. Up river, to the north near the bridge of boats, large bodies of men with their colours flying could be seen. The garrison was called to arms at ten o'clock. Half an hour later, the enemy fired a shell which fell in the Begum Kothi. At almost the same moment, a mine was exploded on the south face of the defences, near the Brigade Mess. The outer palisade was blown down for about sixty feet, the verandah of the Martinière post was partly destroyed, and there was a large hole in one of the main walls. This opened, fortunately, on to an empty room, but the door into the next room was blown open. Mr Schilling, who was sitting there with some of the sick boys, hastily slammed the door, and a barricade was erected.

Brigadier Inglis had made his way immediately to the scene of the explosion. As he passed his wife's quarters, he called her to take the children and Mrs Case and her sister into a large store-room at the other side of the courtyard from their room. A number of other women had rushed in to Mrs Inglis with their children when the explosion occurred, and they all crowded into the store-room which, having no windows, was thought to be comparatively safe.

A second mine was exploded at Sago's post, blowing up two men of the 32nd. One of them was hurled into the road outside the defences, but kept hold of his musket and managed to scramble back over the wall without any more injury than a few bruises, despite the shots that were falling all around him. The other man was also unhurt.

The enemy pressed very hard at this point, and Metcalfe was told to go for help to Captain McCabe, who commanded at the Post Office. When he got there, McCabe said: 'Well, Metcalfe, what's the matter at Sago's?' Metcalfe told him, but McCabe replied: 'I can't afford you any help from my post. We are as badly off as yourselves. Go back and tell your officer he must keep the post at every risk.'[9] Then he changed his mind and said he would go himself.

Captain McCabe had risen from the ranks, having been commissioned from sergeant for conspicuous gallantry during the Sikh wars in 1846. He was well liked by everyone, and his presence was generally considered by the men to be a substantial reinforcement in itself. As McCabe and Metcalfe rushed towards Sago's they came across one of the Eurasian volunteers down on his knees, praying. When McCabe saw this, he gave the man a hearty cuff on the ear, knocking him over.

'What do you mean, you damned swab?' he shouted. 'Now is no time for praying when the position is nearly in the hands of the rebels!'

When the two men arrived at Sago's post, the enemy was still pressing hard. McCabe began shouting loudly, as if reinforcements were arriving, and Metcalfe followed his example.

'Number One will advance,' bellowed McCabe. 'Number Two support, Number Three into reserve. Charge!'[10]

The enemy, fearing a sortie, immediately retired.

The mutineers continued to advance at a number of posts, bringing with them scaling ladders, but all were driven back. The garrison was again fortunate in having a large number of muskets, ready loaded, so that when one was discharged another loaded one could be taken up instantly. This meant that as long as the loader maintained the pace, an almost continuous fire could be kept up. It was necessary, for the enemy was constantly reforming and trying another part of the defences. At about five o'clock in the afternoon there was a sudden rush on the Financial post, and some of the enemy got past the outer defences. One of them even grabbed hold of the bayonet of one of the defenders through a loophole, and tried to pull it through. He was quickly shot.

After a lull, another assault was mounted at nine o'clock, but the defenders managed to throw it back on all sides. An hour later, the guns were quiet. Three Europeans and two Indians had been killed, and twelve men wounded. No one knew what the enemy losses were, but they were sure that they exceeded those on the day of the last assault. On the whole, it was generally agreed that, though an assault was very exhausting, it raised the spirits to know that such a small garrison in such a small area could hold out against many thousands of the enemy.

10
WILL HAVELOCK
NEVER COME?

IT WAS now six weeks since the siege had begun, and though the garrison had nothing but contempt for the besiegers, there was little confidence in the early arrival of a relieving force. If it did not come soon, the steady pounding of the area by the enemy's guns would have reduced to ruins the buildings that gave the garrison shelter. In fact, the posts on either side of the Cawnpore Battery, Anderson's house, and Deprat's, were not much more than a heap of stones. The Residency building itself, always a prime target for the enemy guns, was practically deserted. On the day following the second assault, after a number of shots had hit the building, most of the left wing collapsed, burying six men of the 32nd who were sleeping in one of the ground floor rooms. Digging under very heavy fire, the rescuers managed to clear the rubble away from the heads of two of the men. Each was given a large tot of brandy while the diggers continued their attempts to get them out. It took two hours, but they were brought out alive. The other four, buried under the main weight of the walls, could not be reached.

The same day, Major Anderson, the Chief Engineer whose work had done so much to protect the garrison, died of dysentery. Though ill from the beginning of the siege, he had tried to keep going as long as possible; at last he had been forced to hand over the active work to Captain Fulton and take to his bed. He had made his headquarters at the Post Office, and seemed always awake and ready to receive reports from the outposts at any time of the night. The news of his death, however, did not sadden everyone. A Eurasian named Schmidt was delighted. He had taken a dislike to Major Anderson who, one day, had seen him with a fatigue party at the Post Office and had asked him what he was

135

doing there when he should be at his post, as an attack was expected.

Schmidt had replied: 'Who the devil are you to put such a question?'

'I am an officer,' said Anderson.

'Damn officers,' retorted Schmidt. 'We have too many of them here that are not worth their salt, and who are fonder of bullying civilians than fighting insurgents.'[1]

Anderson called two men of the 32nd and had Schmidt put under arrest, although he ordered his release next day. But Schmidt was neither grateful nor intimidated. He declared he would not fight for 'these bullies', and went around the other Eurasians trying to stir up trouble. No one took any notice of him. Calling all civilians 'a parcel of cowards', he went up to his commanding officer, Captain Boileau, threw his musket at the officer's feet, and swore he would never pick it up again. Schmidt begged that he be given a horse, so that he could go and join the enemy if they would have him. He then broke his sword, turned, and walked away.

Captain Boileau ordered him to stop. As such insolence could not be allowed to go unpunished, he was sentenced to be put in irons and received twenty-seven lashes from the whip of the provost sergeant.

When Schmidt was stripped for the whipping, he said to the officer attending: 'Remember, Sir, I am a British subject and a European!'

'Are you, indeed?' said the officer, pretending surprise. 'Well, judging from your face I did not think so, but now that I see your body, I am of the opinion that you are.' Then, just as Schmidt was thinking that he might be allowed off, the officer added: 'However, lay on, my lads.'

Schmidt went to hospital, had his back dressed, and when it had healed returned to his post as if nothing had happened. But he seemed to retain an unreasonable hatred for Major Anderson, who had had nothing at all to do with his punishment. On the day of Anderson's death, Schmidt suddenly cried to the men near him: 'Boys, I have some capital news to give you. Will you cheer if I tell you?'

'Yes, yes, of course,' was the reply.

'Well, then, Major Anderson is dead this afternoon!'

Everyone cried out 'Shame!', and Rees, who was present, only just managed to suppress an inclination to knock the man down. Soon, Rees began to think that a 'higher power' had taken over instead. From the day of Anderson's death, Schmidt became mysteriously ill and seemed simply to be fading away.[2]

The routine went on. The enemy's miners were heard at work opposite Sago's post, and a sortie to blow up the mine was unsuccessful, the party only just managing to regain the defence lines without loss. There was nothing for it but to hurry along the construction of a counter-mine. At the Cawnpore Battery, it was not the threat of a mine that caused concern, but the heaviness of the enemy gunfire. It had become so intense and accurate that the garrison could not serve the guns, and the battery had to be abandoned except for one lone sentry. The guns were left where they were in case the enemy should witness the withdrawal and mount an attack. But on the evening of the 11th a party was able to bring out for repair a nine-pounder which had been damaged by the enemy's shot and men were able to work on the shattered defences.

All that night, the work on the counter-mine at Sago's post continued. The enemy was well aware of what was going on and tried to stop the work by hurling missiles over the wall. The mutineers approached so close that they could even attempt to set fire to some of the outhouses by fixing tallow on the end of long bamboo canes. But the sentries slashed off the ends as soon as they appeared. Next morning, the men in the counter-mine could hear the picks of the enemy. A charge was quickly positioned, and at ten o'clock the warning was passed to neighbouring posts that it was about to be exploded. One of the officers with the engineers tossed a brick bat at the house hiding the enemy shaft, to discover whether the miners were still there, and received a shower of stones in return. The charge was immediately fired, and a great mass of earth and rock shot into the air. When it had settled, the garrison could hear the groans of the enemy miners buried in the debris. They raised a loud cheer, and despite answering musketry fire were able to pick off the enemy survivors as they emerged dazedly from the house.

On quieter nights, the enemy could be heard talking, especially if they had been roused from sleep, perhaps by the mob of dogs which used to collect around the defences and make a terrible noise. At Anderson's post the mutineers' conversation could be heard distinctly.

One would say: 'Don't you see they are coming? Look out.'

Another would reply: 'Who are you to give me orders?'

'Do as you like,' responded the first, rather mildly. 'The white sahibs will soon come and cut your head off.'

137

'Do you think they are likely to spare you more than me?'

So the argument would go on.

'Come, if you are going to threaten me, I shall run off to the hills!'

'Do you think you'll be safer in the hills than anywhere else?'[3] The listeners used to find it all quite entertaining.

The women and children had little to divert their minds. Mrs Inglis, at least, knew what was happening, for at breakfast every day her husband would give her and her companions the latest news. Not that there was very much. Some twenty letters had been sent out with various messengers, all in the hope of reaching Havelock and, above all, returning with a reply.

Someone found a few potatoes lying in a corner, and Mrs Inglis had them served for dinner, as a special treat. It had been more than a month since they had eaten any. Mrs Inglis's household, in fact, ate fairly well, though the diet was monotonous. They still had their servants and their goats, even though three of the latter had been taken by the commissariat butcher for meat. But there was nothing to spare—or, at least, nothing that was going to be spared—for others, however unfortunate.

One day a woman with a little baby in her arms came up to the door of Mrs Inglis's room and asked if she were 'the brigadier's lady'. She had a very touching story to tell. Her husband had been an overseer of works before the siege, and had recently died after being shot in the lung. The shock had dried up the mother's milk and there was no other milk to be found. Three of the woman's children had already died, and she was so frightened that she would lose the baby, now all that remained of what had once been a happy and loving family, that she had come to beg some of the goats' milk from Mrs Inglis. It upset Mrs Inglis to have to refuse her.

Mrs Bartrum had been able to move from her room at the Begum Kothi to Mrs Ommanney's house. At the end of the first week in August there were only three left of the original inhabitants of her old room, and she felt that if she did not get away from it she would go out of her mind. Bobbie was getting stronger again every day, but the food available was not the most nourishing for a sick child, though one woman at Mrs Ommanney's house was able to give her a little milk every day. Katherine shared part of a room with a young woman who had just lost her only child and was still grief-stricken. Fortunately, she was still able to cook, and was quite good at it. Katherine was not. It was her task to go out as soon as it was light in the morning and collect wood for the fire. This was getting scarce, and was often too wet to light. A soldier of the 32nd one day broke down some railings for her. But although fuel was no longer short, Katherine's problem was chopping the railings up into sticks; she had no tool other than a kitchen knife.

Katherine's hands, too, were covered with boils, which seemed to get worse as the siege went on. Dr Darby, who came to lance them for her, told her that she must not work with her hands. But Katherine had no time to be idle. She filled her day by helping with the cooking and washing, fanning the flies and mosquitoes from her child's face, and talking to him about his father. She could never stop thinking of her husband. Was he alive? Was he coming with the relieving force? Was there ever going to *be* a relieving force? Had people in England forgotten them, were they leaving them to die?

On August 14 a report came in that Havelock was still dug in at Unao, awaiting more men before attempting to take the road to Lucknow once again. No one knew what to believe. Next day there was even more confusing and dispiriting news. At about nine o'clock in the evening, Angad arrived back. He brought with him a letter from Colonel Fraser Tytler, addressed to Martin Gubbins.

'Dear Sir,

We march tomorrow morning for Lucknow, having been reinforced, and we shall push on as speedily as possible. We hope to reach you in four days at furthest. You must aid us in every way, even by cutting your way out, if we cannot force our way in. We have only a small force.

B. Fraser Tytler, Lieut-Colonel.

Mangalwar, August 4.'[4]

The letter was thus more than ten days old, and Angad reported verbally that he had been detained by mutineers after leaving Havelock's lines with it. On being released, he had returned to Mangalwar to see if there was a later letter from Fraser Tytler—but found that Havelock's force had gone. Angad learned that, after inflicting another defeat on the mutineers at Bashiratganj, Havelock had found his communications in danger of being cut by another force of mutineers, and had therefore re-crossed the Ganges and fallen back on Cawnpore. There was, however, at

10 *The breach in the Sikh Square*

least some good news. According to Angad, reinforcements were actually on the way up country to Havelock and should arrive about August 20. As soon as they arrived, Havelock would undoubtedly set out again for Lucknow.

Perhaps the most disturbing part of the news was the discovery that Fraser Tytler, and presumably General Havelock, had obviously no idea of the situation inside the Residency. A sadly depleted force, with many wounded and sick, as well as women and children, could not possibly cut its way out. Havelock's Intelligence must be virtually non-existent if he was not aware of the large numbers of enemy troops in the city of Lucknow itself. Any break-out would mean hand-to-hand fighting in narrow streets, and the reasonable certainty of defeat.

At a meeting at which Gubbins was present, it was decided that an accurate statement of the position, both inside the defences and in the city, must reach Havelock before he made an attempt at relief. Inglis drafted a letter for Angad to take out. It was directed personally to the General, and written—as the other had been—in Greek characters.

'My dear General,

A note from Colonel Tytler to Mr Gubbins reached us last night, dated Mangalwar, the 4th inst., the latter paragraph of which is as follows: "You must aid us in every way, even by cutting your way out, if we cannot force our way in". It has caused me much uneasiness, as it is quite impossible that with my weak and shattered force I can leave my defences. You must bear in mind how I am hampered, that I have upwards of 120 sick and wounded, and at least 220 women, and about 250 children, and no carriage of any description, besides sacrificing 23 lacs, 230,000 rupees, and 20 guns of sorts. In consequence of the news received, I shall soon put the force on half-rations, unless I hear again from you. Our provisions will last till about September 10. If you hope to save this force, no time must be lost in pushing forward. We are daily being attacked by the enemy, who are within a few yards of our defences. Their mines have already weakened our post, and I have reason to believe they are carrying on others. Their eighteen-pounders are within 150 yards of some of our batteries, and from their position and our inability to form working parties, we cannot reply to them, and consequently the damage done hourly is very great. My strength now in Europeans is 350, and about 300 natives. Our men are dreadfully harassed, and owing to part of the Residency house having been brought down by round shot, many are without shelter. Our native force, having been informed, on Colonel Tytler's authority, of your near approach some twenty-five days ago, are naturally losing confidence; and if they leave us I do not see how the defences are to be manned. Did you receive a letter and plan from me from the man Angad? Kindly answer this question.

Yours,
J. Inglis, Brigadier.

To Brigadier-General Havelock
Commanding relieving force.'[5]

The letter stated the position with reasonable accuracy, except in the crucial matter of provisions. To suggest that the defenders could only hold out until September 10, and then only by going immediately on half rations, seemed to Gubbins unnecessarily pessimistic—an estimate which might mislead Havelock into attempting a relief without sufficient force. Inglis, however, would not alter the letter, and alleged that the rest of his staff agreed with this view. That night, Angad went out with the letter unchanged.

Gubbins, in fact, had put his finger on an important failure of efficiency. Despite Sir Henry Lawrence's instructions to keep a proper and accurate control over the food supplies, no one on the staff actually knew what the precise situation was. No attempt had been made to produce a summary of the provisions stored in various parts of the Residency area. The officers in charge of the commissariat were aware that large stocks existed. In fact, the Deputy Commissioner of Lucknow, Simon Martin, had been ordered by Lawrence to lay in sufficient supplies to sustain 3,000 people for six months—and he had carried out his instructions. Nobody on the staff, however, asked for figures, and he did not volunteer them. Neither did Lieutenant Keir, who had taken over the grain store from the commissariat officer, Lieutenant James. Before the siege, both the civil and military authorities had brought in supplies, and such was the petty bureaucratic relationship between the two that neither enquired from the other what was going on.

The real problem was not shortage of food, but lack of variety, insanitary conditions, and constant tension. None of the senior officers had ever been besieged before, and they therefore knew nothing of the problems and were totally unprepared when faced by them. There *was* one man in the garrison who had gone through the experience before. This was Dr Brydon, who, fifteen years earlier, had not only been the sole survivor of a force which had

143

retreated from Kabul in Afghanistan, but had also survived the siege of Jalalabad by the Afghans. No one seems to have asked his opinion or advice, even before he was severely wounded in the last week of July. The staff did not even take its own advice, for though Inglis had said in his letter to Havelock on August 16 that he would reduce rations, he waited a further nine days before doing so.

On August 25 the rations of *dal* and meat were cut, the men's by a quarter and the women's by a half. The men were to have twelve ounces of meat a day, the women six, and the children from six to two ounces according to age.

In the meantime, the shelling, mining and counter-mining went on. There was some resentment at the virtual abandonment of the Cawnpore Battery, at least for all practical purposes, as the guns were not fired. In order to inspire confidence, the Brigadier slept one night in the battery. There still remained the constant menace of the sharpshooters on the roof of Johannes' house. The killing of Bob the Nailer had done nothing to lessen the effectiveness of the enemy marksmen. The only final solution to the problem would be to blow up the building. Lieutenant Innes of the Engineers was instructed to draw up the necessary plans.

From sightings made from the roof of the Martinière house, Innes was able to calculate the size of Johannes' house, so that a suitable amount of powder could be estimated as well as the distance it would be necessary to tunnel. The house was fifty feet long and forty feet away from the Martinière wall. It was decided that the shaft for the mine should be dug down from a line of former shops next door to the Martinière and only thirty-four feet from Johannes' house. Innes planned a mine driven out from the shaft for fifty feet, which would bring the end sixteen feet under the house. Branches dug right and left for twelve feet would be filled with gunpowder. That should be sufficient, it was decided, to bring down the whole structure. The plans were approved and work began on August 17. So that secrecy could be preserved, only men of the 32nd were used as diggers, and to prevent a premature collapse parts of the tunnel were lined.

The enemy had not been idle either. Noises had been heard by the defenders near the Sikh Square. A counter-mine had been started. In this case, Sikhs were used as diggers and paid two rupees for each night's work. Soon, mine and counter-mine were nearing each other. Lieutenant Hutchinson laid his charge and was tamping it in when there was a burst of firing overhead. Rushing from the gallery with the Sikh diggers, Hutchinson

144

heard the enemy's own charge of powder go up. Fortunately, it had not been properly laid and most of the discharge went back into the enemy's diggings.

Captain Orr, who commanded at the Sikh Square, was sure that this was not the only mine the enemy had dug. The engineers assured him that the noises he could hear were not hostile miners, but the trampling of horses tied up nearby. The explanation, which seemed not unreasonable, was accepted, but between five and six on the following morning, August 18, as Captain Orr, his second-in-command, Lieutenant Mecham, and two sentries, were standing on the roof of a building at one of the outside corners of the square, there was an immense explosion. Mecham, Orr, and one of the sentries were blown backwards into the square and suffered only a few bruises. The other sentry, Band Sergeant Curtain, was hurled into the road and immediately set upon by the enemy, who cut off his head.

The explosion was so powerful that it brought down the house. Trapped in the ruins were six Eurasian drummers and a sepoy. There was also a great breach in the defences. The garrison withdrew behind a wall, leaving a gap about thirty feet long completely undefended except for musketry fire from the roof of the Brigade Mess, and their own from behind the wall. When the dust had settled, the enemy, seeing the defences unmanned, swarmed across the road towards the breach. But there was some hesitation about entering the Sikh Square, especially after one of their leaders was brought down by a shot from the Brigade Mess. Another man took his place, waving his sword and calling for an advance. He, too, was shot, and his men remained near the ruins of the house but would move no further.

By now, the whole of the garrison had been called to arms. Brigadier Inglis arrived on the scene with the reserve, now down to eighteen men. The enemy's fire was heavy, though there was no sign of a major attempt to advance through the breach. The reserve erected cover from planks, boxes and doors, and then opened fire while a couple of nine-pounder guns were brought up and a hole made in the wall of the square for them to fire through. These and a twenty-four pound howitzer were brought to bear on the breach.

From the back of the square, some of the drummers caught in the collapse of the house could be seen trying to crawl free. The enemy firing was too strong for any of their comrades to go to their aid, though a volunteer did make his way under covering fire, returning with the news that at least one man was still alive.

145

He was caught under a beam, and the volunteer thought he might be cut free with a saw. A saw was brought, and the same man set out again, only to be driven back, leaving the saw behind.

The situation was stalemate. The enemy moved no further into the breach, but kept up a heavy fire. The guns, alone, did not seem capable of dislodging them. The men of the garrison remained discreetly behind the inner wall of the Sikh Square. In the afternoon, Inglis decided that things could no longer be left as they were. Night would soon be coming down, and it would be virtually impossible to retake the breach. Some heavy half-doors were therefore brought to act as bullet-proof shields. Holding these in front of them, Inglis, his secretary Mr Couper, and another civilian, and three officers, made their way down one side of the square while several European soldiers moved quickly down the other. Reaching the breach, each man laid down his door so that it overlapped the next one, thus erecting a barricade behind which the rest of the garrison could move forward. No survivors could be found in the ruins, and the bodies were incorporated into the new defences which were built up during the night with earth and sandbags.

Seeing that the enemy had withdrawn from the breach, Inglis decided to make a sortie. With a party of the 32nd led by Captain McCabe, he made for the nearest house across the road. There he came face to face with an enemy sentry brandishing a large sword. Inglis's pistol misfired and McCabe hurled a hand grenade, but the sentry fled before it exploded. Behind the advance party came Captain Fulton with two barrels of gunpowder. A few moments later, the house was blown up.

The next day, further sorties were made, blowing up more of the smaller houses. Gubbins found the planks and beams dislodged by the explosions very useful for repairing defences, and some of the Indians at his post would wait for Captain Fulton to set off his charge and then run out and quickly salvage what they could, under the protection of the clouds of dust.

Inglis considered that day the most dangerous the garrison had had to face. The breach had been very large. It showed what enemy mines could do. That night he sent out with a messenger a copy of his last letter to General Havelock, adding a postscript. 'Since the above was written, the enemy have sprung another mine which has given us a great deal of trouble and caused some loss. I trust that you will lose no time in coming to our assistance regardless of the statements contained in any letters which may reach you from Mr Gubbins. Military men are unanimous regarding our case.'

Next day, the demolition parties were out again. The men were getting very proficient at their job. If there was a door to be knocked down, a bayonet with a sack of powder on the end was driven into the wood, a short fuse was lit, and the door blown in. An open door would have a grenade thrown through it, just in case any of the enemy were inside. The advance party cleared the house of the enemy. Then came one of the engineers, more often than not the ubiquitous Captain Fulton followed inevitably by a Sikh named Hukum Singh, a huge man who carried a barrel of gunpowder without even noticing the weight. Fulton had become extremely expert. He could blow a wall *away* from the entrenchment, if it was so near that it might otherwise collapse on the defenders. He was always the last to leave the house, and the explosions always seemed to take place at the exact moment he crossed the palisade to safety.

In what was almost a separate world, the women and children, the sick and the wounded, spent day after day in ignorance of what was going on, fearing the worst but trying to be indifferent to it. Children died. Others lay sick and near to death. Mrs Dashwood, whose husband had been killed early in the siege, sat by the body of her dead son. Her other son was desperately ill with fever and dysentery, and she was expecting a third child. Next door to Mrs Inglis, a child died terribly of cholera; his mother, who had been frantic during the child's illness, became perfectly calm at the moment of death. She asked for a box to bury the child in, but Mrs Inglis had nothing large enough, and the child was sewn in a sheet and taken away to await the daily burial party.

On the 20th, the mine to Johannes' house was finished. While the men were carrying in the powder—four charges of one hundred pounds each—there was some excitement at the Baillie Guard. A party of the enemy managed to creep up to the gate and pile a large quantity of wood and straw against it, which they then set alight. The flames leapt up the gate, but Lieutenant Aitken forced it open and Indian water carriers were able to put the fire out before much damage had been done. Loopholes were then made in a wall overlooking the gate, and a sentry was posted.

The charging of the mine continued throughout the night. Just after dawn on the 21st, everything was ready. As soon as the explosion occurred, two parties were to make sorties, one to the left and the other to the right of Johannes' house. The enemy was quiet, but when the garrison opened fire they stood to, and could be seen in Johannes' house and the adjacent building, carrying lights and making a great deal of noise. As the day lightened, the long fuse was lit. To the waiting men it seemed an age before the explosion came, yet it was barely a minute. A single loud report —and the walls of Johannes' house collapsed inwards in a cloud of brickdust and mortar.

The detachments, twenty-five men of the 32nd in each, slipped quickly through the defences and made for their targets. Lieutenant Browne and his party went for the two guns which had been causing a great deal of damage, and found that, despite the explosion, one of the enemy gunners was still lying there asleep. Browne fired at him with his pistol, which did not strike, and the man ran off. The party found it impossible to spike the guns, however, as the touch holes were so large that even two spikes did not fill them. It was not long after Browne and his men got back to the Residency that the guns opened up once again.

The second party, under Captains Fulton and McCabe, was more successful. Its target was what had been Johannes' shop. When they reached the verandah they found all the doors securely bolted, but Captain Fulton, laying his back against one of them and his feet against the verandah wall, brought the whole door frame and door down with a crash. Inside, the floor was crisscrossed with trenches—filled with the enemy. Into one of these trenches, with pieces of the door flying around him, fell Captain Fulton. After him came McCabe and the rest of the party. The enemy rushed out of the building. Two barrels of gunpowder were then brought in by the triumphant detachment and put in place. The party was ordered out, Fulton prepared to light the fuse, and a few moments later Johannes' shop joined the ruins of Johannes' house.

In fact, it had been a very satisfactory day for the garrison. At last they had disposed of the snipers' post, and at a cost of only two killed and three wounded, though one of the latter died during the night. Lieutenant Innes, who had gone almost without sleep for sixty-four hours, without warning dropped into so heavy a sleep that he could not be roused for two days.

The enemy, as if shocked by the garrison's successes, fired only a stray shot or two that night. Brigadier Inglis took his wife and Mrs Case for a short walk, as far as Ommanney's house. Even the ruins and the smells could not diminish their pleasure in being released from their little courtyard for a while. But everything was shadowed by the question that was uppermost in everyone's thoughts. 'Will Havelock never come?' It was, by now, the fifty-second day of the siege.

148

11
AUCTIONS
AND ALARMS

ONE OF the most depressing types of event for the garrison in the Residency was the frequent public auction of the belongings of those who had died. But these auctions were necessary. It was the only way a man could get hold of a shirt or a pair of trousers to replace garments that were now in rags.

Considerable ingenuity had already been exercised. One officer took the cloth from the Residency billiard table and had a suit made up from it by one of the Indian tailors who had remained behind. Mrs Inglis thought he looked rather smart in his Lincoln green. Another had cleverly acquired part of the large sheet laid down on the Residency ballroom floor in those almost forgotten times when dances were held there. From this he had had a number of shirts made. But, generally speaking, a man could only replenish his wardrobe from another man's property. The prices often ran very high, reflecting the most pressing needs of the garrison. Three flannel shirts would go for £10.50, but a very elegant dress uniform once raised only £1.20.

Not everyone found the auctions of dead men's shirts and trousers a melancholy affair. Lieutenant Anderson was saddened occasionally by the mirth and jollity displayed by many of those who attended. How little, he moralised, did people reflect on the truth of the words: 'In the midst of life we are in death.' Those men joking about the fit of a dead officer's coat would probably be having their own effects sold at the next auction. Anderson found it difficult to understand how the surviving one of two men who had been the best of friends in life could actually bid for his dead friend's boots or for a coat soaked with his blood.

Other articles than clothes were auctioned. Sometimes there were even a few bottles of wine or some canned food. Bidding would run high on these occasions. When Sir Henry Lawrence's effects were auctioned in August, prices soared. As settlement was not expected until next payday, bidding was reckless. Few of those present expected to be alive when that day came round. Most things went for more than ten times their pre-siege price. Brandy fetched between £14 and £16 a dozen, beer from £6 to £7, and sherry £7 for the same quantity. The really high prices were given for foodstuffs. Two small tins of soup went for £5.50, tinned hams for from £7 to £7.50 each, and a quart bottle of honey for £4.50.

Most food, however, never saw public auction. A flourishing black market existed in flour, clarified butter (always rancid), sugar, Indian tobacco, and even pickles. Prices were not quite as high as those at auction, since the sellers demanded cash on delivery and no credit was ever given. Rees, who had run out of money, was forced to give up tobacco and do what the ordinary soldiers did, smoke tea leaves or those of the neem and the guava fruit trees. After a few days of this, Rees became so desperate for real tobacco that he sold his gold watch for 250 rupees, and, for as long as cigars were available for one rupee each, rationed himself to one a day. By the end of August the price had risen three times, and Rees was forced to reduce his smoking.

But there were quite a number of people who seemed to have stocks of what had become luxuries. People to whom, at the beginning of the siege, Rees had given all sorts of little luxuries from his own and M. Deprat's stores, afterwards refused him a handful of flour, a teaspoon of sugar, or a few leaves of tea. It was usually the well off who were most selfish, Rees found. A poor sergeant's wife or a common soldier would occasionally give him 'something that, though in the everyday course of one's life one would scarcely say a "thank you" for, is now prized above gold, pearls, diamonds, and rubies'—all of which were apparently now to be had for a 'few rupees, for a cigar, a glass of brandy, or a little tobacco'.[1]

There was still no firm news of the relieving force. Inglis continued to send letters out, but most never reached their destination. Inglis was particularly worried about the loyalty of the Indian soldiers. On August 25 he sent out yet another copy of his letter to Havelock of nine days earlier, with the addition of a second postscript in which he expressed his fears. 'We have . . . the most alarming reports of the disaffection and plots of our native troops inside, who are wavering in their fidelity owing to your return across the Ganges.'

There had, indeed, been more desertions, but every desertion relieved the Residency of a potentially dangerous inmate. The Sikh troopers were the most suspect. They were in communication with the city. Talking with other native soldiers within the entrenchment, they would say that Angad was lying and that there were no reinforcements on the way. They suggested that Angad never actually left the entrenchments at all, but was concealed by the Brigadier who then pretended that he had gone off carrying letters to General Havelock.

Gubbins and others, to offset these rumours, used to talk to the Indian soldiers on their posts about how British troops were hurrying to the rescue from Bombay, from China, from England. How the mutineers' supplies of ammunition would soon be exhausted. How *could* the rebel cause be successful?

Any man whose fidelity was doubtful was stationed at a post from which escape would be difficult. At night many of the defenders followed Gubbins's example and made their servants sleep under the eye of a European sentry. In order to add at least one incentive for staying, no pay had been given to the Indian soldiers and camp followers since the beginning of the siege. Some of the levies raised by Gubbins, however, had managed to acquire quite a large amount of cash. They had been working on bastions and in the mines, and had been paid as they finished their shifts. Gubbins decided that they must give the money into his keeping, and he would issue receipts. However, a number of the Indian soldiers had been asking for at least some of their pay, and it was thought unwise to refuse them. When the pay was issued, the pensioners and many of the soldiers refused to take it, saying they had no use for it. This was regarded by the authorities as a proof of loyalty.

Inglis was nevertheless upset by a report that had come to him through a Mr Phillips, who worked in the Military Secretary's office. He stated that he had been approached by an Indian who told him that a plot to take over the garrison was ripening. He gave details of the plan of attack. The Sikhs were to enter Gubbins's enclosure in twos and threes, ostensibly to ask him about pay. The Indian artillerymen, at a pre-arranged signal (which the informant did not disclose), would then turn their guns on the Europeans at the post. This was to be followed by a general rising which would coincide with an attack from outside. Asked for his views, Gubbins replied that he thought the whole affair highly improbable, especially as Mr Phillips refused to give the name of his informant. As a precaution, however, and as a sop to Inglis's fears, he agreed that the Sikhs should be ordered not to enter his enclosure. But he thought it would also be wise to insist that the name of Phillips's informant should be revealed and that the man should be closely interrogated. This was not done, though restrictions on the movements of the Sikhs were imposed.

This alarm coincided with the Muslim feast of Muharrum, always in Lucknow a time of considerable excitement, when the deaths of the martyrs Hassan and Husain, the grandsons of the prophet Muhammad, are commemorated. The city was loud with processions, and the garrison wondered whether the festival might be a prelude to another assault. It was necessary for everyone to remain particularly alert. However fatigued and depressed the garrison might be, the authorities felt there was no excuse for laxity. The Brigadier had already warned the post commanders to keep their men up to scratch.

'I have been instructed,' wrote Captain Wilson, 'to call your attention to the careless and indifferent manner in which the soldiers of H.M.'s 32nd Foot perform their duties when on sentry. On several occasions the Brigadier has spoken to the men himself, and this morning he found an important post without a sentry and on inquiry he was told that the man had gone to the rear. The Brigadier is fully sensible that the duties at present evolving on the men are fatiguing and harassing, but at a time when so much vigilance and alertness are required for the safety of the garrison it behoves every soldier to be most watchful, and therefore the Brigadier wishes you to speak personally on the subject to the men under your command.'[2]

Some sentries were more touchy than inattentive. Captain McCabe, making his round of inspection one day, came across a sentry who did not challenge him, having been told that McCabe was on his rounds.

'Are you the sentry?' demanded McCabe angrily.

'I am, sir,' was the reply.

'And why the devil didn't you challenge me?'

'Because I knew it was you, sir, and that you would be coming this way,' the sentry answered. This was too much for McCabe.

'You should have fired, sir,' he exclaimed. 'You are not supposed to know anyone outside of your post especially at night, sir.'

At this, the sentry—another Irishman—lost his temper.

'Then by Jesus Christ the next time you will come this way by night, I will accommodate you. I will shoot you, right enough!'[3]

McCabe went on his way and never troubled that particular

sentry again.

The enemy had begun to keep up a regular fire once more, and there were signs that new batteries were under construction. One of these was opposite Gubbins's post, about five or six hundred yards away from the outer defences. Inglis and his staff went down to look at it. The appearance of a larger number of men than usual on the wall must have attracted the eyes of the enemy gunners, and Inglis, seeing that they were about to fire, shouted 'Stoop!', and himself bent down. A roundshot came crashing through the parapet, covering Inglis with dust. He, however, jumped up again, and called out: 'All right!' But a sergeant of the 32nd shouted back: 'No, it's not all right, sir.'[4] An officer and one of Gubbins's servants had been killed. Inglis ordered the engineers to try and silence the new battery.

This was easier said than done, for the battery was a powerful one. Protected by a substantial wall, and firing through loop-holes cut in it, were a twenty-four-pounder and a twelve-pounder gun. This was not all. Another gun had also been placed in a position which could not be reached by the defenders. A nine-pounder had been hauled up on top of a house, the roof of which was on almost the same level as Gubbins's. The armament available at Gubbins's post consisted of a single nine-pounder, but under pressure Inglis agreed to let the defenders have a larger gun. This meant deepening the bastion and raising the parapet, all of which took time. Fortunately, one of the artillery officers came up with an idea.

Lieutenant Bonham had put together a weapon made from a mortar, with a wooden frame mounted on wheels. This rather primitive device was nicknamed 'The Ship'. Its elevation was controlled by driving in wedges, and it could be made to fire horizontally. The Ship was set up and Bonham, by a careful adjustment of his wedges, was able to score a number of direct hits on the wall protecting the major battery, bringing much of it down. Though the mortar could not fire a shell powerful enough to wreck the guns, it kept the gunners away from them while the new emplacement was being constructed in the Residency.

Naturally, the mortar could not be kept firing all the time, and the enemy were quick to take advantage of the lulls. They repaired the wall, and even succeeded in firing the guns while they were doing so. Gubbins's house suffered considerably, especially the upper storeys. Other enemy batteries also concentrated on this target. The heavy shot, weighing over twenty pounds, came right through the walls, and the upper rooms had to be abandoned.

153

The defenders usually picked up the shot so that it could be sent back from one of the Residency guns. But on one occasion they were unable to find it. Some days later, one of Gubbins's female servants was trying to move a small trunk in an upper room, but found it too heavy. When it was opened, the shot was found nestling on top of the contents.

The evacuation of the upper storeys of Gubbins's house caused some inconvenience to those who had been living there. A number of people had to be re-housed and found refuge in Ommanney's house and the Begum Kothi. Those who remained in the lower storey were rather crowded. The rooms occupied by the ladies were small and low-ceilinged, and the men either slept outside under the verandah, which was not very safe, or in the room in which the garrison took its meals. There was a number of desertions from the post, including that of a young Indian messenger who Gubbins believed would have gone out of his mind if he had remained.

It was still raining heavily, though the showers were not as frequent as before. The diggings would often be flooded by a sudden downpour, holding up the work for several hours. This was particularly worrying at the Brigade Mess, where a counter-mine was being driven out. On the 28th it was discovered that the enemy's tunnel had passed the head of the counter-mine. The direction of the defenders' gallery was changed, and Captain Fulton, who was down there digging by himself, suddenly broke through into the enemy mine. Luckily, there was no one there at the time, though a lantern and candle were still alight. Fulton called for powder, laid the charge up the enemy's own mine, and blew it up.

There were also, once again, sounds of mining at Sago's post, and a new counter-mine had to be begun.

But there was still no sign of relief. Only the children, perhaps, had adjusted to the new life—those, anyway, who were not sick. They played games. War games, naturally. An officer would over-hear one four-year-old say to another: 'You fire roundshot and I'll return shell from my battery.' Another child, angered by his playmate, was heard to shout: 'I hope you may be shot by the enemy!' Others, playing with grapeshot as in other times they would have played with marbles, would exclaim: 'That's clean through his lungs', or 'That wants more elevation!'[5]

At midnight on the 28th, Angad returned. He had taken so long because he had been unable to cross the Ganges opposite Cawn-pore, since the mutineers held the north bank of the river, and had to cross much higher up. This time, however, he had brought a letter from General Havelock himself.

'My dear Colonel,
   I have your letter of the 16th. I can only say, hold on, and do not negotiate, but rather perish sword in hand. Sir Colin Campbell, who came out at a day's notice to command, on the news arriving of General Anson's death, promises me fresh troops, and you will be my first care. The reinforcements may reach me in from twenty to twenty-five days, and I will prepare everything for a march on Lucknow.'[6]

When Mrs Inglis heard what Havelock had written, her first reaction was: 'All is over with us, we can't hold out till then.' But Inglis, despite his pessimistic forecasts about supplies, now seemed, at least to his wife, hopeful that the garrison could last out.

Angad's other news was partly reassuring and partly alarming. He reported that one of the most important rebel leaders, and the one alleged to have been responsible for the massacre of the women and children at Cawnpore, had been defeated by Havelock at Bithur, some fifteen miles from Cawnpore. The long-awaited reinforcements from Allahabad and Calcutta had at last reached Cawnpore, and preparations were going ahead for the drive towards Lucknow. It was also said that Delhi would be recaptured by the British in about three weeks' time, and this meant that more troops would become available. All this was good news. But Angad also said that the enemy outside the Residency was preparing another assault, this time with at least 11,000 men. The attack would take place in a few days, and the enemy was boasting that traitors within the Residency would help in it. Angad complained that it was easier to get through the enemy lines than it was to get through the outer defences of the Residency, and that he was always expecting to be shot by a British sentry.

The news from outside raised hopes among some, though the thought of at least another three weeks without relief was hardly reassuring. Others listened to the report that a new assault was planned, and were frightened. One, a Eurasian named Jones—a fair-skinned, European-looking man, very fond of brandy, and more so of opium—had left his wife and children in the city. This had not appeared to worry him much at first, and he had been appointed sergeant in charge of the outhouses near the racquet

155

11 *Listening for mining*

court. There he was in command of a number of Indian Christians who had once been employed as drummers in the band of the king of Oudh. After the report that the festival of Muharrum would be followed by an attack on the Residency, he decided to desert. On the 29th, after removing a barricade, he and ten of the drummers slipped out of the entrenchment, leaving the hole in the defences unguarded. The next night, a number of servants also deserted, one of them taking a double-barrelled rifle with him. It was thought that they had deserted only because of the shortage of opium.

On the last day of August, the enemy opened fire from a battery with a very heavy gun, a thirty-two pounder, the Residency gunners estimated. This was now in position near the old clock tower, and barely a hundred yards from the Baillie Guard gate. Several shots from this gun went right through the gate as well as the waggons with which it had been barricaded. To oppose this, the defenders also began on a new battery, between the Treasury and the Baillie Guard gate. It was dug by Indian soldiers under the supervision of engineers. In order to take an eighteen-pounder gun and a twenty-four-pound howitzer, a large hole had to be made. The area was found to contain a number of corpses, and these—putrid and decayed—had to be removed and reburied before the work could go on. The Indian soldiers, all of them high-caste Hindus, might reasonably have been expected to refuse to handle the bodies—but they did not.

That same morning, Mrs Dashwood unexpectedly gave birth to a son. Mrs Harris only just managed to get the doctor in time. He said he had never known such an expeditious affair. Mrs Dashwood's only other surviving child was still very ill and it was difficult to find anyone to help with the nursing. At last she found the widow of a sergeant in the 32nd who was willing to assist.

Mrs Inglis's children—with their goats' milk and the tender care of three women and servants—though not in the best of health were at least better off than most. Johnny always looked very well, with rosy cheeks that were much commented on. Mrs Inglis used to allow him to play with some of the Sikhs, who seemed to be very fond of him and gave him chupattees out of their meagre rations. Mrs Inglis encouraged the friendship in the hope that, if things came to the worst, it might be the means of saving Johnny's life. If, indeed, he survived other dangers. On the first day of September, there were five babies buried.

The Reverend Mr Harris had gone back to his burial duties at the graveside after the reproof from Inglis. With the number of casualties increasing, he even had to dig the graves himself. As he read the burial service, bullets would sweep across the burial ground and the sound of grapeshot would drown his words. One night, he arrived at the cemetery to find a private of the 32nd lying there with his head shattered by a roundshot. Mr Harris added him to the others, and went on with the service. Circumstances, he reflected, made all men a little callous.

As Mr Harris already knew all too well, it was becoming difficult to find men to carry out necessary fatigues. It was not only a question of digging graves, but of handling stores, repairing works, and digging mines. Sensibly, the authorities now decided to allot more of the exhausting tasks to the Indian troops, who seemed to be suffering less from the diet and conditions inside the Residency than the Europeans. Those conditions remained much the same. The flies were as thick as ever and the stench as nauseating. Among the men, tempers were frayed, and the women bickered among themselves. These arguments were usually over cooking or servants, and never came to much. If anything, they varied the monotony.

Mr Gubbins, despite all his preoccupations at his post, was still pestering Inglis about the appointment of Chief Commissioner and the prohibition on separate communication with General Havelock and the governor-general. On September 2, after complaining in writing to Inglis, he received a letter from Captain Wilson informing him that the Brigadier had shown to senior officers of the staff a letter which Gubbins had asked to have forwarded, in which he criticised Inglis's assessment of the situation in the Residency. The general opinion of the staff was that, if anything, Inglis had underrated the gravity of the situation. Mr Gubbins was—Wilson was sure—aware that his despatch 'was calculated to convey to General Havelock that there was no necessity whatever for his immediate advance'. Under such circumstances, Wilson went on, 'the Brigadier is of the opinion that both the General and the Government of India will agree that he was right in refusing to allow a despatch so calculated to mislead to be forwarded to that officer who has however been informed that you have been prohibited from corresponding with his camp'.[7] After this, Gubbins wasted no more time on penning complaints.

Gubbins's draft had been prepared in response to the letter from Havelock. He was not shown Inglis's actual reply, but he would certainly not have agreed with its generally pessimistic tone. The letter went off by runner after dark on September 1.

'My dear General,

Your letter of the 24th has duly reached me, in reply to mine of the 16th ultimo.

I regret your inability to advance at present to our relief; but in consequence of your letter I have reduced the rations, and with this arrangement, and our great diminution in numbers from casualties, I hope to be able to hold on from the 20th to the 21st instant. Some stores we have been out of for the last fifteen days, and many others will be expended before the same date. I must be frank, and tell you that my force is daily diminishing from the enemy's musketry fire, and our defences grow weaker daily. Should the enemy make any determined efforts to storm this place, I shall find it difficult to repulse them, owing to my paucity in numbers and the weak and harassed state of the force. Our loss, since the commencement of hostilities here, has been, in Europeans alone, upwards of 300. We are continually harassed in countermining the enemy, who have above twenty guns in position, many of them heavy ones.

Any advance of your force towards this place will act beneficially in our favour, and greatly inspirit the native part of my garrison, who hitherto have behaved like faithful and good soldiers.

If you can possibly give me any intimation of your intended advance, pray do so by letter. Give the bearer the pass-word "Agra", and ask him to give it to me in person, and oblige me by forwarding a copy of this to the Governor-General.'[8]

It was fairly obvious that Inglis had not consulted the engineers —or had not taken their advice. Captain Fulton, for example, was convinced that, with his system of counter-mine and listening posts, the enemy would never succeed in blowing a breach in the defences. Not that the enemy had given up. On September 2, they had mined to within thirty feet of the Financial post, but they were observed when the smoke from their lamps was blown upwards from a well-shaft. A counter-mine was driven quickly outwards, loaded, and fired while the enemy miners were still at their digging. On the north face of the defences, which had been fairly free from mining operations, it was difficult to listen for sounds of enemy digging from inside the defences. Lieutenant Birch who, though an infantry officer, was attached to the engineers, went out with some officers after dark to examine the area for traces of mining operations. The sentries had been warned that a party was out, but when the guard was changed one of the reliefs was not informed.

As Birch approached the entrenchment again, the sentry fired and Birch fell with a bullet in his stomach. As the others picked him up and tried to assure him that the wound was not fatal, Birch smiled sadly and said: 'I know it's all over with me.'[9] He died during the night, leaving a pregnant widow and a young brother and sister. His father, who had commanded the 41st Native Infantry at the outstation of Sitapur, had been murdered by one of his own men.

September had opened without rain, and though the sun was still very hot during the day the nights were distinctly cooler. The ground was drying up and the pools disappearing, when the rain began again. Despite Captain Fulton's beliefs, the enemy still continued mining, and there were fears of a general assault. At sunrise on September 5, the enemy could be seen moving in strength around the positions. The reports of the lookouts led to an estimate of at least 8,000 infantry and 500 cavalry. The garrison was called to arms.

The enemy opened up with an intense artillery barrage on all sides. At ten o'clock, two mines went off, one at Gubbins's post, where on the previous night a sentry had reported sounds of digging which neither Gubbins nor another officer was able to hear. The explosion was so powerful that it was thought that the new battery had been destroyed, but when the smoke and dust cleared, it became clear that the crater was some distance away. The enemy attacked the parapet with an immense scaling ladder, but were picked off with musket fire and helped on their way with hand grenades. The other mine was sprung at the Brigade Mess. This, too, was some distance from the defences. An attack here was also repulsed.

The heavy gun near the clock tower opened up, but the new battery for the eighteen-pounder and the howitzer had just been completed, and Lieutenant Aitken and his Indian soldiers scored a direct hit. The soldiers were delighted. 'We load it,' they said. 'Aitkeen sahib fires it.'[10]

After an hour or so, the assault petered out, though the guns kept up a steady fire from the nearby houses. The enemy could be seen for some time afterwards, transporting their wounded across the river. In the Residency, only three Indian soldiers had been killed and one European wounded. It was thought that most of the attackers had been mercenaries in the employ of some of the rajas and landowners who had joined the mutineers. This was taken as a sign that the trained sepoys had gone off to confront Havelock's force.

There were the usual hairsbreadth escapes, but none quite so fortunate as when a shot from an enemy eighteen-pounder

161

entered through one window of the hospital and travelled down a crowded ward before finally subsiding on to the floor. Only two men were hurt, very slightly.

But there were other deaths inside the Residency that day, and new lives. Mrs Couper gave birth to a boy—the smallest child, thought Mrs Case, that she had ever seen. And Captain Graham, confined to bed with a fever, picked up his pistol and shot himself in the head. He left a young widow who had given birth to a child only a few days before, having already lost one child during the siege.

Part 3

❦

THE FIRST
RELIEF

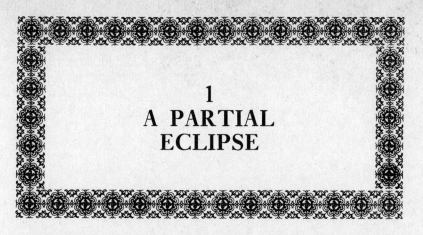

1
A PARTIAL
ECLIPSE

AFTER THE assault of September 5, the next two days were unusually quiet. There was no shelling, and very little musketry.
This seemed sinister to some of the garrison, for it was assumed
that if the enemy was not active around the defences then it
was up to some mischief elsewhere. But at least this meant a
respite for the defenders. At one post, the men were able to spend
their time reading, or composing satirical rhymes about the self-
ishness of their betters, and scratching caricatures on the wall.
A member of the garrison who considered himself something of a
poet wrote in pencil on the walls of the stairs a resounding poem
of praise for the defenders, and a threat to the enemy.

> 'All honor to those,
>   Who, encompassed by foes,
> Grew stronger in courage and might:
>   All honor to them,
>   Who, like brave Englishmen,
> Are ready, aye ready, to fight!
>
>   All hail to the dead,
>   Who by treachery fled
> From husbands, from parents, from friends.
>   There are brave hearts still here
>   Who your memory revere,
> And will trample the heads of the fiends!
>
>   You wretches without,
>   Who go sneaking about,
> A terror to none but the weak,

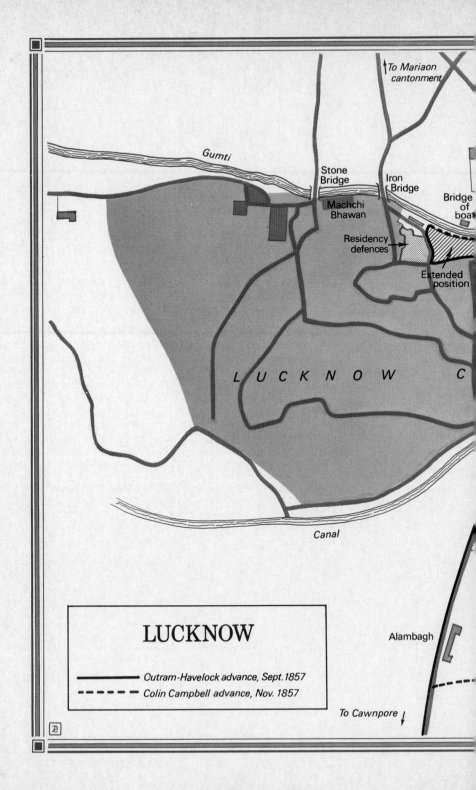

To Mariaon
cantonment

Gumti

Stone
Bridge

Iron
Bridge

Bridge
of
boa

Machchi
Bhawan

Residency
defences

Extended
position

L U C K N O W   C

Canal

LUCKNOW

——————— Outram-Havelock advance, Sept. 1857

– – – – – Colin Campbell advance, Nov. 1857

Alambagh

To Cawnpore ↓

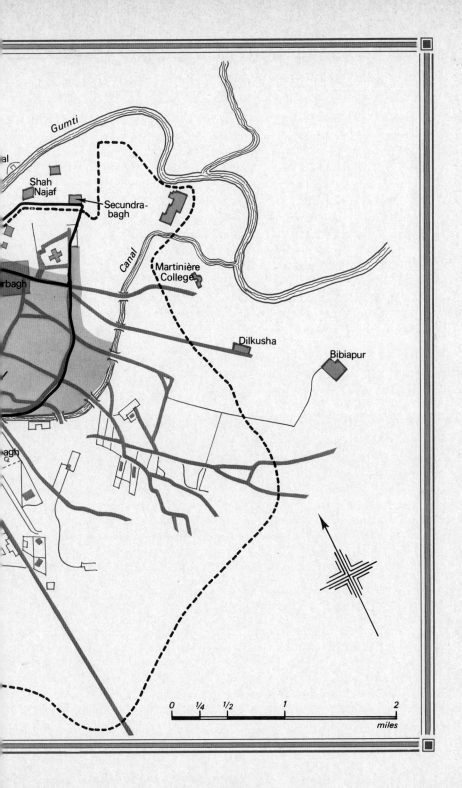

Gumti

al

Shah
Najaf

Secundra-
bagh

Canal

Martinière
College

bagh

Dilkusha

Bibiapur

bagh

agh

0   ¼   ½   1   2

miles

Beware of the wrath
Which your acts have brought forth—
'Tis the vengeance of Britons you seek!

Think not that your babes
Shall redden our blades,
Or their mothers have reason to care;
For an Englishman's pride—
It is known far and wide—
Is the innocent always to spare.

The aged he'll respect,
And the feeble protect,
And the simple he'll pass them with scorn;
But the vicious—ah! they
Shall remember the day
That an Englishman's vengeance was born.'[1]

But a lull also inspired carelessness. When the bullets and shot were whizzing about, every man kept his head down, but when they stopped caution was abandoned and it was easy for enemy marksmen to pick the defenders off. Mr Rees was convinced that the garrison lost more men on a quiet day than they did during an assault.

At the beginning of September, Rees had moved to Innes' post. There was greater honour in being attached to this exposed position, but there was also a room where a man could get some sleep. Rees had found it impossible to sleep at the guard post at the fodder stores, to which he had been assigned in August. The mosquitoes, the fleas, the stench from the slaughterhouse nearby, were bad enough, but the enemy was also constantly throwing incendiary shells at the area in the hope of setting fire to the fodder. Even if there was more fighting at Innes' post, on balance it was a better place to be.

Enemy silence usually meant that mining was in progress. Early in the afternoon of September 6, Captain Fulton led a party of Indian soldiers from Innes' post in an attempt to destroy a house which the enemy had occupied and was beginning to loophole. The house commanded the defences at Innes' post, and it was now decided that it must, somehow, be destroyed. Fulton and his men went down the side of the bastion on a scaling ladder and reached the house without incident. Two barrels of gunpowder were placed in position, and the order was given to retire. Fulton lit the fuse and ran for the ladder, which was only a few yards

168

away. But when he reached it he found that the soldiers had not mounted and were, instead, wasting time collecting wood. Instead of going up himself, he rounded up the sepoys and forced them up the ladder ahead of him. Before he had even put his foot on the first rung, the powder exploded, and he and one of the sepoys were buried under the debris. Fortunately, neither was seriously hurt, though Fulton's arm, which had been hit by a piece of beam, was severely bruised.

Next day, the enemy could be seen in large numbers moving about on both sides of the river. In the morning, an infantry regiment, with band playing and colours at the head, marched across the bridge of boats followed by at least a thousand matchlockmen of the rajas' forces. Otherwise, everything remained unnaturally quiet. But not for long. On September 8, the enemy guns opened a breach in the defences at the Martinière post nearly ten feet in width. No attempt was made at assault, and the garrison was able to fill in the gap. The defenders were very much on the alert again. The sound of picks near the Sikh Square and the Cawnpore Battery was heard. At the former, two new counter-mines were started, but at the Cawnpore Battery a counter-mine had been ready and waiting since early in August. This was duly exploded, blowing up the enemy mine and, as a bonus, bringing down the fronts of a number of houses on the far side of the road.

Poor Mr Rees, who had gone to Innes' post partly in search of a roof over his head, found part of his shelter removed. For two days an enemy eighteen-pounder had been battering at the house, and on September 11 succeeded in bringing down two of the sides. The enemy had now returned to its usual routine of harassing the garrison. In place of an all-out assault, it was a wise policy. A sudden burst of cannon and musket fire would be accompanied by loud and confused shouting, the braying of bugles, and the rattling of drums, as if a general attack was about to take place. The garrison, on these occasions, could do nothing but turn out, whatever the time and however unlikely a genuine attack might be.

All this further tired men already exhausted by the work on the counter-mines. Yet the real danger to the security of the garrison lay in the possibility that enemy mines might make a really practicable breach in a number of places simultaneously. Captain Fulton, in spite of his injured arm, was constantly directing new diggings and going out on demolition sorties. A shaft had been seen in the churchyard, which lay just outside the defences on the west face. The earth was open, and after the enemy had been driven off it was discovered that a gallery led from the shaft to the church wall. Fulton's arm was so tender he could scarcely move it, and a young corporal of the 32nd did the first reconnaissance. Inside the mine were found one sepoy's jacket, three pairs of shoes, and three baskets. Two barrels of powder brought down the roof of the mine and the walls of an adjacent building. 'It's a great thing,' wrote Captain Fulton in his journal that night, 'that we have no scarcity of powder and they are such cowards outside.'[2]

The enemy did not lack technical ingenuity. The baulks of wood fired from their funnels in the ground continued to land with their frightening whistling noise, and, in view of the general dilapidation of the buildings, were sometimes heavy enough to bring down a wall. Incendiary devices grew in sophistication, though not always in effectiveness. One day, a contraption made up of five iron tubes filled with some inflammable mixture and tied up in a canvas sheet landed on open ground. The cover burst open, and fire belched from the tubes.

There was still no more accurate news from outside. During the night of the 12th, a grasscutter with one of the native cavalry regiments came through the defences. He told Inglis that Havelock had crossed the Ganges with 4,000 men. He also alleged that many of the mutineers had left the city, not to attack Havelock's force, but to enjoy their loot in the quiet of their own villages. The besiegers now consisted mainly of the rajas' troops. The news seemed to raise Inglis's spirits, which in turn reassured Mrs Inglis, already desperately worried about her children who were ill despite all the precautions she had taken.

For Inglis, there always remained the nagging fear that his Indian soldiers would either mutiny or desert. The official optimism of their officers, as time went by began to sound hollow. During September it was decided that further precautions must be taken. If the sepoys deserted, the existing defence perimeter could not be held by Europeans alone. Efforts were made to complete a system of inner entrenchments which could be held by the diminished force if the worst came to the worst and the outer defences had to be abandoned. The problem was really one of morale. Nothing could be done if even the Europeans began to despair.

Lieutenant Innes found that the Indian officers at his own battery did not believe a relieving force was actually coming. Angad, they were sure, had invented the tale for money. Innes insisted that the letters were written in a hand that was known to the officers of the garrison, which could not possibly have been counterfeited by Angad, and this seemed to satisfy the Indians' doubts. A little later, recounting the story of the Indians' fears to a European, Innes was surprised to hear the man reply that he was inclined to agree with them. 'Havelock may come near,' he said, 'but how can he make his way against the large force hemming us in, through the streets or other routes which they are certainly barricading? Also, he will probably have other forces to tackle; we hear nothing of Delhi. Ten to one our small army there has been wiped out and the enemy may pour down an army from there onto Havelock's or any other British troops that may be keeping the field here.'[3]

About this time, Rees was distressed by the fate of his old friend, the merchant M. Deprat. Deprat had behaved with great courage and audacity throughout the siege. Sometimes he was foolhardy in a way 'that only a Frenchman or a madman would think of'. He would push his head over the defences and shout in broken Hindustani: 'Come on you cowardly sons of defiled mothers, are you afraid to advance? Are you men or women?'

One of the enemy would recognise him. 'Cursed dog of an infidel, I know you. You are Deprat the Frenchman, living near the iron bridge. We'll kill you yet',[4] and a hail of bullets would whistle past Deprat's ears.

Perhaps the mutineers had a particular hatred for Deprat. According to Rees he had been approached just before the siege by an emissary of one of the principal civilian leaders of the rebellion with an invitation to command Indian troops against the British. Deprat had rejected the offer and, because of his own imperfect Hindustani, had called upon Rees (who spoke it well) to make it quite clear to the emissary that he would have nothing at all to do with the rebels. This declaration he reinforced with the threat that, if the messenger were still around in half an hour, he would have him hanged.

Despite his audacity, Deprat had been convinced that he would survive the siege. 'I deny,' he said to Rees on one occasion, 'that there is a Providence. Just see the justice of your Providence. Here is a good man like Polehampton dead, and a rascal like myself still living, and likely to get out of it too. I am sure I shall not be killed.'[5] He was hit in the face shortly after, by a bullet which shattered the bones of the cheek.

Father Bernard, one of the Catholic priests in the Residency, apparently thought Deprat a heretic who did not deserve a Christian burial. He was persuaded to go to the graveyard, but did no more than mumble a few words in Latin and then leave.

171

Fortunately, Mr Harris was there, and the burial service he read for a dead Protestant officer was taken as intended for Deprat too.

Deprat's death was followed by that of the indefatigable Captain Fulton. For some time, Gubbins's post had been suffering severely from the enemy's guns. Inglis would not authorise the garrison's own guns to continue firing for any length of time because of the enemy's habit of picking up the roundshot and using it themselves. At Gubbins's post, an artillery officer was permitted to spend only two hours each day in the battery, during which he was to fire one shot every twenty minutes. When the allotted time was up, no more firing was allowed. Major Apthorp, who commanded the post, was constantly asking for a continuous cannonade, as this was the only way the enemy guns could be effectively silenced. Six shots a day, even from an eighteen-pounder, caused little damage unless there was a direct hit—and this was rare. The enemy, however, kept up their fire all day and succeeded in bringing down the earthworks defending the battery as well as in shattering the shutter which had been erected to defend the gunners against musket fire. This meant that the garrison had always to be repairing the defences, at great danger to themselves. At last Apthorp was given permission to carry on a continuous cannonade, and Lieutenant Alexander of the Artillery was sent down to supervise the gunners. On September 14 the cannonade was begun. After twenty shots, Alexander had succeeded in bringing down the walls of earth and stone around a twenty-four-pounder gun, which could be seen, its muzzle pointed in the air, abandoned by the enemy.

That afternoon, Captain Fulton dined with Gubbins and heard of the success of Alexander's cannonade. This, however, had put out of action only one of the batteries facing the post. When the meal was over, Fulton and some other officers went down to the battery to view the effect of Alexander's shots. From above the gun emplacement, which was always evacuated after a firing session was over, Fulton could see with the aid of his telescope that the enemy had returned to the damaged bastion and was trying to repair the walls. Calling to Alexander, Fulton set off towards the gun emplacement, presumably with the intention of firing a few more rounds, but as he approached the embrasure one of the guns in the remaining enemy battery opened up. A nine-pound shot struck Fulton—carrying away the back of his head, but leaving his face, like a mask, still on his neck.

Captain Fulton's death was regretted by all. After a period at the beginning of the siege when he had been convinced that there was no hope for the garrison, he had begun to radiate an absolute conviction that not only would Havelock's force arrive, but that it would find the defenders of the Residency still keeping out the enemy. Though he believed, without foundation, that the Brigadier had no very high opinion of him, he hoped that his work in defending the Residency would lead to promotion, which, as he had no private income, would mean a more comfortable life for his wife and children who were safe in Simla.

Nowhere was Fulton's death more mourned than at Gubbins's house. Gubbins himself felt somewhat responsible, for he had asked Fulton whether there was nothing he could do to knock out the second enemy battery. That battery still continued to pound at Gubbins's post. Musket fire still entered through the ever largening holes in the barricades inside Gubbins's house.

These barricades had been constructed out of wardrobes and other furniture, but also out of books, which had given good service to the defenders. Lardner's *Encyclopaedia* had stopped a musket ball within a hundred pages or so. An illustrated copy of the poems of Lord Byron, though totally destroyed in the process, stopped a cannonball dead. It was a pity, thought Gubbins, that every door and passage could not be protected by ponderous tomes. At least most of Gubbins's books were modern and replaceable. At Deprat's house, however, a priceless collection of oriental manuscripts, and dictionaries of 'every language spoken on earth, from the patois of Bretagne down to Cingalese, Malay and ancient Egyptian'[6] had been destroyed by musket fire.

Behind the defences, the strange life of the non-combatants went on. Soap became unobtainable, even for large sums. A piece about an inch square had been selling for nearly £1. There were still Indian washermen, but their charges were exorbitant and the washing was done without soap. Mrs Case's sister, Caroline, began to wash clothes herself, but the day she chose was so rainy and windy that they would not dry. Some of the ladies were horrified to find lice in their hair.

The weather was, however, improving, and by the middle of September the rains had stopped. This meant that the pools of water dried up and left a terrible smell, but Dr Fayrer said he had never seen such a healthy September in all his years in India. Certainly, though there were still cholera and smallpox, neither reached epidemic proportions. If they had, all would have been over for the garrison. The unbalanced diet was still affecting people's skins. The slightest bump would produce a large bruise, the result of blood flooding the tissue—a symptom of scurvy.

173

12 *The Residency Billiard Room*

Mrs Dashwood's children seemed to be thriving in spite of everything, and the Inglis children were well again. But not everyone was so lucky. Mrs Soppitt, wife of a lieutenant in the Oudh Infantry, whose baby had died of cholera early in July, wrote: 'Mrs Marriott nursing Katie, who is wasting away. Poor little orphan. At times when seeing children gradually fading away, I feel thankful that my poor boy was spared a slow death.'[7]

The drain on the garrison was beginning to make things difficult, especially for the gunners. There were now so few of them that only half the guns and mortars could be manned simultaneously. When any volume of fire was required, teams were forced to run from battery to battery. The rations, too, had been cut, though there was still bullock meat and plenty of wheat for chupattees. The beer and rum rations had been cut by half, and even the black market seemed to be drying up. Mrs Inglis managed to get some tea and coffee at twenty times the normal price. An occasional luxury still appeared. One lady recorded in her journal on September 15: 'Bought a bullock's heart at a fabulous price. Mrs Ogilvie, wife of a doctor who was a personal friend of Sir James Outram, gave me a sheep's head.'[8] At Dr Fayrer's, an unexpected treat consisted of a quarter of mutton and a suet pudding dripping with the contents of a bottle of patent sauce which had been saved by an officer of the garrison for just such an occasion.

And there was still no news from Havelock. On September 16, Inglis could wait no longer. He had been keeping Angad in the Residency in case it became necessary to send Havelock special information, but it was now absolutely essential for the garrison to know what was happening. Angad agreed to go out again for the usual fee of £500. A letter was prepared, partly written in Greek characters, and rolled tightly in a quill. Some of the ladies wondered where Angad concealed it, as he wore so few clothes. In fact, there was no absolutely safe place. If the enemy had his suspicions aroused, he might easily discover a letter hidden in a hollowed staff, in a nostril, or in the rectum. The greatest safety for Angad lay in an appearance of innocence.

At ten o'clock that night, Angad slipped out through the defences, carrying Inglis's letter. 'My dear General,' he had written:

'The last letter I received from you was dated the 24th ultimo, since when I have received no news whatever from your camp, or of your movements, but am now daily expecting to receive intelligence of your advance in this direction. Since the date of my last letter the

176

enemy has continued to persevere unceasingly in their efforts against this position, and the firing has never ceased night or day. They have about sixteen guns in position around us, many of them 18-pounders. On the 5th instant they made a very determined attack, after exploding two mines, and succeeded for a moment in almost getting into one of our batteries, but were eventually repulsed on all sides with heavy loss. Since the above date they have kept up a cannonade and musketry fire, occasionally throwing in a shell or two. My weekly losses continue very heavy both in officers and men. I shall be quite out of rum for the men in eight days, but we have been living on reduced rations, and I hope to be able to get on pretty well till about 1st proximo. If you have not relieved us by that time, we shall have no meat left, as I must keep some few bullocks to move my guns about the position. As it is I have had to kill almost all my gun bullocks, for my men could not perform the hard work without animal food. There is a report, though from a source I cannot implicitly rely on, that Man Singh has just arrived at Lucknow, having left part of his force outside the city. It is said that he is in our interests, and that he has taken the above step at the instigation of British authority. But I cannot say for certain whether such is the case, or whether he is really in Lucknow at all, as all I have to go upon is bazaar rumour. I am most anxious to hear from you of your advance, to enable me to reassure my native soldiers.'[9]

The arrival of the Raja Man Singh in Lucknow, if the report was true, could be regarded either as reassuring or frightening. He was one of the most powerful of the Oudh landowners, but he had not declared either for the mutineers or for the British, preferring, it seemed, to wait and see which way the rebellion was going. Sir Henry Lawrence had offered him large rewards if he would come to the aid of the British in Lucknow, but he had pleaded that he had neither enough followers nor sufficient guns to stand up against the mutineers. Now, however, it was rumoured that he had with him a substantial force. His appearance at Lucknow was therefore a source of both hope and anxiety for the garrison.

In the morning of the 18th there was a partial eclipse which lasted for almost three hours and almost entirely obscured the light of the sun. The enemy was particularly quiet during that time, as if he was afraid it was a bad omen. The Indians in the garrison maintained that it meant there was going to be a famine.

177

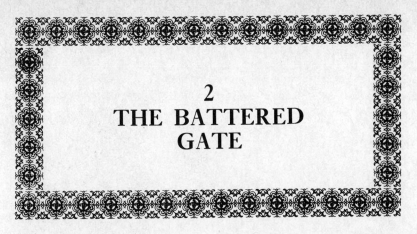

2
THE BATTERED
GATE

ON THE 21st, the rain returned once again, with such a high wind that Mr Rees was nearly blown off his feet as he stood sentry. It rained so heavily that it came through the ceiling of Mrs Inglis's quarters. The occupants moved the boxes and chairs from one part of the room to another, but soon the whole floor was so wet that it began to look like a lake.

The rain did not seem to hamper the enemy. Two new batteries were sited, one of them with a thirty-two-pounder which was so well fortified with huge wooden beams and a high earth parapet that even the 'Ship' mortar was unable to put it out of action. It was left to an eighteen-pounder gun sited at the Post Office to play such havoc with the parapet that the thirty-two-pounder was exposed, and marksmen at the Financial post were able to pick off two of the enemy gunners.

About eleven o'clock on the following night, under the protection of a shower of rain—which did not, however, prevent his being fired on by the enemy—Angad came rushing through the defences. This time he brought a letter, not from General Havelock, but from Sir James Outram.

'*To Colonel Inglis,*

North Side of the River,
September 20, 1857

The army crossed the river yesterday, and all the material being over now, marches towards you tomorrow, and under the blessing of God will now relieve you. The rebels, we hear, intend making one desperate assault on you as we approach the city, and will be on the watch in expectation of your weakening your garrison to make a diversion in our favour as we attack the city. I beg to warn you

179

against being enticed to venture far from your works. When you see us engaged in your vicinity, such diversion as you could make without in any way risking your position should only be attempted.

Yours sincerely,
J. Outram.'[1]

This was most heartening news, though Inglis did not tell the garrison that he now expected the relieving force to arrive in only a few days. Instead, he announced that the garrison was certain to be relieved within two weeks. This caused great excitement among both British and Indian soldiers. Mrs Inglis thought she could already hear the sound of the force's guns. Each boom seemed to say: 'We are coming to save you.'[2] Katherine Bartrum wondered whether it could really be true and, if it was, whether her husband would be with the force. Would they meet once more after all the weary months of separation?

Angad reported verbally that the besiegers now numbered about 15,000, and the relieving force was composed of 5,000 Europeans and 1,000 Sikhs. He also said that Delhi was still being held by the mutineers. As for Raja Man Singh—while Havelock had remained on the north side of the Ganges on the road to Lucknow, Man Singh had stayed in his own fort on his estate at Shahganj, recruiting and training men. When Havelock retired on Cawnpore, Man Singh had concluded that the British would never recover, and had therefore joined the mutineers. Angad carried a private letter for one of the officers of the garrison from a cousin serving with Havelock's force. This said that many reinforcements were coming from England and that, although there had been some trouble on the Bombay side, the whole of southern India was quiet.

Though the rain continued heavily during the night, it began to slacken about three o'clock in the morning, and by midday on the 23rd the clouds had blown away and the sun was shining brightly. The sound of gunfire could be heard distinctly, coming from the direction of Havelock's march. By early afternoon the firing was heavier and, without doubt, only a few miles away. The enemy was active in the city and on the other side of the river. Large bodies of men were moving along the roads, and many waggons passed, loaded with ammunition. At five in the afternoon there was a fresh sound of guns. The experts were convinced that they were no more than three miles from the Residency.

The garrison could hardly contain its excitement, though the officers were constantly making their rounds to see that there was

180

no lessening of alertness. Angad was so pleased that he went to the Sikh Square and danced around, snapping his fingers and demanding: 'Who is the liar now? Who has been inventing tales?'[3]

The night was unusually quiet, but the garrison found it difficult to sleep or rest. Next morning, enemy cavalry could be seen leaving the city, and at half past eight the guns opened up again in the distance. They sounded further away than the day before. The engineers, however, thought that they were at the Alambagh, a pleasure garden near the city. The Indian troops were not convinced. Even Angad was silent. Activity in the city was increasing, and it was obvious to the garrison that, whatever was happening to Havelock's force, the mutineers were preparing to block the streets, loophole the houses, and generally make any progress as dangerous and as deadly as possible.

At 8 p.m. the enemy suddenly opened fire on the Cawnpore Battery and gave every indication that an attack was imminent. There were further alarms during the night and the whole garrison was under arms until dawn. At daylight, the guns could be heard once again, and this time there was no doubt. They were drawing nearer. The defenders at Gubbins's post were listening intently when, without warning, a sepoy appeared over the top of the entrenchments, catching the sentry completely by surprise. When he raised his musket to fire, the sepoy stopped him by handing over a letter, which turned out to be an old one written by Outram before the force crossed the Ganges. The sepoy had been forced to take a more circuitous route than Angad, and his additional information about the relieving column amounted only to what the garrison already knew, that it had reached the suburbs of the city.

Brigadier Inglis immediately wrote a letter to Outram and sent the sepoy back with it. Angad had already told Inglis: 'Now I have got back three times, I will go no more, but live or die with you,'[4] and had not been pressed to take any more risks. In his letter, Inglis warned Outram that he could expect no real help from the garrison. Were a sortie to be attempted, 'I should run the greatest risk of losing my post. The enemy sepoys and matchlockmen with guns, some of large calibre, are now,' he went on, 'moving through the streets in your direction. I will shell them to the utmost. We can reach from 16 to 1,800 yards down the Cawnpore road on either side as you approach us, and are much on the alert.'[5]

At about half past eleven, the firing in the distance ceased. The lookouts in the Residency could see no sign of the advancing force, but it was obviously there, as crowds of civilians emerged from the city with bundles on their heads, making for the north over the bridges. Soon the civilian refugees—which is what the garrison took them to be—were joined by sepoys, matchlockmen, and troopers from the Irregular Cavalry. The crowds on the bridges became so thick and confused, the waggons, elephants and horses crushing together, that some of the cavalry could be seen urging their horses into the river. Convinced that the enemy was in flight, the defenders turned every available gun on the bridges. The guns on the Redan Battery scored a number of direct hits on the bridge of boats, which parted in the middle. The cries of those thrown into the river could be heard above the noise of the guns. But not for long. Not all the mutineers were in flight. The enemy guns opened such a heavy fire on the Residency that Gubbins thought it the worst cannonade the garrison had had to suffer. There was a perfect hurricane of shot and shell, and fragments were falling everywhere, even on places towards the centre of the area which had never been hit before.

The bombardment went on for nearly three hours, but early in the afternoon gunfire and musketry could be heard towards the east. Havelock was apparently making a wide detour in order to avoid fighting in the cramped and easily defended streets. Inglis had the mortars brought to bear in Havelock's general direction, so that they could lay down flanking fire. Still the lookouts on the Residency tower could see nothing..Despite the enemy fire, many of the garrison had gone up on to such roofs as remained, and all were straining ears and eyes for any sign of Havelock's men. The women and children had been told to keep under cover, but it was almost impossible for them to remain quiet. Strict orders had been given to the defenders that they were not to leave their proper posts. Mr Rees felt too excited to obey the command, and quietly stole off to the terrace of the Residency, where he hoped for a clearer view. He was unlucky, for he could see nothing but smoke and hear nothing but the crack of musketry.

It was nearly four o'clock before the anxious officers on lookout could discern European troops in the suburbs of the city. They could be seen moving along the south bank of the river near the Moti Mahal, a palace of the former king, about a mile away from the Residency perimeter. An hour later, the sound of musket fire could be heard in the streets. Now, Havelock's men were not visible, but the enemy were—standing on roofs and firing down into the streets below. Naturally, there was hideous anxiety within the Residency. Nothing could be done to help Havelock. A sortie was out of the question, and the guns could not be fired in case they should hit the relieving force.

A few minutes after five, the lookouts could clearly see men of the force making their way up the long street leading to the Baillie Guard gate. A body of Europeans and Sikhs, led by mounted officers, came at the head. The terrain was extremely difficult. The road itself was criss-crossed with enemy trenches which slowed the men down. The houses on either side were loopholed for muskets, and a hail of bullets was taking its toll. There was no stopping to pick up the wounded as the men ran forward, shouting and firing. They were greeted by a great roar of shouting and cheering from the Residency, from the men on the roofs, from every pit, trench and battery, from behind the sandbags piled in the shattered houses, even from the hospital, where many of the sick and wounded crawled out to add their feeble voices to the welcome.

The Baillie Guard gate, battered with roundshot and riddled with bullets, was heavily barricaded and backed with a bank of earth which took some time to remove. Generals Havelock and Outram, who were with the advance party, made their entrance through an embrasure at Aitken's battery, near the gate, and were soon followed by a stream of men—staff officers, soldiers of the 78th Highlanders, and Sikhs. Despite the rigours of the advance, the two generals seemed to Inglis's aide-de-camp to be almost immaculate, in their shooting coats and solar topees, while the garrison and its commander looked more like bandits than soldiers. Hurriedly, he despatched an orderly to fetch Inglis's sword. The Brigadier had not worn it since Chinhat.

Inglis's first words to Havelock were: 'We hardly expected you before tomorrow.' To which the general replied: 'When I saw your battered gate, I determined to be in before nightfall.'[6]

It was the eighty-seventh day of the siege.

3
GOOD NEWS
AND SAD

WHEN THE Baillie Guard gate was finally cleared and opened, the rest of the force, which had remained in the streets outside the Residency, came rushing in—tired and dirty but, to the garrison, looking excessively healthy.

General Outram made for Dr Fayrer's house, and soon the enclosure was full of soldiers, shaking hands with the ladies, lifting the children high in the air. There were tears in many of the soldiers' eyes. 'God bless you! We thought to have found you only bones!' The pipers of the 78th struck up a tune. When one of them learned that Mrs Anderson came from Edinburgh, he cried: 'So do I, and from the Castle Hill!'[1] The ladies produced water, and later, tea without milk or sugar, and the men distributed tots of rum which they had saved from their ration. Almost incredibly, the relief force had brought no supplies, though they had expected to find the situation inside the Residency considerably worse than it was.

That night, the garrison did its best to entertain its saviours. Believing that evacuation would now take place, they brought out carefully hoarded stocks of wine and food. The officers dining at the Brigade Mess were astonished at the quality of the meal they were offered. They had thought the garrison would be eating horses, even rats. General Havelock was given not only beef cutlets, but mock turtle soup and champagne.

Not all the garrison joined in the celebrations. Some had died at the moment of relief—among them, Schmidt, the man who had been so pleased at the death of Major Anderson and had then been struck by a mysterious disease. He had lingered on until the force reached the Residency. Rees found some satisfaction in his fate. 'To die neglected and unnoticed in the midst of rejoicing' seemed

185

apt. 'Many think, and think justly, that his death was a direct punishment of Heaven.'[2]

It was news the garrison wanted, news of the outside world, of happenings at Cawnpore and Delhi, of the fate of relatives and friends. To everyone's horror, Angad's story of the massacre at Cawnpore was confirmed in the most terrible detail. Lieutenant Delafosse of the 53rd Native Infantry described how, after General Wheeler's surrender, the little garrison with its sick and wounded had been allowed to march out, with their weapons, to the river, where a number of boats were waiting. The sick and the women had been carried in palanquins supplied by the rebel leader, and the children were carried in the arms of some of the mutineers who, only the day before, had been trying hard to kill them. But when everybody was on board the boats, the rebels had raked them with grapeshot and musket fire. A single boat had got away, with four survivors. One of them had been Lieutenant Delafosse.

The women and children who had been taken from the boats again with the other survivors had been allowed to live for a little while after the men had been shot. But when the rebels heard that Havelock was approaching, the women and children were butchered and their bodies thrown down a well.

For those of the Residency garrison who had still hoped that their relatives in Cawnpore might have survived, all pretence was over. Captain Evans, who commanded the battery at the Residency churchyard, had lost his wife and two children. Dr Darby, who had been so kind to Katherine Bartrum, learned that his wife had given birth to a baby in the shelter of a gun in Wheeler's entrenchment; wife and child had both been massacred. A young bandsman of the 32nd, named Symes, was told this his mother, stepfather, sister and brother had all been killed.

Every tale of torture—all of them based on hearsay—was believed. There were few in the garrison who did not approve of the revenge which had been taken on Indians, particularly by Brigadier-General Neill. At Cawnpore, Neill had discovered the room where the women and children had been kept. It was covered with bloodstains. He had immediately issued an order which was put into effect without delay. 'Every stain of innocent blood,' ran the order, 'shall be cleared up and wiped out previous to their execution, by such of the miscreants as may be hereafter apprehended, who took an active part in the mutiny, to be selected according to their rank, caste, and degree of guilt. Each miscreant ... will be taken down to the house in question ... and will be

186

forced into cleaning up a small portion of the blood stains; the task will be made as revolting to his feelings as possible, and the Provost-Marshal will use the lash in forcing anyone objecting to complete his task. After properly cleaning up his portion, the culprit is to be immediately hanged, and for this purpose a gallows will be erected, close at hand.'[3]

There was news, too, of happenings elsewhere. Two days before the relieving force had broken its way through into the city, Outram had heard that Delhi had fallen to the British. The Punjab, which had been a British possession for only nine years and was the homeland of that martial race, the Sikhs, was safe, thanks to the foresight and courage of John Lawrence, Sir Henry's brother. There had been a massacre at Jhansi, but the hill stations, including Simla, were quiet. Those anxious for more personal news from other parts of India and from home would have to wait a little while. A waggon loaded with letters and newspapers had been left at the Alambagh outside the city. Only a few personal letters had been brought in by the members of Havelock's force. Lieutenant Innes was one of the lucky ones. He was stopped by a private of the Highlanders and asked where might be found the officer named on a letter he had carried from Cawnpore; Innes discovered the letter was addressed to him.

Naturally, the garrison wanted to know what had happened in the city that day, and why the relieving force had not been able to come earlier. They heard how Havelock, after winning action after action against forces several times the size of his, had been compelled by casualties and disease to fall back on Cawnpore. With his effectives reduced to less than 1,000 men, he had had no alternative but to dig in at Cawnpore and wait for reinforcements to arrive. These had been delayed by a mutiny at Dinapur in Bihar, which had diverted the reinforcements since the mutiny threatened communications with Calcutta. Havelock had been further hampered by a lack of maps. All he had was a ten-year-old rough sketch of the road to Lucknow.

While Havelock lay at Cawnpore, he had learned that he had been superseded in command by Major-General Sir James Outram. Outram had arrived at Cawnpore on September 15, bringing some reinforcements with him. On his arrival he had performed what most people considered a rare and noble act of generosity. Outram had been appointed by the governor-general to both the supreme military and civil power—as Chief Commissioner of Oudh, and as officer commanding all troops in the area between Calcutta and Agra. At Cawnpore, Outram issued the following order:

'The important duty of relieving the garrison of Lucknow had been first entrusted to Brigadier-General Havelock, C.B., and Major-General Outram feels that it is due to that distinguished officer, and to the strenuous and noble exertions which he has already made to effect that object, that to him should accrue the honour of the achievement.

Major-General Outram is confident that this great end for which Brigadier-General Havelock and his brave troops have so long and gloriously fought will now, under the blessing of Providence, be accomplished.

The Major-General, therefore, in gratitude for, and admiration of, the brilliant deed of arms achieved by Brigadier-General Havelock, and his gallant troops, will cheerfully waive his rank in favour of that officer on this occasion, and will accompany the force to Lucknow in his civil capacity as Chief Commissioner of Oudh, tendering his military services to Brigadier-General Havelock as a volunteer.

On the relief of Lucknow, the Major-General will resume his position at the head of the force.'[4]

With Outram's arrival, Havelock's force had numbered just over 3,000 men, nearly four-fifths of whom were European infantrymen. On September 18th, the vanguard had crossed the Ganges and after a number of minor but brisk engagements had reached the outskirts of Lucknow five days later. At the Alambagh, about four miles south of the Residency, Havelock had found himself faced by about 10,000 of the enemy, with some 1,500 cavalry in support. A heavy artillery barrage and a quick advance had turned the enemy's flank and driven the main body into retreat. The problem then facing the force had been—which was the quickest and safest way to the Residency?

Three routes had been discussed. The first was directly along the Cawnpore road, from the Charbagh bridge over the canal south of the city, direct to the Baillie Guard gate. The second was to make a long detour to the north, approaching the Residency across the iron bridge. These two possibilities had been abandoned, the first because of the dangers of fighting through the narrow streets of the city, the second because the rain had softened the ground so much that the heavy guns could not have been moved across country. A third plan suggested by Outram had been adopted. This was to cross the Charbagh bridge, then to make for the group of palaces which lay to the east of the Residency. This would still mean some street fighting but, it had been thought, less than on the Cawnpore road.

On the morning of September 25, the force had been drawn up ready to move. The heavy baggage, the sick and the wounded, were to be left behind at the Alambagh. This was a large park surrounded by a high wall with turrets at various points along it. Inside the walls were a large palace and a number of smaller buildings. To defend the position there were some 300 men and six officers, with a few small guns. Havelock insisted on taking a battery of twenty-four-pounders with him.

The first brigade had hardly moved off when it met heavy enemy fire. 'The enemy,' Outram reported, 'had on that occasion flanked his road under cover of long high grass, and a murderous fire was poured on the column from a double-storeyed house, full of musketeers, and from the loop-holed walls of the large surrounding gardens, from two guns that raked the road from the right flank, and another that commanded the front.'[5] This was before the Charbagh bridge had been reached. Neill had ordered a cavalry charge to clear a way across the bridge, but a shower of grapeshot left only one man alive, Havelock's son, Harry. The main force rushed forward before the enemy gunners could reload, and secured the bridge. The way into the city had been closely fought. Outram had wanted to occupy one of the palaces and wait there for the rearguard to come up, but Havelock insisted on going forward. 'There is the street,' Havelock had said. 'We see the worst—we shall be slated, but we can push through and get it over.' Outram replied, angrily, as if he thought Havelock questioned his honour, 'Let us go on, then, in God's name.'[6] Leaving the rearguard behind, and with the two generals at its head, the force moved through the narrow streets, suffering heavily from enemy fire. Brigadier-General Neill was killed by a shot through the head. Havelock, however, was untouched, as was Outram, although he had earlier in the day been wounded in the arm. But the casualties were very heavy. A few moments after he had reached the Residency, a little girl saw tears running down Havelock's cheeks and asked her mother afterwards what he had been saying. Her mother told her that Havelock had been repeating over and over again the words: 'My brave soldiers! My brave soldiers!'[7]

Though the first column had made the Residency, the whole of the force did not enter the defences that night. A second column, led by Lieutenant Moorsom, who had been stationed in Lucknow before the Mutiny and knew the city, arrived a little after the first. Moorsom had taken a different direction and found the

13 *View from the Highlanders' Post*

streets heavy with enemy fire. When he and his men finally reached the Clock Tower, they found their way blocked by the enemy battery sited there. In the dusk, the enemy gunners' portfire could be seen distinctly, and the men were able to drop to the ground only seconds before a shower of shot was hurled over their heads. An officer led a party forward to take the gun before it could be reloaded, but when they reached the emplacement they found it abandoned. As the column moved forward in the direction of the Baillie Guard gate, the Highlanders suddenly saw dark faces in front of them. Taking them for the enemy, the Highlanders rushed forward with their bayonets. The men were actually a detail of sepoys who had been taken out by Lieutenant Aitken with picks and shovels to level the enemy battery. Three of the sepoys were wounded, and one was heard to cry out in Hindustani as he fell: 'Never mind, it was fated. Victory to the Baillie Guard.' Others, more sensibly, called for their officer. Aitken came running up, shouting: 'For God's sake, don't harm these poor fellows. They've saved all our lives.'[8] Fortunately, the Highlanders were stopped before anyone was actually killed. The survivors went on to level the battery, and to bring in the enemy gun and their own wounded. Aitken and another detachment remained behind to occupy a courtyard of the Tehri Koti, one of the nearby palaces, in order to give some cover to the remainder of the relieving force.

The moon had now risen, and though some scattered detachments continued to make their way to the Residency, others bivouacked in the streets and in the Tehri Koti. The rearguard, under the command of Colonel Campbell, with the heavy guns and the men who had been wounded during the day, remained behind in the Moti Mahal. During the night, the streets were empty and there was no sign of the enemy. Nevertheless, no attempt was made to bring the rearguard inside the defences.

This left some of the people of the garrison separated from relatives. As the men came in, wives and sisters and brothers anxiously scanned their faces and asked after loved ones. Katherine Bartrum, rushing out with the others, learned from the first officer she met that her husband *was* with the relieving force; they had shared a litter on the previous night. Picking Bobbie up in her arms, she ran down the road to the Baillie Guard, hoping to see Dr Bartrum among the men coming in there. After a while, she heard that he was with the heavy guns and would not come in until the following morning, with the rest of the rearguard. That night she could hardly sleep, her joy at the thought of seeing her husband safe after four months of separation was so great.

Others, too, found it difficult to rest. Mrs Inglis was kept awake by the Sikhs in the square next to her quarters. It seemed to her that this was more a time for solemn thankfulness than for revelry, but she felt that she could not grudge the poor men their enjoyment. 'They had suffered and fought well, long and nobly.'[9] Mr Rees joined in dancing a hornpipe with the Highlanders and learned of a new use for the bagpipes. While coming through past one of the palaces, a piper had lost his way and found himself confronted by one of the enemy cavalry, his sabre raised to cut the Highlander down. The piper's musket was empty. But 'a bright idea struck me,' he told Rees. 'All at once I seized my pipe, put it to my mouth and gave forth a shrill tone, which so startled the fellow that he bolted like a shot, evidently imagining it was some infernal machine. My pipe saved my life.'[10] Rees did not get to bed until after three in the morning.

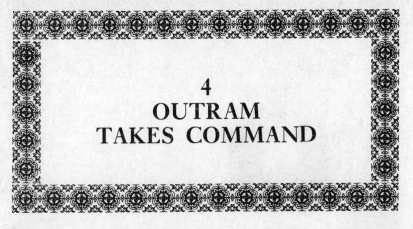

4
OUTRAM
TAKES COMMAND

ON THE morning of September 26, Outram took over the command both of the garrison and of the relieving force. Before he did so officially, he was observed by Dr Fayrer wandering around with his coat in his hand. He showed Fayrer two bullet holes in the sleeve, and asked him: 'Do you think Mrs Fayrer or one of the ladies could mend this for me?' Mrs Fayrer was delighted to help, and her husband found a uniform cap with a gold-banded peak which was almost the right size, which replaced the hat Outram had lost during the rush to the Baillie Guard gate. Outram's wound was not serious, and he soon grew impatient with the people who came to enquire about it. 'Oh, damn the arm!'[1] Fayrer heard the general reply to one questioner.

There still remained the problem of getting the rest of the relieving force inside the Residency defences. Outram was particularly worried about the wounded. So, too, was Havelock, as his son Harry was with them. Havelock's nephew by marriage, Bensley Thornhill, who had never met his cousin, volunteered to go out and guide the rearguard and wounded into the Residency. His offer was accepted.

Thornhill made his way along the river bank, avoiding the palaces, and was fired on at only two points. This was, obviously, the best and most protected way to move the wounded. Thornhill found them with the rearguard in the Moti Mahal, where they had spent the night. The wounded, all of them seriously hurt, were in covered litters, there being about fifty of these, each with two or more native bearers to carry it.

The litters were formed up into a convoy with an escort of 150 men, and moved off under Mr Thornhill's leadership. After leaving the gate of the Moti Mahal, there was a dangerous stretch of forty yards of broken ground that had to be crossed before the shelter of a large, masonry-built house was reached. The escort and the litters were bunched together and the convoy made a run for it. As they left the gate, the enemy opened up a heavy fire, but there were few serious casualties and the protection of the house was reached. While the convoy reformed, the enemy guns opened up, some of the roundshot tearing through the walls. After about half an hour, the next move was made. Again the convoy had to cover ground that was broken, this time by a small ravine with about three feet of water in it. Through this the convoy waded, pursued by grapeshot. On the other side, a long stone wall sheltered them from the enemy's fire. As they moved from behind the wall, Thornhill lost his bearings and took a wrong turning, into an open square surrounded by houses. They were now following the route used on the previous day by the main force. In fact, Neill had been shot down as he passed through the arched way the convoy was now using. The movements of the convoy had obviously been carefully watched by the enemy, for the moment the advance guard came into the square, they closed in, opening a deadly fire from their muskets at what was almost pointblank range.

Many of the escort were immediately shot down, but some, with a number of litters, pushed on across the square. Two of the leading litters reached the Residency safely, but only because Private Ward of the 78th Highlanders held his gun on the bearers and would not let them drop the litters. In one of them was Harry Havelock. In the square, Thornhill realised his mistake and tried to turn the remaining litters back. Rushing through the archway, he was shot in the arm, and a moment later another musket ball grazed his forehead. It was impossible to turn back the litters already in the square—the bearers had quickly abandoned them and made off. But one of the doctors managed to get the bearers to take up the litters at the rear and, turning back, found the right way to the river bank and reached the Residency safely. So, too, did Thornhill, though he was so badly wounded that he died a few days later.

Between thirty and forty litters had been dropped by the bearers in the square itself. The enemy rushed into the square armed with swords, while fire was kept up from the houses on three sides, aimed at the remainder of the escort—desperately trying to shelter. Surgeon Home of the 90th Light Infantry at first stayed with the wounded, though he could see little hope of getting them away, but he then saw some stragglers from the escort making for

196

one of the houses in the square and decided to join them. The building he found himself in formed the right-hand side of the archway through which the convoy had first entered the square. The party he discovered there consisted of two wounded officers and three wounded men, and eight unwounded men. He himself was as yet unhurt. Their action had been observed, and the enemy closed in, not only from the front and sides, but also from the rear. The doorway was under fire, and only the marksmanship of Private McManus of the 5th Fusiliers prevented the enemy from rushing the house. Standing behind a pillar which was solid enough to give him shelter, McManus fired steadily for half an hour. His shots were so effective that, not only did he kill many of the enemy, but frightened the rest into taking immediate cover as soon as he raised his musket.

While McManus was thus holding off an attack, the others were trying to barricade the house. There was some timber and sand, but nothing with which to make sandbags. Around the doorway, however, were a number of native corpses. The clothes were pulled off and used for holding sand, while the bodies themselves were dragged near the door to form a shield. Still, the enemy pressed forward, one of their leaders shouting that there were only three Europeans left inside the house. At this, all fourteen of the defenders raised a loud cheer, which put an effective stop to the intended rush.

Many of the wounded in the litters left in the square were too weak to look for shelter, and these were shot or cut down by the swords of the enemy. In one of the litters nearest to the house being defended was an officer of the Madras Fusiliers, while in the house was one of his men, Private Ryan. Ryan decided he could not leave his officer to a certain death without at least making an attempt to rescue him. He asked if anyone would help him and Private McManus, though wounded in the foot, volunteered. The two men rushed out into the square. Reaching the litter, they tried to lift it, but found it too heavy for them. They therefore lifted Captain Arnold out, and carried him between them to the house. Neither of the soldiers was wounded, but Arnold was hit in the thigh. The two men also managed to bring back a wounded private, but he, too, was hit again and died a few moments after reaching the house.

Dr Home thought that all the party had to do was hold out for an hour or two, and that they would then be relieved when the rearguard marched past on its way to the Residency. The defenders kept up a steady fire through the doorway, and from a window overlooking the square. An hour passed, during which two of the defenders were so badly wounded that they could no longer hold a musket. Private Hollowell of the 78th Highlanders, with a fortunate shot, killed the leader of the attackers. He appeared to be quite an old man, dressed in white with a red sash round his waist, and carried a sword and a shield. There was a lull in the firing. Home and his party broke through a blocked window into another part of the house, from which they could get a better view of the streets away from the square. These were deserted— or so it seemed—except for the headless bodies of some of the wounded.

While the survivors were trying to think up a plan of action, there was a loud rumbling noise in the square. Home was convinced that the enemy was bringing up a gun, but it turned out to be only a bulletproof screen on wheels. The situation was developing dangerously. Sounds of feet on the roof were followed by the dropping of plaster, and through the holes in the ceiling lighted straw was thrown into the rooms below. After a hasty discussion, three of the most seriously wounded defenders were picked up by the others and a break was made from the house to a line of sheds across the nearest corner of the square. On the way, though none of the sound men was injured, one of the wounded officers was hit again. There were now only six men capable of firing a gun, though four more were fit enough to keep a lookout.

When the enemy saw that the house had been abandoned, a number of them came forward and, creeping up to the litters which had previously been protected by fire from the house, murdered the occupants. One of the wounded officers managed to leave his litter and, though wounded in the legs by musket balls, succeeded in getting out of the square, evading pursuit, and eventually meeting up with the rearguard. The cries of the wounded were so terrible that the injured men of the defending party asked Home to shoot them if it turned out that the only way for the others to escape was to abandon them. However, it looked as if no one would leave the sheds alive. The enemy had begun to break holes in the roofs, and were soon firing down on the men inside. Home and another man broke through one of the shed walls and crept out to reconnoitre a possible way of escape. They discovered a small mosque which seemed solidly constructed and would offer better shelter, but they were soon forced to retreat. Home carried back with him two pots of water which he had found on the way.

By now, it was getting dark. Home told off nine men to mount guard in threes. Overhead, they could hear men moving about on the roof. Lying near the doorway were a number of corpses, including that of a horse. Some of the wounded were delirious. There seemed no chance of rescue. In the square, the litters had been set on fire and the moans of the dying could clearly be heard. The enemy stopped shooting, and gathered round a large fire near the archway into the square. The defenders, too, stopped shooting. Ammunition was getting low, so low that there was only enough to give seven rounds each to the six men still able to handle a gun.

At about two o'clock in the morning, there was firing nearby and the enemy could be heard running along the roof. Home was convinced that help was at hand. The firing must, he thought, be coming from a party sent to find them. The men raised a cry 'Europeans! Europeans!', and, with a cheer, shouted again: 'Charge them! Charge them! Keep on your right!' But the firing suddenly stopped. After a while, it was clear that no help was coming, and Home—slipping out from the sheds—found the enemy still gathered around the fire as if nothing had happened. What was to be done? There was no possibility of escaping, of passing the men at the fire and trying to make either for the rearguard or the Residency. Making for the river also seemed out of the question, especially in the dark. Home tried to persuade the others at least to give it a try. The only alternative appeared to be to wait for death. But only two of the men were willing to follow him. Home found that, in any case, he could not have borne to leave the wounded behind—or to have shot them in cold blood.

Dawn found the men resigned to death, but soon there was again the sound of firing. It seemed too far away to be reassuring. Then it grew nearer, and Private Ryan suddenly shouted: 'Oh, boys! Them's our chaps!' At this everyone cheered and kept on cheering and shouting until they heard an answering cheer. Home called out: 'Keep to the right! Keep to the right!' and ordered his comrades to fire from the loopholes. A moment or two later, Lieutenant Moorsom appeared at the door of the shed, and before long Home and his party had been moved to the shelter of the Chuttur Munzil palace. The earlier firing, they learned, had come from a detachment sent out from the Residency to take the gateway of the square; but the officer in charge had not realised that there were any survivors in the surrounding buildings, and, finding the enemy in too great strength for him to enter the square, had retired to await reinforcements.[2]

The rearguard, which Home had hoped would relieve them, had also had its troubles. The quiet night had been followed by intense enemy activity. The shock of Havelock's arrival had soon worn off and the mutineers were now determined to ensure that his rearguard, at least, should not reach the Residency. Opposite the Moti Mahal stood a large, modern palace with many buildings, known as the Kaisarbagh. This was now held in force by the enemy. The party led by Lieutenant Moorsom which had come to Surgeon Home's relief had formed part of a larger detachment of 250 men of the 5th Fusiliers and a number of Sikhs. The fire from the Kaisarbagh had been so intense that all his party could do was occupy a line from the Moti Mahal to the Chuttur Munzil palace and wait for reinforcements. The rearguard, with those wounded who had not gone forward with Mr Thornhill's convoy, remained in the Moti Mahal with two heavy guns and a large number of ammunition waggons.

At about midday on the 26th Outram sent out Colonel Robert Napier, the Engineer officer who had accompanied the relieving force, with a hundred men of the 32nd under Captain Lowe, a hundred of the 78th under Lieutenant-Colonel Stisted, and some Indian cavalry. Napier, who had been wounded the day before, had volunteered to lead the reinforcements. He had wanted to take with him a couple of guns, but Captain Olpherts of the Bengal Artillery persuaded him to leave these behind, taking instead a team of bullocks to bring back the rearguard's heavy guns. Outram gave Olpherts permission to destroy the guns if he found that he could not bring them into the Residency. To guide Napier's force went Thomas Henry Kavanagh, a civilian who had been superintendent of the Oudh Chief Commissioner's office.

As the force moved down the river bank it was clear that it would not be possible to bring the guns back that way. The ground was too soft and broken for the heavy carriages to negotiate. It was thought that the most practicable route would be through the open courtyards of the palaces lining the river front. Leaving a detachment to keep communications open with the Residency, Napier pushed on with the remainder of his men and joined up with the rearguard, with the loss of a few men wounded. As soon as it became dark, the wounded and the ammunition—loaded on camels—were sent along the river bank. They reached the Residency without incident. It was particularly important that the ammunition should reach the defenders, because the relieving force was equipped with the new Enfield rifle—the introduction of which had been one of the sparks which had fired the Mutiny. Compared with the old smooth-bore musket, known affectionately as 'Brown Bess', the rifled barrel of the Enfield provided a weapon not only of great accuracy but of considerable range. Though

200

there had been some Enfields inside the Residency, the small quantity of special ammunition had soon been exhausted.

While the camels and the wounded were making their way along the river bank, Captain Olpherts was trying to recover one of the rearguard's twenty-four-pounders which had been in action on the previous day but had been left in an exposed position when the enemy's musket fire had become too hot for the gunners. It still lay in an exposed position. Olpherts, who was known by his men as 'Hellfire Jack', was determined that he would neither leave the gun behind nor destroy it. Helped by another artillery officer, Captain Crump, and by Private Duffy of the Fusiliers, he succeeded in dragging it into the shelter of the Moti Mahal wall. In the dark, Private Duffy was able to creep out without being noticed by the enemy and attach two heavy ropes to the gun carriage. These were then fastened to bullocks and the gun was drawn in. During the operation, Captain Crump was killed.

The enemy fire was so intense that Napier decided not to wait until dawn, as he had originally intended, to move the guns and waggons. He divided the force into an advance guard and a rear-guard, with flanking parties to escort the guns and waggons. In this formation, he moved off quietly at three o'clock in the morning of the 27th, while the rearguard opened up on the enemy to distract their attention from the move. The method was effective. The enemy heard neither the jingle of metal harness nor the squeak of wheels. At one point, Napier thought one of the guns was going to get stuck, when its wheel jammed in a dense hedge of thorns, but the gunners managed to push it through. The whole party reached the Chuttur Munzil palace before the enemy sighted it. The enemy then occupied the enclosed garden adjoining the palace and opened fire, but a party of volunteers managed to kill most of the attackers and to occupy the garden. After putting out piquets, Napier turned to his men and, pointing at the main hall of the palace, said: 'There are your barracks, go and rest yourselves.'

During the 26th a number of sorties had been made from the Residency, primarily to enlarge the defensive perimeter. Lieutenant Aitken and a small number of men of the 13th Native Infantry occupied the whole of the Tehri Koti palace. Captain Lowe, before joining Colonel Napier's force, had, with 150 men of the 32nd, cleared an area known as the Captain Bazaar, which lay between the Residency defences and the river. After spiking a number of guns and destroying some mortars, Lowe was prevented by enemy fire from advancing on the iron bridge, and he was forced to turn and join up with Aitken in the Tehri Koti. From there he penetrated to a larger palace, the Farhat Baksh, which the men of the 32nd were soon referring to as the 'Ferret Box'.

Private Metcalfe was one of Lowe's detachment. So was the young bandsman, Symes, who had had so many of his family killed at Cawnpore. When he had heard the news from the relieving force, he had sworn that, given his chance, he would spare none of the enemy, neither man, woman, nor child, but would take full revenge for what had been done at Cawnpore. Metcalfe tried to keep an eye on him, but lost sight of him among the buildings. Asking another soldier if he knew where Symes was, he learned that he had rushed into a nearby house and had not yet come out. Fearing the worst, Metcalfe dashed over and, as he approached the door, heard the sound of a scuffle. Inside, a huge sepoy had hold of the barrel of Symes's musket and was about to slash at the boy with a sword when Metcalfe shot him. Symes exclaimed: 'Oh, Harry, I am a brute!'

'How's that, Jack?' asked Metcalfe.

'Oh, I said when I came out I should spare no one and I fired at a young woman and I'm afraid I killed her and by doing so I have placed myself on a par with the rebels.' Symes was distraught. 'By me killing her,' he went on, 'I will not get my own relatives restored. I am not fit to be called a soldier or a Christian.'[3]

Metcalfe asked Symes to show him the body, and when the two got to the spot they found a number of soldiers bending over something on the ground. It turned out to be the young woman, who was not dead, but had been slightly wounded and had fainted with fright. Some of the men carried her inside the Residency where her wound was dressed and she was allowed to go. A striking contrast, Metcalfe thought, 'to the way our poor women and children were treated, but then we were soldiers—they were fiends'.[4]

Symes, completely recovered from his attack of hysteria, joined a party in an attack upon a nearby Hindu temple in which there were several of the enemy. The officer said: 'Now, lads, we must take this sammyhouse at a rush.'[5] Then, raising his sword, he led the party in a charge. The enemy fled, leaving behind a large quantity of gunpowder spread about the floor. Metcalfe thought they had intended to set it off with a fuse when the British got inside but had been forced out before they were able to light it. Because of the standing orders not to destroy temples or mosques, the officer would not allow the building to be blown up —even with the enemy's own powder. While the other men

202

scouted the area, Symes lay down, not noticing the powder. A piece of burning paper from the discharge of a musket fired by one of the 32nd floated into the room. There was an immediate explosion, and Symes staggered out, badly burned, and was taken hurriedly back to the Residency hospital.

The hospital was crowded with the wounded of the relieving force, and conditions were chaotic. There was not enough space inside the hospital to house all those who needed a bed, and men awaiting treatment were left on the ground outside, surrounded by amputated legs and arms. There was nothing the doctors could do for Bandsman Symes except to make him as comfortable as possible. Metcalfe remained with him. At about ten that night, Symes's two surviving sisters, one of them married to a Colour Sergeant, and the other to a Drum Major, both of whom were out on duty, came to ask about their brother. They were so upset by the thought that he, the last male member of their family, was dying, that Metcalfe had to ask them not to make their brother's last moments so bitter and sad. They went away after Metcalfe had promised to call them when their brother was at the point of death, but they had barely left when the young man died.

Metcalfe hurried off to find the sisters—but when they returned there was no sign of Symes's body. Metcalfe searched for it. The doctors were asked, but said they knew nothing. One suggested that he might have been picked up by a burial party and taken to the cemetery. Metcalfe and the two women walked through the moonlight to the graveyard. The body was not there either. Rushing back to the hospital, they finally found it, being sewn up into a cotton rug by two Indian orderlies. The sisters wanted to see their brother's face for the last time, but the orderlies would not undo their work, even when they were offered money. Thinking that he must perform at least this one service for the women, Metcalfe took out his pistol and cocked it, threatening to blow the orderlies' brains out if they did not undo the rug. He was sorry afterwards. Both sisters became hysterical, and Metcalfe had to drag them away, more dead than alive.

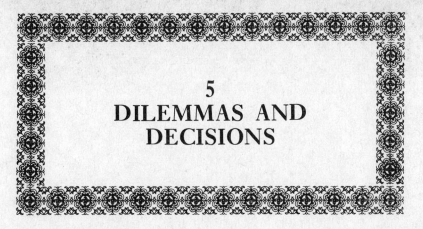

5
DILEMMAS AND DECISIONS

In the Residency itself, September 26 had been a day of confusion and dying hopes, of councils of war, and fears for the future. Early that morning, Katherine Bartrum had washed Bobbie and dressed him in a clean set of clothes which she had been keeping for the day his father arrived to join them. Outside, she met an officer who told her that Dr Bartrum was just coming in and that, when they last spoke, he had been in high spirits at the thought of seeing his wife and child again. Katherine waited, but he did not come. She gave Bobbie his breakfast, and then sat at the door of the house to watch. In the evening, with still no sign of her husband, Katherine took her child to the top of the Residency tower, where she could see the road from the gate. By the time it was dark, he had still not appeared, and Katherine, deeply disappointed, took Bobbie back to their room.

Those soldiers who had not been out on detachment spent most of the day looting in the palaces near the Residency, and by nightfall the ground was covered with piles of plunder. There were shawls and dresses, pieces of satin, silk, and English broadcloth, thin silky carpets studded with pearls and gold thread. Piled on top of richly embroidered velvet saddles for horses and elephants were garments of cloth of gold, turbans of costly brocade, and bolts of the finest muslin. Swords, their blades damascened in gold and silver and their scabbards studded with precious stones, lay next to English clocks. Some of the plunder had been carried in palanquins with rich curtains and gold-plated poles. There were enough cups and saucers and other pieces of china, Mr Rees thought, 'to set up fifty merchants in Lombard Street',[1] as well as scientific instruments, English full dress uniforms, and pistols—mainly from the Tehri Koti palace, which had been the home of

14 *Front view of the Residency*

the ex-king's brother, known as the General Sahib.

Unfortunately, though there was plenty of valuable loot, there was very little in the way of provisions. The garrison could not eat gold brocade, and the small amounts of tea, rice, spices and tobacco that were found soon disappeared. One lucky civilian succeeded in bringing into the Residency a number of boxes of tea, tobacco, soap and candles, and made a great deal of money by selling them in small quantities as soon as it was realised that the garrison was not going to be evacuated after all.

This decision was not arrived at immediately, though already, on the day after the arrival of the relieving force, it was clear that the situation was still critical. It would, of course, have been much worse if Havelock had been delayed any longer. Casualties from enemy fire and from sickness had been heavy, and with Indian desertions—which would certainly have increased every day the relieving force was delayed—the garrison would not have had enough men to hold out for many more days. Of the 1,720 combatants who had been there at the beginning of the siege, 979 remained. 577 of these were Europeans, and 402 Indians. Deaths among the women and children had been proportionately fewer; they at least had had the protection of houses and underground rooms. Nevertheless, sixty-four of the 270 children who had been there at the start of the siege were now dead, while three of the 240 women had been killed and eleven had died of disease.

Havelock had left Cawnpore with 3,179 officers and men of all arms, and a horde of Indian servants, grasscutters, grooms, drivers, and other camp followers, without which no army moved even in times of rebellion. Before it reached the Alambagh, the force had lost over 200 killed and wounded. At the Alambagh, Havelock left 531 men, including sick and wounded, and over 4,000 camp followers, as well as the artillery bullocks, camels, heavy baggage, supplies of food and drink, treasure, and a large quantity of rifle and gun ammunition. When the casualties of September 25 and 26 were counted, it was found that 535—mainly Europeans—had been killed or wounded. Among the dead was Dr Robert Bartrum.

Katherine did not discover this until the afternoon of the 27th. All that morning she had been sick with anxiety. Then Dr Darby came to see her. His face was kindly and sad. Katherine said: 'How strange it is my husband is not come in.' 'Yes,' he replied, 'it *is* strange,' and turned and went out of the room. Then the thought struck her that something had happened, and they did not want to tell her.

208

Robert had been killed on the threshold of the Residency. He had been on his way to help a wounded man. A Dr Bradshaw, who had been with him, told Katherine that he had warned her husband he was exposing himself too much. 'Oh, there's no danger,' he had replied, and a moment later was struck in the forehead. He fell across Bradshaw, saying: 'It's all up with me,' and died instantly. His body had been placed in a litter, but what happened after that no one could say. Katherine could not understand why God had forgotten 'to be gracious'. She thought of their son. 'Poor little fellow, how often had I said to him, "Papa is come; now baby will get quite well."' But she tried to comfort herself with the thought that 'Robert had fought the good fight, he had finished the course'. She knew that he would 'rise again at the last day'. Now there was only the child to live for. Mrs Pole-hampton, herself a widow, came to her and the two women sat together, scarcely talking, their understanding needing no words.[2]

Outram was faced by a real dilemma. His instructions from the governor-general had been to rescue the garrison of the Residency, even if this meant the evacuation of Oudh, but if the garrison could hold out he was to remain in Lucknow, if he so decided, provided he could maintain his position without early reinforcement. Outram had hoped that, as the relieving force approached Lucknow, the people would rise against the mutineers —a view shared by no one else in the force, nor, apparently, by the citizens of Lucknow. Before reaching the city, he had considered the possibility of evacuating the women and children from the Residency, and holding the town with three of his regiments. This was now obviously impracticable. Whatever the situation, Outram was determined not to remove British forces from Oudh. If he did, the people would be convinced that British rule was at an end.

Information reaching Outram disclosed that most of the mutineers had in fact left the city during the early evening of the 25th. All that then remained were the mobs, and the mercenaries of the rajas and landowners. But in the morning of the 26th, when the British wounded had been caught and butchered, some of their heads were sent out after the sepoys to show that all was by no means lost. The majority of the mutineers were induced to return.

The extension of the defensive position around the Residency was put in the hands of General Havelock, who had been appointed to command the new defences while Inglis remained in charge of the old. Havelock extended the line to include the palaces, gardens and other buildings to the east by which the relieving force had approached through the town. This was not an easy line to defend, and it was soon closely invested by the returned mutineers.

Before the end of September, a number of sorties were mounted, designed primarily to destroy or capture as many of the enemy's guns as possible and to destroy their emplacements. The first of these, on September 27, was badly organised. The aim was to destroy an enemy battery sited in the gardens of a house to the south-east of the Cawnpore Battery. The force consisted of a detachment of the 32nd and another of Madras Fusiliers. With them went a party of artillerymen, whose task was to spike any guns that might be captured. Unfortunately, Major Stephenson, who commanded the party, seemed incapable of imposing discipline on his men, who rushed forward without waiting for orders, and lost their way in the lanes leading to the enemy's battery.

The forward party succeeded in capturing a number of guns on the way, but the demolition men were slow in arriving. The method used for destroying the guns was to charge them with gunpowder, seal the barrel with clay, and then fire the charge, thus bursting the barrel. The men, thirsty in the still hot sun, had drunk all the water they had brought with them for the purpose of moistening the clay, and none was to be found nearby. The guns had to be left untouched, and the party was forced to retire through a hail of deadly fire from the surrounding houses. The Fusiliers lost four killed and seven wounded, and the 32nd, three killed and five wounded.

Among the dead was Private Cuney, the bandsman whose exploits had made him famous among the old garrison. Though frequently wounded, he had seemed to bear a charmed life, and would get up from his hospital bed to volunteer for action. This occasion had been no exception. Cuney and his constant companion, Private Smith, had been out in an earlier sortie and Cuney had injured his hand. But hearing that Smith was going out with Stephenson's party, Cuney took his arm out of the sling, pretended he was cured, and joined in. Both men were this time brought in dead. Cuney's death added an extra element to the growing depression of the old garrison, for there was as yet no indication of what Outram had decided to do. That night, twenty-five bodies were sent to the graveyard, and the enemy's fire was as heavy as it had ever been.

Next day, as parties of soldiers consolidated their positions in the outer defences, Outram sent a letter to Major McIntyre, the commander of the force remaining at the Alambagh. He would not, wrote Outram, be able to spare men to open up a line of communication between the Residency and the Alambagh for at least three days. In the meantime, McIntyre was to hold his position and act with caution. 'Should you be assailed,' wrote Outram, 'you will be able to hold your own. The only damage they can do you is by firing shots into the garden, but I trust the four guns left with you will soon silence such fire.'[3]

That night, the rumour spread that Outram had decided to evacuate the women and children from the Residency. But it was only a rumour. Outram was communicating his designs to no one but his God. His secretary, Mr Money, saw him in the early hours kneeling on his cot in prayer.

It was obvious to all that Outram was wrestling with his dilemma, though he was continually genial (except to those who continued to enquire after his injured arm) and did his best to keep his anxieties to himself. After the near fiasco of the passage through the town on September 25, he did not trust Havelock's opinion, and though he listened to his deputy's views he was not to allow them to influence him again. Yet it was Havelock who was the more experienced soldier. Indeed, despite his rank, Outram had virtually no experience of high command, though he had served in many campaigns. For much of his service in India, he had been detached from the army on what were known as 'Political' duties—relations with native princes, the pacification of new territories—areas of action which attracted many of the best young officers in the East India Company's army. This draining away of the best talent had left the army almost entirely to the command of the mediocre, whose incompetence had contributed much to the causes of the Mutiny as well as to the initial successes of the mutineers. Outram had proved himself a man of courage and intelligence, but he had a weakness for romantic and heroic gestures. His combination of hard-headedness and daredevilry had earned him, nearly twenty years earlier, the name of the 'Bayard of India', a knight *sans peur et sans reproche*. Lately, he had developed an ambition to win one of the new Victoria Crosses, which the queen had instituted as a reward for deeds of valour at the close of the Crimean War in 1856. But 1857 in Lucknow was a time, not for heroics, but for the careful weighing of facts.

While Outram was involved in his calculations, the defenders were settling in to their enlarged defences and keeping up their sorties against the enemy. On September 29 three expeditions were made, this time more carefully planned. The first column sent out moved against the twenty-four-pounder gun which had done so much damage to Innes's post.

The column consisted of 130 men commanded by Captain Shute, and included Lieutenant Edmondstone of the 32nd with a dozen of his men. Lieutenant Graydon of the Oudh Infantry acted as guide. Edmondstone and Graydon were at the front of the column, but Captain Shute 'thought the rear was the best place and there he stuck'. Starting before daybreak, the party marched off in the direction of the iron bridge and got within a hundred yards of it without being seen by the mutineers. One of the men told Edmondstone he could see the guns, and the lieutenant cried: 'Men, there are your guns. Take them!' With the two lieutenants leading, the men of the 32nd ran cheering towards the guns. There was a burst of grapeshot and then the gunners fled. The guns were spiked, and the party then turned down a lane towards their next objective. Here, the enemy opened up with muskets from some of the houses, and Edmondstone proposed taking the lane at a run, so as to reach the site of the guns which were the party's main target. The men who had arrived in Lucknow with the relief force were reluctant. Edmondstone gathered his own dozen men of the 32nd around him. They were 'awfully disgusted' with the newcomers, muttering, 'Did you ever see such a cowardly set?' Edmondstone gave the word, and the 32nd 'sprang forward directly', the others bringing up the rear. Three guns and two mortars were taken, but not before the guns had fired grapeshot into the attackers. Preparations were then made to blow up the barrel of the twenty-four-pounder, and the party retired into the houses surrounding the site to await the explosion. With the gun barrel burst and the other guns and mortars spiked, the force prepared to retire up the lane again. But although orders had been given to a subaltern to take possession of the houses at the entrance to the lane, so as to cover the party's retreat, he had failed to do so.

A heavy enemy fire opened up from these houses. The party 'doubled up the street, intending to charge the houses and scrag the sepoys', but half way up Edmondstone was hit in the head by a bullet and fell half senseless to the ground, only to be trampled on by men of the 5th Fusiliers. When he called out: 'Lift me up for I think I can walk,' they paid no attention. Aided by one of his own men, Edmondstone contrived to reach the head of the lane. There, Graydon, in spite of being wounded, managed to get a small group of men together and charged into the lower storeys

212

of the houses occupied by the enemy. But though both Graydon and Edmondstone begged the other men to follow, and take the upper storeys, 'they had no appetite for that sort of work'. Even when their own officer ordered them to go, he 'did not offer to lead them so they would not stir'.[4]

At this stage, Edmondstone could go on no longer and returned to the Residency to have his wound attended to. It was a bad business, he thought, when you could not count on British soldiers to back you up. At least the twenty-four-pounder had been destroyed and a few guns and mortars put out of action. But the casualties, ten dead and twenty wounded, in the end, had been too high for such meagre results.

The other sorties, too, were marred by serious casualties. One party was commanded by Major Apthorp, who had been in charge of Gubbins's post. The party set out from the Sikh Square, with the intention of causing as much damage as possible to enemy gun emplacements, mines, and the houses which gave cover to snipers. In these aims the party had some success. An eighteen-pounder gun which had been doing considerable damage to the Brigade Mess only the night before was destroyed. Two mine shafts discovered close to the gun emplacement were also destroyed, and several houses were entered, cleared of the enemy, and then blown up.

While this was going on, Gubbins himself and a party of the 32nd were posted on the top of one of the bastions, keeping up a steady fire on the enemy in order to distract them from observing the movements of Major Apthorp's men. Gubbins could see the enemy firing from the ground floor of a mosque which was very solidly built and was also protected by other buildings from fire from Gubbins's post. This was pointed out to Lieutenant Maitland of the Royal Artillery, with the suggestion that, if the tops of the minarets at the corners of the mosque could be brought down, they would cause many casualties. A nine-pounder gun was brought up, and with three shots Maitland brought down both the minarets. They crashed on to the main building, which collapsed on top of the enemy. Major Apthorp's party returned to the entrenchment at about 11 a.m., having lost four killed and seven wounded.

The third sortie was made from the Brigade Mess. The column was led by Major Simmons of the Fusiliers and Captain McCabe. Inglis protested strongly to Outram about the continued use of the men of the 32nd. It was they who had carried the burden of the defence of the Residency, and now they and their officers were

213

being expected to go out in the forefront of action. But Outram insisted. The men of the 32nd knew the terrain, he said. Though in fact they knew little about the area outside the old defensive position, there was nothing Inglis could do, and each of the sorties was spearheaded by a squad of men from the 32nd.

The party left the Brigade Mess at dawn and, forming up in the shelter of a wall, were able to rush the crew of an eighteen-pounder gun, known in the garrison as the 'Lane gun', which had been pounding the upper storey of Gubbins's house and had almost reduced it to ruins. The gun was captured, the enemy gunners firing two rounds before running away. As a party was entering one of the houses nearby, Captain McCabe was shot through the lungs. He died two days later. The ground floor of the building was taken in a very short space of time, but some of the enemy still remained on the upper floor. Private Metcalfe, who was with the 32nd detachment, joined another private in bringing up two ladders and placing them against the upper windows. Metcalfe was a small man, just over five feet in height. The other private, Tom Carroll, stood over six feet tall.

As Metcalfe climbed up the rungs of his ladder, he kept his feet —though not his head—on a level with Carroll's. Carroll was through his window before Metcalfe. The room Metcalfe found himself in was gloomy after the bright sun outside, but Metcalfe could see no one in it. In fact, there *was* nothing there but a very large box. Metcalfe thought it might be a flour bin. Always, like everyone else, on the lookout for provisions to supplement the meagre rations in the Residency, Metcalfe opened the box—and found, to his surprise, that there were three Indians squatting in it. Metcalfe shot one and bayoneted another before they could move, but the third man grabbed Metcalfe's musket by the barrel, preventing him from using the bayonet again.

Metcalfe's opponent had a curved sword, and the only way the private could protect himself was by holding the butt of his musket over his head with one hand while, with the other, he tried to grapple with the man. Seeing this, his assailant brought up his sword and struck Metcalfe's left hand at the knuckle, nearly cutting off his thumb. Metcalfe fell, the curved sword was raised to give him what could only have been a fatal blow, when Carroll rushed in from the other room. Bringing down the barrel of his musket on the enemy's head, Carroll crushed his skull. Seeing Metcalfe covered with blood, Carroll let out a great hoarse laugh, and shouted: 'You little swab, you were very near being done for!' Metcalfe admitted that it was so, but retaliated by showing

214

Carroll the dead men in the box, which 'rather astonished him'.[5]

Leaving that house with a guard, the rest of the party moved on to another. Here Major Simmons was brought down by a musket shot and killed instantly. The losses seemed to be getting too high, even though the enemy eighteen-pounder which had been causing trouble for the Cawnpore Battery was now in sight. Lieutenant Anderson, who had accompanied the column, now sent for reinforcement, asking that an officer with higher rank than his own should come back with the extra men. Outram, who, with Havelock, had been watching the action from the roof of the Brigade Mess, returned a message to the effect that, if Anderson thought that further advance could not be made without additional casualties, he must return, destroying the buildings the column had occupied. Anderson decided to retire. Thirteen barrels of gunpowder completely demolished the buildings. The column suffered two dead and nine wounded.

The sorties to the south at least cleared an area of some three hundred yards from the old defences of guns and buildings. But the price had been high. Mrs Inglis was horrified to see Captain McCabe carried past on the way to the hospital. His death and that of Major Simmons were much regretted by the garrison. Brigadier Inglis was particularly distressed by McCabe's death, and there was little comfort in the thought that he had tried to persuade Outram not to send him and the detachment of the 32nd. Apart from the casualties, Outram was disappointed by the results of the sorties. Those to the south had produced something, but he had hoped that Captain Shute's (and Lieutenant Edmondstone's) sortie towards the iron bridge might have taken the bridge, which would have been the first stage in opening up communications in that direction. His main worry, however, concerned the state of supplies inside the defences. He decided that a sortie must be made down the Cawnpore road in the direction of the Alambagh.

The organisation of this was put in the hands of Colonel Napier, who was recalled from the Chuttur Munzil palace where he had been supervising the construction of new defences. When he returned to the Residency, Napier asked about the exact state of supplies. Inglis had insisted in his letters to Havelock that the situation had been grave, and that assumption had underlain the decision to get the relieving force inside the Residency as quickly as possible. But Napier discovered that the comissariat officers did not appear to know what the precise position was. He immediately ordered a thorough search and a proper accounting.

215

While this was going on, Outram decided that he must establish his communications with the Alambagh. He had already decided —for he had no option—that he could not force his way through the enemy, encumbered by the women and children and the wounded. For one thing, he did not have enough transport. For another, the casualties would be too high to be borne. What was he to do? To leave a few hundred troops to help the garrison defend the Residency, while he himself departed for the Alambagh with the remainder? It was really a supply problem, and not only inside the Residency. A messenger had come through from Major McIntyre in the Alambagh to say that he too was short of provisions. This Outram did not believe. On September 30 he wrote to the governor-general explaining his dilemma. This despatch was to be carried by the cavalry. Fodder was extremely scarce inside the defences, and the extra horses were eating too much. What fodder there was must be reserved for the meat animals.

Captain Barrow, who had come in with Havelock's volunteer cavalry, was to lead, and Lieutenant Hardinge of the garrison was to be the guide. Both the men of the cavalry and those who remained behind were convinced that it would be a dangerous journey to the Alambagh. The moon was full and the sky clear. But the attempt had to be made. At ten o'clock the horses and men set out along the bank of the river. It was so light that they were perfectly visible to the enemy. Before the column had gone far, a heavy fire was opened up on them from directly ahead as well as from the opposite bank of the river. The enemy was obviously fully alert—and making the fact clear by blowing bugles and banging drums. Captain Barrow decided to turn back. Two men and two horses had been wounded by the time the force regained the Residency. One of the men was saved from serious injury by a couple of biscuits he had in his pocket. They were so hard that they deflected a musket ball.

The following day, Napier began operations to open the Cawnpore road. Outram placed at his disposal over 500 men, two engineer officers, a party of men experienced with mines, and some gunners with all the necessary materials for destroying the enemy's guns. Napier's plans were conceived with such care for detail that the officers and men of the force immediately had confidence in his judgement. On the first day, a number of buildings on the road to the south-east were occupied, but the going was so slow that it became dark before the objective—the battery in the gardens which had not been spiked in the sortie of the 27th, and which the enemy had since reinforced—had been reached.

Though the men were anxious to continue the advance, Napier insisted that the assault should be postponed until daylight.

During Napier's advance, some of the men had come across a man who looked like a sepoy, who was climbing out of a dry well as they approached. The man called out to them in English, and they discovered that he was a private of the Madras Fusiliers who had been lost during the unsuccessful sortie. Cut off from his comrades, he had found his way back to the Residency blocked by a large body of the enemy. His best plan, he thought, was to hide in one of the houses until night came, when he would have more chance of slipping through the enemy lines. The house he chose turned out to be occupied by sepoys. Rather than be taken alive, he jumped into a well. This, surprisingly, turned out to be dry. At the bottom was the body of an Indian. For three days and nights the fusilier, only slightly bruised by his fall, remained concealed. The corpse of the Indian was rapidly decomposing and the air at the bottom of the well was almost unbreathable. Yet he dared not come out during the day because of the activity of the enemy around him. At night he struggled as far as the top of the well, always ready to drop down again at the first hint of danger. He had been unable to get either food or drink and had given up hope of survival when he heard the shouts of Napier's force—and was almost shot by them.

The men, especially those who had come with the relieving force, were very quick to shoot Indians, and the fusilier had been lucky. In fact, the men's tempers had become so uncritical that the loyal sepoys of the garrison were given a special armband of bright red cloth to wear when they went out on a sortie. No quarter was otherwise given, and every black face was automatically assumed to belong to an enemy, to be shot or bayoneted to the words: 'Remember Cawnpore!' One captured sepoy, who got down on his knees and begged for his life, was told by a man of the 78th: 'You black rascal, do you think we are going to carry your ugly face all over the face of the blessed earth?'[6] The soldier then drove his bayonet through the man's heart.

When the force was not fighting, it was looking for plunder, even though instructions had been given that looting must cease. Food, however, was not considered to be plunder, and in fact it was what the men—and their officers—looked for first. The men would return from sorties with chickens and other fowls stuck on their bayonets. One British soldier, asked what success he had had, replied: 'Damned the ha'porth we got, sir, but an ould cock and a hen—oh, yes, we *did* get a sepoy or two!'[7]

On October 2, Napier assembled his force again after the men had breakfasted and arrangements had been made for artillery cover from the batteries in the Residency. The enemy put up a barrage of grape and roundshot, but Napier sent out a party which outflanked the mutineers and captured the battery, destroying two nine-pounder guns and a six-pounder. Lieutenant Innes, who was with the force, blew up the adjacent buildings, and the force returned to the Residency having lost two killed and eleven wounded.

On the same day, Outram at last made up his mind what was to be done. He informed Havelock and Inglis of his decision. That evening, Inglis went to visit his wife and, taking her outside into the courtyard, told her that because of the shortage of supplies the relieving force would leave the Residency and attempt to break through to the Alambagh. One European regiment would be left behind. The operation was to be carried out with such secrecy as was possible. The men from the outposts would be withdrawn and a sortie mounted, with the ostensible purpose of bringing in cattle. But the force, instead of returning to the Residency, would make for the Alambagh. Mrs Inglis noticed that her husband did not seem particularly dismayed by the prospect of being left alone again. On the contrary, he was unusually cheerful.

Outram's problem was initially one of time. If the Residency was to be partially evacuated and most of the relieving force withdrawn in what appeared to be a large sortie, preparations would have to be discreet in case the enemy should get to know about it. Yet Outram was convinced that, without some help from outside, he would not be able to move with any sense of security. The number of the enemy in the city and the countryside was believed to have increased to at least 100,000. Outram therefore wrote to Captain Bruce, the head of the Intelligence Department at Cawnpore, asking him to pass on to the Brigadier commanding at Cawnpore certain requests for action.

The Brigadier was asked to 'prepare a detachment of not less than 300 Europeans and two guns, to advance to the relief of the retiring column', which would be commanded by a responsible and experienced officer. The detachment was to be supplied with rockets, 'to give us notice of its position when we are supposed to be in the vicinity'. Outram also instructed the Brigadier to start making preparations for the withdrawal of the garrison in the Residency by calling up reinforcements from Fatehpur, Allahabad and Benares. 'All men that can be spared to be sent to Cawnpore with all practicable despatch.' Outram's message continued: 'Request the authorities at Agra to make known to the General at Delhi the urgent necessity there is for reinforcements being pushed on to Cawnpore as speedily as possible, without which the Lucknow garrison cannot be withdrawn.' Outram hoped that, as Delhi had now been recaptured, 'at least one strong brigade may be spared from there'.[8]

As the telegraph line down the country to Calcutta had been reopened, Outram ordered Captain Bruce to telegraph the commander-in-chief that 'the insurgents are too strong to admit of withdrawing besides this garrison, the sick, wounded, women and children, amounting to upwards of 1,000'. To the governor-general he must communicate Outram's failure to arouse the population of Lucknow and Oudh in favour of the British. 'My hopes of a reaction in the city are disappointed; the insurgent sepoys have inspired such terror among all classes, and maintain so strict a watch, that we have not been able to communicate with one single inhabitant of Lucknow since our arrival. Nothing but a strong demonstration of our power will be of any avail.'[9]

While he was waiting for confirmation from Cawnpore that a relief body was ready to start, Outram continued with the extension of the defensive perimeter around the Residency. The move down the Cawnpore road was also pressed further, this time by the occupation of houses, and then by breaking a continuous way through the adjoining walls and gardens. But this plan to produce a kind of covered way for the retiring force had to be given up when the wall of a large mosque was reached. This had been strongly fortified by the enemy and could not have been taken without considerable loss. The houses which had been occupied were therefore blown up, but an outpost with one gun was sited near the mosque.

Outram had prepared a valedictory order which was to be read to the garrison in the Residency after the departure of the force on its apparent sortie for cattle. In it he explained why the evacuation was necessary, and why the garrison itself, with the women and children, could not for the moment be withdrawn. 'It would have afforded the Major-General very sincere pleasure,' the draft said, 'to have been at liberty to have communicated to the assembled troops in person the message which he leaves with Brigadier Inglis to communicate with them. But the movement requisite to effect a junction with the Alambagh detachment, is one of great delicacy and peril; and its success depends in a great measure on the Major-General's intentions not being perceived until the moment of their execution.' Outram concluded with a statement of his belief that he had 'reinforced the garrison to the full extent deemed necessary by Brigadier Inglis; and with every confidence in the ability of that gallant officer and his glorious Garrison to maintain themselves in their present position, the Major-General bids them each, and all, a hearty God's-speed'.[10]

What effect Outram's order would have had on the old garrison, and especially on the women and children, was not put to the test. On October 4, Colonel Napier's enquiries into the state of the supplies inside the Residency were answered with the discovery that the situation was by no means as desperate as Inglis had made out in his despatches. The vast swimming bath underneath the residency building was found to be packed so full of grain that it was almost impossible to calculate how much it held, but there was certainly enough to keep the garrison and the relieving force supplied for at least a month. This, with the new additions of artillery bullocks, meant that the need for the main body of the force to retire no longer existed. Outram made his decision. The whole force would stay until the final relief came.

When Napier questioned the commissariat officers about the grain supplies in the swimming bath, they disclaimed all knowledge of Inglis's statements about the supply situation, and insisted that no one on the Brigadier's staff had ever asked them for figures.

Part 4

❧

THE SECOND
SIEGE

15 *The Secundrabagh*

1
REORGANISING THE RESIDENCY

ON OCTOBER 7, Outram wrote again to Captain Bruce at Cawnpore. 'Our whole force is now besieged by the enemy, who have increased in number and audacity, which leads me to think the Delhi mutineers must now be here. Our position is more untenable than that of the previous garrison, because we are obliged to occupy the neighbouring palaces outside the entrenchment to accommodate the Europeans, which positions the enemy are able to mine from cover of neighbouring buildings. Still no communication with the town, and little prospect of procuring provisions; the neighbouring streets, into which we have made sorties at much cost of life, containing nothing. We have grain, and gunbullocks, and horses, on which we may subsist a month I hope, but nothing else. No hospital stores, and but little medicine.'[1]

While Outram had been making up his mind, work had gone on continuously not only on extending the perimeter but on repairing the old defences of the Residency. The great number of camp followers who had come with the relieving force supplied an ample reservoir of labour, and gaps in the entrenchments were repaired and new batteries sited. The command of the old area was still left to Brigadier Inglis, and the outer to General Havelock, whose command was now called the 'Oudh Field Force'. The two commanders had their headquarters inside the old defences. Havelock and his staff lodged themselves in Ommanney's house. Every morning, Havelock would make a circuit of the outer defences, a distance of about two miles, before reporting to Outram at his headquarters in Dr Fayrer's house.

The old Residency position was now extended down to the river on the north face, while to the east the Tehri Koti, Farhat Buksh, and Chuttur Munzil palaces had been brought in. Whereas in the first siege, the hospital, Fayrer's house, Sago's, and the Financial Garrison had been exposed to attack from only a few yards away, the enemy's positions were now at least a thousand yards from the old entrenchment. The Baillie Guard gateway, scene of many assaults, now stood in a kind of central space with the battered gate itself defiantly open. But on the west and south faces the old line remained almost the same as before. Only two additions had been possible. The burial mound opposite Innes' post was occupied and fortifications were erected out of Muhammadan gravestones. A number of covered trenches joining the new position with Innes' post were dug, and a small mosque in the direction of the iron bridge was held as a lookout. Mr Rees, who was still stationed at Innes' post, went with the party which occupied the mound. The men assembled at five o'clock in the evening and, with bayonets fixed and muskets loaded, moved silently out and up to the mound. With a sudden cry, they rushed the position and found—nobody. 'We set up a loud laugh and congratulated ourselves on the ease with which the conquest was effected.'[2] The enemy had apparently occupied the mound only when they were mounting an attack on Innes' post.

On the south side, however, the houses occupied by the enemy still remained dangerously near the Residency defences. The line of outhouses near Gubbins's post from which enemy mining parties had been more than once ejected by sortie were occupied, and a new battery on a raised emplacement was constructed and armed with a nine-pounder gun. Taking advantage of the destruction of so many of the enemy batteries, the garrison carried out work on parts of the old defences on the south side which had been reduced almost to ruins before the arrival of the relieving force. The Cawnpore Battery, target of so much of the enemy's heaviest fire, was little more than a heap of earth and had been virtually abandoned by the garrison. It was now completely rebuilt and armed with two eighteen-pounder guns, becoming, as Gubbins said, 'the show battery of the garrison'. To give some outer protection to the east of the Cawnpore Battery and Anderson's house there was the post which had been set up after the failure of the house-breaking operation down the Cawnpore road. Here a party of the 78th occupied the place known as Phillips' garden. Three main buildings on the site had been joined together by breaching the walls. Loopholes were cut on the outer sides, and all the doors and windows were heavily barricaded. The post, according to the usual practice, was christened 'Lockhart's', after its commander.

The range of palaces along the river front at least supplied an outer entrenchment of solidly constructed buildings. Inside them, the defenders lived in slovenly splendour. There was a great deal of filth, and an almost equal amount of luxury. Reclining on silken couches, the men of the garrison ate their meagre rations from the finest porcelain and china. The cooks preparing the men's food over fires on the marble floors, crouched on stools of rare woods, covered with costly damask. All around were shawls from Kashmir, ornaments from Paris, dead sepoys, horses, camels, and the smell of decay. Only the flies seemed to be really enjoying themselves.

The garrison occupied only the lower floors of the palaces. For some reason, the enemy—who managed to bring a few guns into action on the other side of the river—spent most of his time shooting at the upper storeys and the gilded domes, which were knocked about a good deal. The garrison abandoned all rooms facing the river, and barricaded the windows and doors.

The enemy also ran a mine near the Chuttur Munzil. His first explosion there did little damage, but on a second attempt he managed to blow a hole in the garden wall of the palace. Appearing in force at the breach, the mutineers were driven back. On another occasion, they set fire to one of the wooden gates leading into the garden, but again failed to force an entrance. Their third attempt, on October 6, was made after they had blown up a house occupied by an outlying picquet. This time, they entered the palace itself, only to be repulsed with losses of—it was believed—at least 400 dead and wounded.

The enemy's presence in the neighbouring buildings could no longer be tolerated, and for a few days there was a succession of engagements designed to clear them. The fighting was heavy. But at last, with the capture of a small mosque which had been used by the enemy snipers to harass the outlying picquets, the immediate vicinity of the Chuttur Munzil was made reasonably secure.

For the women and children, for the first time since the siege began, there was less constriction. The extension of the perimeter meant that, though there was still danger from the enemy guns, it was possible to walk about the old Residency. Confined to their underground rooms and barricaded houses, the women had known very little of the realities outside. Mrs Germon, like many others, had been keeping a clean dress aside for the day of deliverance. On the second Sunday after the relief, there were a number of religious services. Some of the ladies went to the first of them,

227

held in the Brigade Mess, but Mrs Germon waited for the afternoon service which was held at Dr Fayrer's house. Her husband and a number of other officers attended, although Outram did not. After the service, Mrs Germon was taken by one of the doctors on a tour of the old defences. She was 'perfectly thunderstruck'[3] to see such a mass of ruins, especially at her husband's post, the Judicial Garrison. The building was riddled with bullets and roundshot, the verandah was down, and large pieces of masonry were lying about. Even the centre room, occupied by her husband, had great holes in the walls. She was taken up on the roof, the enemy now being 'too far off to be dangerous',[4] and could hardly tell which were the houses occupied by the enemy and which by us—'there was merely a bamboo stockade between us, and the marvel is they never got in'.[5] She could only be thankful that her husband had been preserved—almost miraculously, in the circumstances—and unwounded. She was able to take a cup of tea with her husband, without milk or sugar, of course, but it 'seemed like Paradise to be alone with him again'.[6] He gave her a beautiful manuscript on gold paper decorated with small green and white beads, which Fayrer thought might have been worked by the ladies of the Court of Oudh. A few days before, Captain Germon had brought her some beautiful china and a splendid punchbowl.

Others, too, found visiting the old defences, as well as those parts formerly used by the enemy in their attacks on the Residency, something of a revelation. Mr Rees, walking round the old entrenchments and into the new positions, could not withhold his admiration at the enormous labour the enemy had put into their operations. Before their batteries, they had dug trenches, some of them twenty feet deep and three feet wide. Ladders had been placed at various spots so that men could go down and listen for sounds of the garrison's counter-mining. Deep trenches seemed to run everywhere, acting as protected communications around most of the old perimeter. 'How we resisted it all,' thought Rees, was 'truly a wonder. The right hand of the Lord is manifest in all this plainly enough, for in spite of all our courage, we could never have kept them out.'[7]

Captain Sanders, who had been stationed at the Financial post, was more struck by the enemy's 'want of pluck'. When he looked at his post from what had been the enemy side, he was convinced that 'you might have driven a buggy into the compound'.[8] The verandah wall was so damaged that he could walk over it with ease. The general impression was that the garrison had been both very lucky and carefully watched over by Divine Providence.

Outram, at least, recognised that the old garrison had shown great courage, whatever help it had received from the incompetence of the enemy. Such courage had to be rewarded. The day after Outram made the decision to stay, he issued a highly complimentary statement to the old garrison. First, he pointed out that, as Brigadier Inglis had been delayed by 'incessant and arduous duties' from submitting an immediate report on the events of the siege prior to the arrival of the relieving force, he had himself been unable to comment officially on the gallantry of the garrison. Now, however, he was happy to 'tender to the Brigadier and to every individual member of the garrison, the assurance of his confidence that their services will be regarded by the Government under which they are immediately serving, by the British nation, and by Her Gracious Majesty, with equal admiration to that with which he is himself impressed'.[9]

Outram was convinced, he said, 'that the annals of warfare contain no brighter page than that which will record the bravery, fortitude, vigilance, and patient endurance of hardships, privations, and fatigue, displayed by the garrison of Lucknow, and he is very conscious that his unskilled pen must needs fail adequately to convey to the Right Honourable the Governor-General of India, and His Excellency the Commander-in-Chief, the profound sense of the merits of that garrison which has been forced on his mind by a careful consideration of the almost incredible difficulties with which they have had to contend'.[10]

Outram reminded the garrison that a governor-general of India had once given the title 'illustrious' to the garrison of the town of Jalalabad, which had held out against siege during the Afghan war almost twenty years earlier. For Lucknow 'some far more laudatory epithet, if such the English language contains' would have to be found. At Jalalabad, the defenders had not had to suffer incessant attacks. But, at Lucknow, an enemy vastly superior in numbers had been driven back when it tried to break in, and the garrison had also for almost three months been 'exposed to a nearly incessant fire from strong and commanding positions', held by an enemy 'possessing powerful artillery, having at their command the whole resources of what was but recently a kingdom, and animated by an insane and blood-thirsty fanaticism'.[11]

The Major-General was pleased that, on his own authority, he was able to hand out rewards to the Indian troops who had remained loyal throughout such trying times and with so many inducements to desert. All were raised in rank, so that there were no native privates left in the Residency. A number of the sepoy officers were awarded the Order of British India, and the pensioners who had given such loyal service were told that their pensions would be doubled. The Sikhs, whose fidelity had been suspect throughout the first siege, were—save for a few exceptions—given nothing. Neither, at least for the time being, were the British soldiers. Outram could 'do no more than give his most earnest and hearty support to the recommendations of the Brigadier' and felt that the governor-general would 'fully and publicly manifest his appreciation of their distinguished services, and that our beloved Sovereign will herself deign to convey to them some gracious expression of royal approbation of their conduct'.[12]

This gave little satisfaction to the Europeans, and some did not in the least like the thought of waiting for their rewards. 'Damn those black fellows,' was the widespread opinion. 'There they go as usual, petted and rewarded, while we gets nothing.'[13]

Outram praised the Europeans and Eurasians, civil servants and private citizens, and assured them that when the governor-general heard of their bravery he would find congratulating them 'one of the most pleasing acts of his official life'.[14] Rees, for one, would have preferred something more tangible.

The civil service volunteers were called together a day or two after the issue of Outram's congratulatory order and told that, owing to the 'vigilance, gallantry, zeal and valour thay had displayed in the defence of the siege, they were to receive three months' gratuity'.[15] It was paid out immediately. But the private citizens, who had behaved just as well, could not even borrow money. Rees, who had gone through all his own funds, managed to get a loan of seventy-five rupees, but was annoyed that he should be paid nothing for his labours when others, who had done no more, were made a gift of as much as fifteen hundred rupees. Money had again come into its own, for since the occupation of the palaces it had become possible to buy such things as clothes. Mrs Harris, the chaplain's wife, was able to purchase seven pairs of stockings from a soldier. Much of the loot, however, was of less immediate value. There were jewels and shawls, rolls of silks, and decorated swords and daggers, as well as books, pictures, and clocks. The authorities declared all plunder (except crockery) the property of the state, and appointed prize agents to gather it together. The rumour was soon heard that, with the treasure already in the Residency, the state had come into possession of valuables worth nearly £1 million.

Unfortunately, there was little to be found in the way of food,

230

and what there was soon disappeared. After Outram's decision not to try to break out, rations were reduced. European troops were now to have twelve ounces of meat, about half of which was usually bone; one pound of ground wheat; four ounces of rice; and one and a half ounces of salt. The women were allowed only half this amount of meat and three-quarters of the ground wheat, one and a half ounces of rice, one ounce of grain, and half an ounce of salt. The sepoys' rations were cut back severely, and the camp followers suffered worst of all, being allotted only a pound of wheat, two ounces of grain and a quarter of an ounce of salt a day.

The meat, as before, was obtained by slaughtering the gun-bullocks, and was very tough. It had been hoped that Havelock would have brought in with him a few bakers so that proper bread could be baked, but he did not, and chupattees remained a staple food. Many of the newly-arrived men found the coarse flour used for making the chupattees caused diarrhoea and dysentery. There were still no green vegetables or fruit, and scurvy was increasing. One officer who jumped off a low wall and bruised his leg found the whole leg turning blue. What was particularly irritating was the fact, soon common knowledge, that the relieving force had brought with it large supplies of rum, tea, coffee, sugar and tobacco, but that all these had been left behind at the Alambagh, only a few miles away. With so many more men in the garrison, the price of these commodities on the black market soared even higher than before.

The lack of tobacco was still, perhaps, the worst privation the soldiers had to face. Small cheroots were available at three rupees each, but there were not many of these to be had, even by people who could afford them. On one occasion when Captain Maude, with a well-aimed shot, successfully knocked out an enemy gun which was annoying the garrison at the Redan, Outram came down to the post and said to Maude: 'I have heard of your feat of arms, Maude, and I now give you the highest award it is my power to bestow.'[16] He then handed over a Manilla cheroot, which was gratefully accepted as a fitting tribute.

Outram was still concerned about the detachment in the Alambagh, though communication by runner was now functioning smoothly and without interference from the enemy. Though there were plenty of what had now come to be thought of as luxury provisions in the Alambagh, flour and meat were comparatively short. On October 7, Outram had sent a note to Major McIntyre by the hand of a pensioner who owned a small estate, and would 'do his best to procure you supplies'. Outram warned McIntyre, however, that he must 'arrange with him to introduce what he gets in such a way as to make it appear that you looted his carts on passing near your post. Otherwise you would get no second supply. He might be instructed to bring his carts into the vicinity of the Alambagh, when you would creep out and rush upon him with a cheer, and pretend to plunder, taking him and the banians [dealers] with him (to whom the grain belongs) prisoners, and, when out of observation, paying them most liberally in hard cash, from the public treasury, five rupees for every rupee's worth of supplies, and sending them off again with the carts after dark, with instructions to repeat the experiment. It is obviously necessary to manage it so that our friends must appear victims'.[17]

The subterfuge turned out to be unnecessary. That same day McIntyre was able to report that a convoy of supply waggons had come from Cawnpore, escorted by 270 men with two guns. The journey had been made without incident.

Though the arrival of supplies at the Alambagh took one worry off Outram's mind, it did not ease conditions inside the defences. As well as a shortage of provisions, there was also a scarcity of medical supplies. The wounded brought in by the relieving force and those who had been injured in sorties after its arrival had put a tremendous strain on the hospital and its staff.

The numbers in need of attention had doubled in a day, and the wounded had to be accommodated wherever there was room. Many were left outside in the litters on which they had been carried. The whole of the hospital area smelt as it had always smelt, of vomit and blood. All round lay piles of soiled linen, bottles of physic, blue powder papers, pill boxes, dirty wine glasses, and cups with the remains of draughts and drenches, as well as plates covered with the reddened salt into which leeches disgorged the blood they had sucked from fever-struck men. Indoors, the doctors probed for bullets with their fingers, used long razor-edged knives to slit the skin of arm and leg in preparation for the amputation saw. All these operations were carried out within the sight and hearing of other patients. All knew that amputation meant a slow death from gangrene or necrosis of the bone.

But after a few days the presssures eased a little. A large room was taken over in the Begum Kothi as an additional ward, and two sizeable tents were erected outside the hospital. Even with these additions, there was still overcrowding, but some of the more general discomforts were relieved by the plunder taken from the palaces. Now, there was plenty of bedding, and more than enough linen for bandages and swabs.

232

There was still very little chloroform, however, and sick men could not eat the harsh ordinary rations. Arrowroot, tapioca and milk were in very short supply.

Some of the stench of decaying bodies and other matter was reduced. The fact that the weather was getting colder had something to do with this, but the real change was brought about by Dr Ogilvie, the Sanitary Commissioner, who had asked for and been given as much labour as he needed to clear away the filth and carcases of men and animals which littered the approaches to the old entrenchment. This was of benefit to everyone, though it took some time before there was an appreciable diminution in the numbers of flies and mosquitoes. Early in October, for example, Mrs Inglis was unable to walk because of badly inflamed mosquito bites on her foot, and Dr Scott was convinced that, had it not been for the good nursing she received from Mrs Case's sister, Caroline, she might have lost her foot.

The reorganisation inside the Residency continued. The magazine was overhauled, and all supplies of ammunition were carefully counted and graded. Many of the relieving force had been armed with the Enfield rifle, and though they had managed to bring in some quantities of the special ammunition, these soon diminished. The men were very reluctant to return to the old smooth-bore musket, so a factory was established to make cartridges for the Enfield. Fortunately, one of the officers of the old garrison had a bullet mould for the new weapon. Other men, however, would not give up the old musket, swearing—with some truth—that it was quicker to load and that, in close fighting, speed often made the difference between life and death.

The expansion of the defensive area, which allowed some freedom of movement inside the Residency, encouraged a number of women to volunteer to help at the hospital. Every morning, braving the stray bullets that still reached the centre of the position, they would make their way from their quarters to wash the patients' faces, or read the Bible to the dying. Their attentions were much appreciated by the sick and wounded. So were the regular daily visits by Outram, who was always to be seen about, even when the gunfire was heavy, genial and radiating confidence. One day in the hospital a seriously wounded soldier looked up at him and then at one of the women nurses, and said proudly: 'We've saved them, sir.'[18]

Conditions in the hospital improved even more when it was decided that the upper storeys might be used again. This extra space, and the opening of some of the barricaded windows and doors, brought in more light and air and gave those in the upper rooms a view of the city. Mr Gubbins, too, was able to ease some of the pressure on the hospital by accommodating some wounded officers in the upper storey of his house. Now that the enemy batteries nearest the house had been put out of action, the danger had decreased and the upper rooms could be brought into use once again. Parts of the house were still too badly damaged to be occupied. The dining room, whose domed roof had been regularly pierced by roundshot, remained unusable.

Among the officers who moved from the hospital to Gubbins's house were Lieutenant-Colonel Fraser Tytler, Lieutenant Have-lock, Lieutenant Bonham (inventor of the famous portable mortar), and Major Vincent Eyre, a hero of the Afghan war. Eyre told Gubbins the story of another siege, that of a small house at Arrah in Bihar, where sixteen Europeans and fifty Sikh police-men had held out against a large force of mutineers for eight days until Eyre went to their relief. Gubbins felt that there was some reassurance in this tale of what Eyre, now himself besieged, described as 'one of the most remarkable feats in Indian history'.[19]

2
FOOD, CLOTHES
AND VICTORIA CROSSES

THE EXTENSION of the Residency perimeter produced one serious, not to say dangerous result. After the enemy had recovered from the initial shock of having their old gun emplacements destroyed, they erected their guns on new sites from which they had much greater success in hitting the inner defences. Before, the guns had been so near their targets that more shells passed over the area than actually hit it. Now, with the guns further away, the number of direct hits began to increase. It meant that some restrictions did, after all, have to be placed on free movement in the area. Mrs Inglis, who had been allowing the children to take the air near Ommanney's house in the mornings, had to stop them. Her husband did not think it was safe.

At least life for Mrs Inglis and her two friends remained reasonably comfortable. They still had a few private stores, now mainly consisting of arrowroot—but nothing could have been more nourishing, they thought—and Mrs Case had been given a share of a box of provisions packed by the late Brigadier-General Neill for some of the ladies of his acquaintance. There had been sago and arrowroot, candles and wine. Mrs Case received some of the arrowroot and sago.

But food for many in the garrison was still not only a problem but, in some cases, a constant quest. It was said of one officer who was continually volunteering for dangerous sorties that his only motive was the hope of finding food in some of the houses that were attacked. He was certainly a large man, and had suffered much from the smallness of the rations.

One day Private Metcalfe, recovered from the wound to his hand, volunteered for a sortie against an enemy gun. Three of the party knew exactly where the gun was sited, Metcalfe himself, and two other privates, Kelly and Ryan by name. Each had decided he would be the first to get to the gun and therefore win the commander's commendation. Private Ryan took a wide circuit, trying to avoid the walls of gardens and houses. Kelly and Metcalfe found themselves faced by a brick wall. Kelly started to break his way through it with the butt of his musket, and as soon as there was a hole large enough Metcalfe scrambled through and ran on, without waiting for his comrade. When he arrived at the emplacement,.however, he found that the gun had been dragged away. He scratched his initials in the gun tracks and then turned to view his surroundings. Soon, he found himself in a yard in which there were some large baskets which turned out to contain game fowl. Picking two up and tying them together, Metcalfe left before the others arrived. On his way through a shed, he found an earthenware container full of flour. Undoing a length of turban cloth which he had tied round his cap, Metcalfe spread it out on the floor and began to pour the flour into it. As he did so, a bugler appeared, and said to him warningly: 'Harry, you'd better throw away that flour!'

'Why, George?' asked Metcalfe.

'It might be poisoned, Harry, you know.'

'Poison here or poison there, George,' replied Metcalfe, 'I'll stick to it. I might as well die of poison as die of hunger.'[1]

Metcalfe got back to the Residency, still in possession of his two birds, at about five o'clock in the evening. He was immediately asked how much he wanted for them, and was offered what he thought to be fabulous sums. But he was not prepared to sell. One he gave to his friend Mrs Harris, the wife of the chaplain, and the other to a lady with four children whom he felt sorry for. They had been reared in 'the lap of oriental luxury', but, 'poor little things',[2] were deprived of all they had been used to before the siege. With the flour he managed to make some rather coarse unleavened bread, which he found very sweet and certainly not poisoned. He no longer had to feed Bustle, because he had found it impossible to supply the dog out of his reduced rations and had been reluctantly forced to ask Mrs Harris if she could take him back. Somehow, Mrs Harris had contrived to find enough to feed him.

The enemy, it seemed, was well aware of the shortage of food inside the defences. As well as their usual firing, blowing of bugles, and banging of drums at all times of the day and night, they had invented a new line in psychological warfare. They would hold chupattees and chickens on top of long poles, shouting to the nearest of the defenders that they would soon be dead of starvation.

, The only thing the enemy seemed to be short of was ammunition. One day, one of the guns lobbed over a smoothing iron. On other occasions, it was found that they were firing lengths of telegraph wire—the $\frac{3}{8}$"-thick iron rods then used as 'wire' making severe wounds on impact.

One of Outram's first acts after entering the Residency had been to set up an Intelligence Department under Captains Garnegie and Alexander Orr. Its main function was to find out what was happening in the city. The information it produced confirmed, in the main, rumours that had been current in the Residency before the relief. It was indeed true that the mutineers and their supporters had set a young son of the ex-king of Oudh upon the throne. The boy was said to be only eight or ten years old; his mother was the power behind him. It was reported that she had donated £50,000 from her personal funds for the construction of a defensive wall around the city, and that she was more militant than many of the men. To one chief who had seemed to be faint-hearted in support of the new king and the rebel cause, she was said to have sent a pair of women's trousers with the suggestion that he should put them on and take himself off to his proper place—a harem. It was reported that a council of state had been set up under the new chief minister, a man who had always been thought to be a friend to the British. The council consisted of members of the royal family, some of the largest landholders, and representatives of the mutineers.

Mr Rees, who was an old friend of Captain Orr, heard from him that the mutineers and their civilian allies had everything highly organised, with generals and brigadiers in command of the army. But 'these great dignitaries were never treated with that respect and obedience we ourselves had commanded'.[3] The sepoys, he was told, *elected* their officers, and these officers elected their commanders, though they did so in the name of the king. But if any officer displeased the rank and file, 'a debating assembly would be immediately held by the privates, at the conclusion of which, they would usually signify to their officers, either that they would be degraded, or, what suited their cowardly and sanguinary minds better, they attacked and fired on their victim.'[4]

Perhaps the most distressing news was that the enemy had some European prisoners, in the city of Lucknow itself. It was not at first known who they were, but there were women and children among them and they had been lodged in the Kaisarbagh palace.

16 *Dilkusha House and Park*

The defenders believed they must be a party of survivors from the outstation of Sitapur, who had gone for protection to a friendly raja and had instead been sent to Lucknow in chains. At the end of October this assumption was confirmed when Captain Alexander Orr, one of the heads of the Intelligence Department, received a letter from his brother, Patrick, bearing the signatures of six of the prisoners—of whom Patrick was one. With him were his wife, Sir Mountstuart Jackson and his sister Madeleine, Lieutenant Burnes, and Sergeant-Major Moreton. There were also two children, a daughter of Captain Patrick Orr, and another little girl named Sophie Christian. The letter said that the party was being well cared for, and did not lack food or clothes, but Alexander Orr was convinced that the letter had been written under dictation. It was assumed that the enemy were keeping the prisoners as hostages for potential use in the future. Certainly, nothing could be done to rescue them. The Kaisarbagh was too well fortified and defended, and any attack might result in the murder of the prisoners. It was appalling to imagine their situation: 'constantly in dread of their lives, in the hands of savage and remorseless barbarians, in the hearing of our guns, knowing assistance was near, and yet unable to obtain it, they must indeed have been leading a miserable existence.'[5]

The women and children in the Residency were, at least, better off than the poor prisoners in the Kaisarbagh, for, although conditions were by no means comfortable, there did seem to be real hope of an end.

Katherine Bartrum, however, had almost ceased to care. She found she could no longer 'look on the bright side of anything . . . All looks so dark and there is no sweet hope now of meeting my husband whenever relief may come'.[6] She concentrated her mind on taking care of Bobbie, who was getting stronger every day, so that when it *was* all over, she could take him to England, where he would be 'loved and cared for for his father's sake'.[7] She would occasionally take the child out for a walk but there were still shots flying about. One evening, a servant who was with her was wounded in the side by a musket ball which glanced across Bobbie's leg. Fortunately, there was only a slight graze and it did not turn septic.

Katherine had a few more comforts than before the arrival of the relief force. Her husband had brought with him two of their old servants, and these now stayed with her doing the harder work. She still found enough to occupy her. The weather was getting colder and warm clothes were needed. She herself had

240

only one black dress which she hoped would last the siege. The problem of washing clothes remained. There was still some soap available—at a price, but not a price Katherine could afford. Instead, it had been discovered that a mixture of water and coarsely ground lentils or grain was not too bad a substitute. Unfortunately, neither lentils nor grain were plentiful, and it was sometimes a question of whether to eat them or wash with them.

The shortage of soap had naturally made it difficult for the garrison to keep down vermin. Mrs Germon had taken strong measures against the lice which, even in Dr Fayrer's house, could not be kept at bay; 'light infantry' was the ladies' name for the pests which destroyed their peace and comfort. Most of the men had their hair cropped short, so that their heads were as bald as an egg. There was, at least, plenty of water, and officers had their servants scrub them down as if they were horses. One day, one of the relieving force—a rather elegant young man who had joined direct from England and had managed to keep himself looking unusually clean—remarked that he thought it odd that the officers had shaved their heads. He was told with great gravity by someone who had a Classical education that the reason was *pediculina* (from the Latin *pediculus*: a louse). The young officer, who obviously had not had the same advantages in life, thought this was some kind of brain fever, or choleraic attack. He was soon enlightened. 'Beastly,' he remarked, and suggested that those who suffered had only themselves to blame. At this, one of his companions cried: 'Come! Fetch a rake and let's draw his covert!' A comb was brought and a find made. Next day, the young officer appeared looking much like everyone else—a monk, one of his comrades remarked, in a very odd monastery.[8]

Mrs Germon, who had been in charge of supplies at Dr Fayrer's house until she was confined to bed with dysentery, recovered enough to take up her duties again. The reduced rations made it very difficult to produce anything eatable for the seventeen occupants of the house. There seemed to be even more bone in the meat ration than there had been before. The eternal stew of meat and rice, with a few chupattees, had become even less palatable now that the salt ration was so small. There was still tea to drink, but still no sugar or milk. There was little wine, and less beer— the celebrations at the end of September had seen to that. The commonest drink was a brew of charred chupattees and water, and a large jug of this was always put on the table at mealtimes. One Sunday there was a special treat. Dr Fayrer had contrived to shoot one hundred and fifty sparrows, which were made into a curry. Mrs Germon could not bear to taste it, but most people found it delicious.

Many were not as fastidious as Mrs Germon, and a great deal hungrier. Rees, arriving at a post to visit a friend and finding the breakfast dishes still on the table, could not resist picking up an already well-stripped bone and gnawing it clean. At the Martinière post, as the boys were queueing up for their dinner, a piece of a shell blew the pot containing the stew to pieces scattering the hot food all over the boys. Rather than waste any, they scraped it off their shirts and trousers. Officers, while on duty, diverted their stomachs by conjuring up visions of meals to be ordered as soon as they reached Calcutta. One young ensign dreamed permanantly of sausages and iced champagne. Others saw mirages of fresh cream and butter, rich milk and eggs.

Of eggs there was, in fact, a real scarcity, even for the upper ranks of the besieged. Though some of the hens kept by the garrison continued to lay, many had ceased, and been eaten. Mrs Inglis had kept one non-layer since early in the siege, but at last it was decided that it must go. But on the day the execution was to take place, young Johnny Inglis rushed in crying: 'Oh, Mama, the white hen has laid an egg!'[9] As Colonel Campbell of the 90th, who had been wounded when with the rearguard of the relieving force, had been taken into the Inglis's quarters, Mrs Inglis thought he should have the egg. To everyone's surprise the little white hen continued to lay an egg every day until the day after Campbell died. It never laid again, but no one had the heart to kill it for the pot.

Such happenings were, of course, unusual, but there could be occasionally pleasant surprises. On the birthday of one of the Martinière masters, he suddenly produced a plum cake which he claimed he had been preserving for just such an occasion; though it was small, every one of the boys had a piece. Mrs Hamilton Forbes could not stop the tears springing to her eyes when, one day, her husband's orderly appeared smiling and presented her with two glittering cubes of rock salt. Mrs Soppitt was given a glass of sherry by Mrs Ogilvie, the wife of the Sanitary Commissioner; it was the first she had tasted for months and she thought it put a little life into her. She could not help thinking that 'people are becoming generous with brighter prospects before them'.[10]

Brighter prospects there might be, but the present was still gloomy. At least Outram considered it so. In the middle of October he wrote to Brigadier Wilson at Cawnpore: 'The commissary has just informed me that after the strictest scrutiny, he finds that our attah [ground wheat] and bullocks (we have nothing else) will last only till the 18th proximo, on half rations for natives and three-quarters for Europeans. No possibility of our obtaining supplies unless previously relieved.'[11] Brigadier Wilson must have found this letter rather confusing—if, that is, Captain Bruce had told him of the contents of a letter he had received from General Outram, dated only five days before. According to this, the commissariat officers, also after the 'strictest scrutiny', had reported that the grain would only last until November 6, that the meat would not last even as long as that, and that rice rations could be kept up for only four more days. 'Unless,' Outram had written, 'unless, therefore, the Delhi troops come speedily to our aid, we must starve.'[12]

Some of the women, not so fortunate as the aristocracy quartered at Gubbins's or Fayrer's houses, sacrificed their own meagre rations so that their fighting husbands might have more. Thomas Henry Kavanagh would return to his wife to be greeted with: 'There, dear soul, you must be tired and hungry, and I have cooked that horrid bit of beef so nicely for you!'

'But, dear wife,' Kavanagh would reply, 'have you eaten any?'[13]

His wife invariably told him that she had already eaten, not knowing when he would come. It was a long time before he found out that, more often than not, she had foregone her share for his sake. A doctor, seeing the face of one such self-sacrificing woman covered with ugly blotches and sores, prescribed a change of diet —only to receive the tart reply: 'I wonder you don't prescribe a change of air!'[14]

A change of air was what everyone would not only have prescribed but willingly taken. Yet there was still no firm sign of relief. There was, however, some comforting news. On October 9, a runner came in with the information that the British had now retaken the whole of the city of Delhi, after bitter fighting in the streets and palaces. The old King of Delhi and his principal wife were prisoners, and a column commanded by Brigadier Greathed had marched for Oudh. The runner brought information from the Alambagh, which was apparently not closely invested by the enemy. Supplies, certainly, were getting in. This was good news, especially as Outram had not given up hope of opening up communications between the Residency and the Alambagh, perhaps even of evacuating some troops there. In any case, it would serve as an essential staging post when the time of final relief came.

On October 11 Outram wrote that the Alambagh must be held

at all costs. He no longer feared that the Europeans there would be without supplies, but if the vast number of camp followers—so essential to the movement of a relieving force—were to be prevented from deserting, then they too must be carefully looked after. Those among them who were Muhammadans and could therefore eat beef were to be given some of the European ration. The others, of course, would draw on the rations supplied specifically for them. Any plundering of the stores, he instructed the officer commanding at the Alambagh, must be dealt with severely. 'The Provost Marshal will inflict fifty lashes on any man caught in the act of plundering our own stores . . . The troops should be warned that the commanding officer has received my orders to direct the Provost Marshal to hang on the spot the next man found thus offending and that the order will be carried out.'[15]

There were also problems of discipline inside the Residency, though Outram had no intention of dealing with them as harshly as those in the Alambagh. In any case, in one breach of discipline he had in mind, the punishment was almost built into the crime. Divisional Orders issued early in October requested General Havelock to 'take the strictest measures to prevent the men of the different Brigades from going outside the picquets on any pretence. The bodies of five men belonging to the Artillery, who had gone out, it is supposed in search of liquor, two days ago, were found without their heads.'[16]

Men went out looking not only for food and drink and valuable loot, which despite the appointment of prize agents was still being taken and concealed. The relieving force had come in without any clothes other than those they were wearing. Unfortunately, the palaces of Lucknow, though they produced a number of expensive dress uniforms, were not very rich in ordinary shirts and trousers. As October grew older, the weather became colder. Between the old garrison and the new, competition for clothes became intense. An old shirt, which had belonged to Captain Fulton and was covered with mud from the mines, changed hands at an auction for £4·50. Even Outram was forced to acquire a new jacket. His secretary, Mr Money, was able to get hold of an almost new broadcloth coat which had belonged to Mr Ommanney, the Judicial Commissioner. Just in time, Money stopped his chief from wearing it on a visit of condolence to the widow.

The appearance of the new garrison soon began to resemble that of the old. Among the broken Doric columns and the ravaged gardens of the Residency, the inhabitants looked like so many Robinson Crusoes. The green baize from the Residency billiard table had worn well, even if it was now being worn by a different person. White drill fabric had been dyed with mixtures of inks from the offices. Strange shooting jackets and ruined uniform coats were worn over pyjamas made from embroidered curtains. There were patches in plenty, some of them exotic, some plain. Mrs Germon mended her husband's 'unmentionables' with a piece of the Reverend Mr Harris's sacrificed cassock. Headgear was even more extravagant and varied. There were shakos, forage caps, leather helmets, great topees wound around with turban cloth, large wide hats, some once white, others of rubbed fur. There were even a number of tall, still elegant, silk hats.

Cold nights produced the sight of officers and men huddled in rich quilts, a hole cut out for the head, and a string tied round the waist. Socks and shoes were more of a problem. Some people were lucky, and actually possessed both, though they did not necessarily match. One officer had discovered a new use for red tape, and had bound it around his legs; Kavanagh's comment was that 'it always tied one's *hands* before!'[17] The Indian soldiers were worse off—though, of course, as Mrs Germon reflected, they were used to wearing less, anyway. But her husband, Charlie, asked her to make a coat for his senior Indian officer and produced some cloth for the purpose. Mrs Germon took the best part of a day to cut it out and begin sewing it together. On her wedding anniversary, she had it ready for a fitting. Also, as a special treat, she cut out and made up a black silk necktie for her husband. She was so overcome by the gift of two lumps of sugar and a pint of champagne that Charlie had been keeping for the occasion that she quite forgot to ask whether the coat fitted or not.

She summoned up her memories of married life. Of the hotel in Barrackpur six years before, when they had celebrated their wedding earlier that day with a grand dinner. Of Lucknow and the Residency before the deluge. It was hard to think that the battered houses had once looked like elegant Italian villas designed by Palladio, their verandahs deep and heavy with flowers, the long windows gaily shuttered against the sun. Where now there was only ravaged mud, like a field ploughed by a giant, there had once been formal gardens—at this time of year beginning to live again with flowers. But Mrs Germon did not think that recalling past days made either herself or her husband discontented, 'only thankful that our lives had been so mercifully preserved through such awful scenes'. No one could see the battered state of Charlie's outpost 'without feeling that he has been most miraculously preserved'.[18] Together they walked to Dr Fayrer's

245

house. By about half past eight in the evening, Mrs Germon was in bed, her wedding anniversary over.

For someone else in the same building there were other pre-occupations. Outram, his eyes on the Victoria Cross for himself, was still concerned with seeing that others were recommended for it. He could not make the recommendations because he had not been in military command of the relieving force. This fact was, indeed, important, because it was to form the basis of his own claim. He had served during the march to Lucknow as a volunteer under General Havelock. However, he was now considering others. With his eternal cheroot in his hand, he dictated a letter to Havelock. It was a pleasing duty, he wrote, to recommend two names for the high distinction of the Victoria Cross. He had witnessed these men's valour himself but, as he carefully pointed out (for the record), he had on that occasion been under General Havelock's command. These men could therefore 'only through yourself receive the reward they justly merit'. The two men, Outram informed Havelock, were Captain Maude of the Royal Artillery, and—Lieutenant Havelock.

Captain Maude had shown his worth at the Alambagh during the advance on the Residency, and Outram was sure Havelock would agree with him that Maude had 'fully and honourably earned a right to the Cross which our Gracious Sovereign has instituted as a reward "For Valour"'. In the case of Lieutenant Havelock, Outram was aware that Havelock might be embarrassed, but he hoped that he might 'without giving offence, beg you, as a friend and comrade, as well as my official colleague, not to allow the name of this gallant young officer to militate against his just claims'.[19]

Outram need have had no fears. Havelock not only agreed about the fitness of Captain Maude, but about that of his son. 'It must of course afford me peculiar satisfaction,' he wrote in reply to Outram's letter, 'that the behaviour of my son in action has attracted your attention.' He knew that the younger Havelock would never accept the recommendation if it came from his father alone. But as the suggestion had come spontaneously from Outram, 'every such scruple may be laid aside, and the value of the decoration will be much enhanced to him, by its being virtually awarded by an unprejudiced judge, as well as by one, I trust you will permit me to add, whose proved gallantry and devotion to the service peculiarly fit him to judge of these qualities in another'.[20]

246

3
UNDERGROUND
AND OVERGROUND

OF THE two generals in the Residency, Havelock was now virtually unemployed. Since Outram had taken over command, he had very little to do. The defence was mainly a matter of engineering, and after his morning rounds Havelock could return to his headquarters for the rest of the day.

The campaign to relieve the Residency had exhausted Havelock both mentally and physically. He was now sixty-two, a veteran of many wars and attacks of ill health. In Calcutta, when he had been appointed to command, they had laughed at him because he insisted on wearing his campaign medals and his sword at all times. Many people had thought him too old for the job. He himself did not agree. He believed himself to be a really professional soldier, and had studied the campaigns of the world's great generals. He was a hard man, and though his men respected his virtues he was not much liked. Through all the bitter weeks, he had driven himself and his men to victory. Just before the capture of Cawnpore he had written to his wife, far away in Germany: 'One of the prayers oft repeated throughout my life since my schooldays has been answered and I have lived to command a successful action. Thanks to Almighty God who gave me the victory.'[1] His God was a Baptist god, but Havelock just escaped being a fanatic because he had a rather black sense of humour.

Now deprived of active command, Havelock spent most of his time reading accounts of great battles in Macaulay's *History of England*. He dined once a week at Gubbins's house. Gubbins had, in fact, asked him to take up residence there, but he preferred to remain at Ommanney's. He did, however, accept with pleasure the regular gift of a bottle of sherry, 'without which it would have gone ill with me'; his doctor had advised him 'to take something strengthening until we can get upon good diet again'.[2] It was still not clear when that day would come.

Though the enemy had increased its artillery and musket fire, the main campaign was underground. While the enemy tried to breach the walls of the palaces, the garrison was constructing a vast system of counter-mines, under the planning control of Captain Crommelin of the Bengal Engineers. By the end, twenty-one counter-mines had been dug, with two hundred feet of shaft and over three thousand feet of tunnel. Fortunately, the soil was now light and dry, though still firm enough for most of the mines to do without roof supports and casings. As there was some concern over the garrison's stocks of gunpowder, the normal custom was not to blow up the enemy mine but to break into it and drive the diggers away. This so upset the enemy that they began to place their own charges before the mine reached its intended point. It did not mean that they stopped digging.

The sight so familiar to the old garrison—of an officer suddenly dropping to the ground in the middle of a conversation to listen for the sound of the enemy's picks—now also became familiar to the new. So, too, did the unpleasant task of digging shafts and tunnels, and then standing guard in them.

Men of Havelock's force found this unnerving. Frequently, a soldier who had shown nothing but courage and fearlessness above ground ran with panic from the alarming darkness below. Early in October, one man who had been down a tunnel for the first time was scared by a harmless fall of earth and came rushing out. There he was chided by his officer: 'What did you think? That the enemy were coming after you?'

'I suppose so.'

'Well, no one knows better than you that if you think the enemy are there you should go at them and not back from them.'

'I didn't think at all,' confessed the soldier. 'Down below is very different from up above.'[3]

One officer who had been down for the first time emerged with an assumed look of dismay, saying how terrifying it was down there in the darkness. When some of his fellow officers implied that he was afraid, he offered to place a bottle of brandy at the end of one of the galleries. He was prepared to bet £10 that no one who had not yet been down a mine would go and bring it back. There were no takers. But it was not long before all of them were forced to go through the experience. One of them recorded what it was like.

Firstly, the only way down to the gallery was through a deep

248

shaft on the end of a rope. After that, there was nothing but dark-ness and the whine of mosquitoes. As the man moved up the tunnel, his back continually rubbing against the roof, he could hear nothing but his own breathing. Then he caught sight of a gleam of candlelight, which showed up the figure of a man squat-ting down with a cocked pistol in his hand. Without warning, he heard the sound of the enemy's pick, a cascade of earth, saw the gleam of metal in the candlelight, and was half deafened by the reverberations of a pistol. At the same time, the light went out. He took himself back along the tunnel as quickly as he could, with the guard following him. When he emerged, he recognised the guard as Thomas Henry Kavanagh.

This was not surprising. The tall, thirty-six-year-old Irishman, a flamboyant figure with his red-gold hair and beard and fiery blue eyes, was usually to be found at the most dangerous places during the siege. He was a very junior civil servant, a humble clerk, and had almost been dismissed the service eighteen months before the siege began for getting heavily in debt to Indian moneylenders. He owed them £780—more than two and a half years' salary. He was saved from dismissal by the then governor-general, Lord Dalhousie, who had written on his papers: 'Were the mere fact of being in debt to disqualify him . . . I apprehend there would be a large number of vacancies in the service.'[4]

The siege had given Kavanagh a sense of release, for though he had kept his job he still faced paying off his debt. His home had been shabby and his income too small to allow his wife to buy a new bonnet. The crisis, however, seemed to give Kavanagh the chance he had always hoped for—to break out of the drudgery of twenty years of unfulfilled ambition in dusty offices. He was determined to perform some great act of courage that would make his name. He was resolved, he wrote later, 'to die in the struggle rather than to survive it with no better fame than I took in to it'.[5] During the first siege, he had been active with the volunteers, but had made no great mark. After the arrival of the relieving force he had been quick to volunteer to join the parties going out on sorties against the enemy. Now, with the end of such expeditions, he had been appointed Assistant Field Engineer. His chief, Captain Crommelin, kept him continually on the go, and when Captain Crommelin fell sick and Colonel Napier took over, Kavanagh found him the most dangerous man he had ever worked with—'for if you escaped being shot by the enemy, you only lived to be walked to death'[6] by Napier.

Kavanagh's job was to visit and inspect the mines. It was very dirty work, and his old uniform of ancient breeches and jacket could not stand up to the wear. From one of the deserted palaces he brought some lengths of coarse canvas, and with the help of one of the ladies cut himself out a suit. As he peeled the skin from his fingers sewing the harsh material, the ladies laughed at him, but when the suit was finished he found it hard-wearing, and useful for keeping him dry and warm in the dank darkness of the tunnels. The Sikhs who worked with him called him *Burra Surungwala*, The Great Miner.

Down at the end of the tunnel he would sit, abominably cramped, for his long, lanky body barely fitted into the narrow galleries. As he waited for the sound of the enemy picks, his mind would wander, edged by fear. Would the roof cave in and leave him suffocating under mounds of earth? Would the enemy break in and catch him off balance; would his pistol misfire? Yet it was, he convinced himself, a trial by ordeal for something greater. Even the nine hours he had once spent waiting in a mine had been worth it. The enemy pick had been audible, coming nearer and nearer. Silently, Kavanagh had cocked his pistol and waited, scarcely breathing. It was two more hours before the wall crumbled and Kavanagh and the miner were face to face. But only for a moment. The pistol went off and the man fell back, mortally wounded and moaning pitifully. Kavanagh had barely hesitated. He could see the enemy's mining tools, and such tools were in short supply in the Residency. Stepping through the hole between the two mines, he saw that the gallery was unusually large and—more dangerously—not more than a few yards from the shaft. The tools were near the bottom of the shaft, and Kavanagh could hear shouting at the top. A little closer, and he could hear what was being said. Someone was calling for someone else to go down and bring up the wounded miner and his tools. Other men were obviously priming their muskets; Kavanagh could distinctly hear the jingle of ramrods. Suddenly a sepoy appeared. Kavanagh shot him in the stomach before he had time to fire his musket. Kavanagh had no time to reload his pistol, and there was only one round left in it. But he did not even think of retiring. He was wholly determined to take back that set of tools.

Lying on the floor of the gallery, he could actually see the sepoys' feet at the edge of the wide shaft. There was now a great deal of commotion. Shouting up in Hindustani, Kavanagh taunted the sepoys with cowardice, hoping that another of them would venture down into the mine. But the enemy preferred to let off a volley of musket balls into the gallery from the safety of above

250

ground. The smoke effectively drove Kavanagh back to his own mine. But he returned within a few minutes, his pistol fully charged, and accompanied by two Sikhs armed with muskets. Shouting further abuse at the enemy, Kavanagh heard himself in return being upbraided as a traitor, an eater of cow's meat who had sold his soul to the cursed foreigners. Kavanagh's two Sikhs were convulsed with laughter. The enemy had taken Kavanagh for one of the garrison's Indian soldiers.

When Kavanagh informed them that he was a British officer, the revelation was greeted with total silence. When Kavanagh reproached them with ingratitude to their British masters, cruelty to women and children, and warned them that nothing but ruin awaited them and their families, they were still silent.

'Why have you mutinied?' cried Kavanagh. 'What can you expect for the atrocities you have perpetrated?'

The voice of an invisible sepoy floated down to him. 'We are fighting for our religion which you mean to destroy.'

'In what manner have we threatened your faith?'

'By giving us greased cartridges.' The reply came back in a chorus.

But this, Kavanagh tried to explain, had been a mistake. The government had done its best to make that clear. It had never had any intention of disregarding their religious beliefs.

'Did you ever know the British government to make false professions?' he exhorted them. 'Has it not always spoken the truth?'

There was a moment's pause in this strange conversation, which was broken by a thoughtful voice remarking: 'It is true.' Silence fell again, as if everyone was thinking. Then there was the ring of a sharp command. An enemy officer had arrived at the head of the shaft. He ordered the sepoys to fire, but their aim was ragged, and one sepoy called that he 'wished to hear the sahib speak'. Kavanagh, seeing that their attention was diverted, could not resist making a dash for the mining tools. His rush frightened the sepoys back from the edge of the shaft, and he was able to make his way to his own mine with only a couple of shots falling very wide—deliberately wide, he thought. The next thing he heard was the sound of the enemy filling in the shaft with earth.[7]

When Outram heard of the conversation, he remarked without a smile that, as the Articles of War condemned a man to death for conferring with the enemy, he proposed to have Kavanagh hanged. He repeated the statement on a number of occasions,

251

successfully startling those who had not heard it before. Kavanagh was very proud of this peculiar distinction.

Kavanagh was not the only one who was waging a war of nerves against the enemy miners, though he seems to have been alone in his efforts to spread propaganda. Lieutenant Innes, as always at the forefront of any operation, was called one day to the Chuttur Munzil palace where mysterious sounds had been heard in a counter-mine which had been dug outwards from the palace walls. As he listened in the darkness, he could hear the sound of gentle scraping, obviously very near. Sending his sergeant back to the next bend in the gallery, he ordered him to post a chain of men, one at each turn in the tunnel as far back as the shaft. He himself stayed at the place where he thought the sounds were nearest.

As Innes sat in the dark the scraping stopped, and he saw a faint light reflected on the wall opposite him. As he had no light, this could only come from the enemy mine. It took some time to find the hole, which was very small indeed, but as Innes discovered it the scraping began again. When it stopped, he could hear whispering through the wall of the tunnel, and then more scraping. The hole began to grow bigger.

Suddenly, Innes broke down the thin partition of earth. The enemy doused their light and fled back up their gallery, hurried on their way by several shots from Innes's pistol. Innes and his sergeant followed them for some way but could not catch them before they disappeared up the shaft. The enemy began firing down the shaft, and then—apparently believing that they were about to be blown up—poured down quantities of water. Innes and his men replied with laughter and shouts of abuse.

Not all the action was underground. On October 17, the enemy exploded a mine under one of the outposts of the Farhat Baksh palace. This was followed by the breaching of the high wall which protected a post in a garden beyond the Chuttur Munzil, used for forward observation of the enemy's movements. After the breaching, a body of the enemy marched towards the post with colours flying. The men in the post were able to shoot down the leaders, and the force retired, leaving behind twelve bodies.

Particularly active among the defenders at this time were 'Brasyer's Sikhs'—British soldiers called them 'the Sykeses', Havelock preferred 'the Six'. These men had been raised by Jeremiah Brasyer, an ex-gardener with a vast white beard who had threatened to blow all his men to Hell if they ever thought of deserting. Their loyalty was entirely personal. During lulls in the fighting, Brasyer would gravely give his formal permission for the men to get drunk. Somehow, even in the Residency, Brasyer and his men contrived to find the means to this end.

October 20 brought in a message from Captain Bruce at Cawnpore containing news of Raja Man Singh. Ever since the relieving force had made its way to Lucknow, there had been rumours that Man Singh was prepared to negotiate and that he had even offered to escort the women and children from the Residency to Cawnpore. No one, of course, would have risked accepting such an offer, even if it had in fact been made. Memories of the 'safe conduct' offered by another Indian leader at Cawnpore were too recent. Was Man Singh a rebel leader, or a friend? In a letter he had sent to Captain Bruce for onward transmission to Outram, he explained that he had had no wish to take up arms against the British, and that he had in fact only gone to Lucknow to rescue a relative who had been detained there by the rebels. His second appearance in Lucknow had resulted from the news that the British had marched on the city and had defeated the rebels. He had also been told that the British were about to 'disgrace his Majesty's harem', and he had marched to save the female relatives of the ex-king of Oudh—as a loyal subject should, 'for he had eaten the king's salt . . . and could not keep himself aloof from protecting the king's honour'.[8]

Bruce told Outram that he had replied to Man Singh. 'I have received your letter, and enclosure for General Outram. The British do no injury to helpless women and children, however humble their rank, and you ought to have known that those of the King would not have been dishonoured. I have written to-day to General Outram, who is now in the Lucknow Residency, and in the meantime, if you are really friendly to the British Government, you are desired at once to withdraw all your men from Lucknow, and communicate with the Chief Commissioner [Outram]. I have sent to tell your vakeel [agent] that if he likes to come in and see me, he will meet with no injury.'[9] The agent had come in, and after telling Bruce that Man Singh was willing to do what Bruce suggested, had left for Lucknow. But the agent did not arrive at Lucknow, or, if he did, made no attempt to get in touch with Outram. On October 24, Inglis told his wife that there was now no real hope of coming to some agreement with Man Singh, and that all that could now be done was to wait patiently for the coming of the second relieving force.

Information on the movements of the force from Delhi remained somewhat confused, but it was still expected that the relief would arrive around November 7. On October 26, however, word arrived

253

17   *Lying in wait*

that Brigadier Greathed's column had defeated a large rebel force at Agra, and should arrive at Cawnpore by the first day of November. The relieving column was now commanded by Colonel Hope Grant of the 9th Lancers. The concentration of men at Cawnpore could not, it was thought, be completed before November 10, and it would be another five days at least before the force could be expected at Lucknow. Rations were therefore once again reduced. The numbers who now had to be fed amounted to 6,938. There were 2,866 European men, women and children; 755 Indian troops; and 3,317 camp followers and servants.

Outram was very much concerned over rumours that a new and powerful rebel force was about to join up with other mutineers in the region of Cawnpore. This force was said to have come from Gwalior, a princely state whose ruler had managed to keep his men quiet for some time. If this force did join up with the other rebels, the communications of the second relieving force would be in danger. It was more than possible that the commander-in-chief, Sir Colin Campbell, would decide to strike at the Gwalior troops first, before coming on to the rescue of the garrison at Lucknow.

With this possibility in mind, Outram wrote to Captain Bruce on October 28 to say that he had received various letters by a messenger named Kanauji Lal. He had once thought this man's loyalty to be doubtful, but he now said: 'Kanauji Lal has certainly proved himself most zealous and able, has richly earned reward, and shall assuredly obtain it.' In fact, Outram had such faith in him that he proposed sending Bruce a plan and further instructions for the officer commanding the relieving force, that night if possible, by Kanauji Lal's hand. 'If not ready to send by him,' Outram continued, 'I hope it may safely reach Alambagh by other means, there to await the arrival of Colonel Grant, or whoever may be in command of the force. I shall not detain Kanauji beyond to-night, being anxious to prevent the force being hurried from Cawnpore to Alambagh. The latter post, having now been amply supplied with food, and sufficiently strengthened to defy attack, is no longer a source of anxiety; and however desirable it may be to support me here, I cannot but feel that *it is still more important that the Gwalior rebels (said to be preparing to cross into the Doab) should be first disposed of.* I would therefore urge on Brigadier Wilson, to whom I beg you will communicate this as if addressed to himself, that I consider that the Delhi column, strengthened to the utmost by all other troops that can be spared from Cawnpore, should in the first instance be employed against the Gwalior rebels, should they attempt to cross into the Doab [the region between the Jumna and the Ganges], or be tangible to assault elsewhere within reasonable distance. We can manage to screw on, if absolutely necessary, till near the end of November on further reduced rations. Only the longer we remain the less physical strength we shall have to aid our friends when they do advance, and the fewer guns shall we be able to move out in cooperation.

'*But it is so obviously to the advantage of the State that the Gwalior rebels should be first effectually destroyed, that our relief should be a secondary consideration.* I trust, therefore, that Brigadier Wilson will furnish Colonel Grant with every possible aid to effect that object before sending him here.'[10]

Communications with the outside world had been deliberately restricted by Outram, who would not even enclose a personal letter of his own with the official despatches. 'Tell her I cannot write to her,' was Outram's message to his wife in the postscript of a letter to Captain Bruce. 'As our expensive messengers can carry only a quill, private communications have been forbidden for others, and I cannot in honour take advantage to write privately myself.'[11] Others were not, however, quite without resources. Gubbins had been sending messages out for some weeks, though he never heard whether they arrived. Another officer smuggled out a letter to his mother, telling her not to believe that he was dead until she had it on unimpeachable authority. That letter did get through.

All official correspondence was conducted using Greek characters, and this sometimes caused difficulties. On October 30, Outram sent to Major McIntyre a long letter giving suggestions for the relieving column's approach to the Residency, as well as a plan of the city. He asked McIntyre to request some of his friends to prepare a number of English versions, 'written out clear', so that the commander of the force would not be 'confused by the cramped hand and Greek character'[12] in which the instructions were written. McIntyre obviously found some trouble in complying with this request, and wrote to Outram to say that he would prefer future messages to be written in English in the first place. So would the enemy, replied Outram. 'As the only security against their understanding what we write in case our letters fall into their hands, the Greek character *must* be used.'[13]

Outram's suggestions for the movement of the relieving force were not the same as those which he and Havelock had adopted at the first relief. Then, having left the Alambagh, the force had crossed the canal at the Charbagh bridge and made directly into the city by the Cawnpore road. The new force should, Outram thought, make a wide circuit to the north-east, heading for another park known as the Dilkusha and then working round by the Martinière College and the Secundrabagh, keeping as much as possible to open country. After that, it would be a question of cooperation between the relieving force and the garrison, who could help with artillery fire and the exploding of some specially prepared mines. A system of signals was also suggested, and at the end Outram showed that he did not forget the garrison's need for supplies which would help keep up its morale. 'You will, I suppose, leave all the heavy baggage at the Alambagh,' he said, 'bringing only light carts, elephants, camels, and pony or bullock carriages, to the Dilkusha. But I beg you will bring the kits of the European troops here; for the cold weather is coming on, and they have neither greatcoats nor bedding.' There was something else just as important. 'When you advance from the Dilkusha, I hope you will be able to bring on with you a few days' supply of rum, tobacco and tea, for the Europeans (who have been so long without these luxuries), and gram [chickpeas] for our horses. Other supplies, which are less pressing, we can obtain when an escort can go back to the Dilkusha for more.'[14]

Outram had instructed McIntyre to hoist a flag on the roof of the small palace in the Alambagh as an indication that he had received the plan and the despatch. The next morning, the flag was seen flying. An officer present suggested that, since the flag could be seen so clearly, it might be worth erecting a semaphore on the Residency roof and another at the Alambagh so that messages could be sent by that method. The distance between the two points was considerable, nearly three and a half miles in a direct line, and the city was frequently overhung by a dense haze. Nevertheless, the suggestion was taken up. Did anyone know how to construct a semaphore machine? Fortunately, Mr Gubbins's excellent library—what survived of it—contained the answer. It was found under the heading 'Telegraph' in the *Penny Cyclopaedia*.

Major McIntyre was instructed to get Captain Sibley, his second in command—'I know he is a great mechanic,' wrote Outram—to build a semaphore machine to the enclosed design. The one at the Residency would be ready in a couple of days. An additional machine should be made for the relieving force to carry with it for setting up on the roof of the Martinière College. 'The evening before the day on which we propose telegraphing to you,' Outram went on, 'a bonfire will be lit on the highest point of our

258

position (the Residency roof), to enable you to know exactly our whereabouts. A similar illumination on the top of the Alambagh will be proof to us that our signal has succeeded.

'We shall signal at twelve noon, of each day, the time best suited; for the enemy annoy us least at this hour, and our signallers consequently will incur less danger.

'Even should our signals fail from your being too far from us, still do not delay in having two sets of telegraphic apparatus prepared; for so soon as we establish one set of apparatus at the Martinière, and yours also is ready, the signals will be carried on without difficulty.' [15]

All these activities, as well as the latest news that was available, were always communicated to the officers of the garrison, though not in detail, in case there might be some leakage to the enemy. Naturally, spirits began to rise again, even though the food ration was by now extremely small. On October 30 there was a great sale of goods, with brandy selling readily if not at such a high price as some tinned provisions. Rees, who had very little money, was unable to buy anything in competition with those who were better off. After their meals, he and his friends felt 'a deplorable emptiness; overeating is no complaint with us. We live in a great Sahara of wants'.[16] He hoped sincerely that the news of forthcoming relief was true, and not just another false promise to be 'added to the great mass of unredeemed expectancies'.[17]

A few newspapers from Calcutta and some copies of *Home News* had been smuggled into the Residency concealed in bundles of grass. These were avidly read, though they were all much out of date. Katherine Bartrum wondered whether her relatives in England knew what had happened to her. Her husband's name had not been on the first list of killed and wounded which had been sent out, and the news had probably not yet reached England. She hoped Robert's mother would have God's comfort 'when she shall learn the sad truth'.[18] Bobbie seemed to be growing stronger every day, but still had 'an old, sad look; and no wonder, poor child, shut up in this terrible way'.[19] The boy's chief amusement was calling the monkeys who were always running about the roofs of the houses and among the ruins, and could be enticed with the offer of a little food.

There were still deaths, and still the danger of being wounded. One young officer, Charles Dashwood, whose brother had been killed leaving him responsible for the widow and two children, had been injured when his own revolver went off at the beginning of the siege but had managed to play a part with the aid of crutches.

Dashwood was interested in sketching, and was amusing himself making a drawing—in an extremely exposed position—when a roundshot wounded him in the feet. The shot had come from a six-pounder gun across the river, which the enemy moved from place to place. Dashwood had already received warning when an earlier shot from the gun had passed near him, but he did not move away. There was no alternative but to amputate both his feet above the ankle. No chloroform was available for the operation. Despite the sentence of death implied by amputation, the doctors thought he might possibly live to reach England again.

That same day there were three fatalities. A milk goat belonging to Mrs Couper, and two kids from Mrs Inglis's small flock were out grazing when they were stolen and slaughtered by some men of the Madras Fusiliers. Mrs Inglis could not blame them. The men suffered much from hunger at that time. The cold weather and the lack of warm clothes, combined with much work, she thought, gave them 'an appetite which they had no means of satisfying'.[20] It was not unusual for a soldier to offer two rupees for a small chupattee—stealing one, if he had to, but leaving the money behind.

Fortunately, Mrs Inglis was able to spare Mrs Couper a little milk now that she had been deprived of the only goat she had had left. Mrs Couper had always been one of the most consistently gloomy people in the Residency. 'Poor Mrs C—,' wrote Mrs Case in her journal, 'comes to see us every day. She is so desponding and melancholy when she talks of provisions being likely to fail, that it is quite sad to hear her.'[21]

The old garrison was now in its fifth month of siege. On November 6, the 129th day, it was reported that the column from Delhi had already crossed the Sai river and was waiting at Bani for the arrival of the force from Cawnpore before making for the Alambagh. The commander-in-chief had also arrived at Cawnpore and was expected to reach the Alambagh by the 10th at latest, having decided that the Gwalior mutineers, though threatening, would have to wait. Campbell was convinced that Outram's situation in the Residency, with the extreme shortage of supplies he was constantly referring to in his letters, must be relieved first.

With Campbell would move some 3,400 men, including a Naval Brigade under Captain William Peel, with eight heavy guns dismounted from *H.M.S. Shannon* and two rocket launchers on light carts. When they joined up with Hope Grant's force, there would be more than 5,000 men and nearly forty guns. It was very reassuring news.

This information came from Captain Bruce at Cawnpore. There had been nothing from the Alambagh since the flag had acknowledged receipt of the plans and despatches for the commander of the relieving force. There was no sign of the semaphore going up on the roof of the palace. On November 7 Outram sent out a copy of his previous letter. In a covering note, he instructed McIntyre to get the semaphore pole up as quickly as possible. 'When your pole is up, I shall light my beacon the night we see it, and have our telegraph ready for noon, next day. Should there be difficulty in making out the signals at this distance, at all events the telegraph will be of service after the intermediate one is erected at the Martinière.

'I have requested the officer commanding the relieving force to light a beacon fire on the top of the Alambagh at 8 p.m. on the evening before advancing to Dilkusha. To prevent mistakes, a salvo of four or more guns should be fired *twice*. I have requested him to fire a similar salvo three times (five minutes interval) at 2 p.m. on the day of his arrival at Alambagh.'[22]

The enemy was not unaware of what was going on. The news that the Delhi force was near had reached the city on about the 2nd of the month, and it was said that Raja Man Singh, who had been keeping up a desultory correspondence with Outram, had departed at once, with all his men. This was taken within the Residency as a good sign. But Man Singh's defection, if such it was, did not seem to lessen the enemy's activity. Shells still hit the Residency. A soldier's wife was badly injured by masonry which had been sent flying by an enemy missile.

But there was no doubt now that relief was near. Inglis began preparations for the evacuation of the women and children, the sick and the wounded, on about the 13th of the month, the expected date. Everything should be ready, he told Mrs Case. All that the ladies would be allowed to take with them would be a change of clothes, and those they would have to carry themselves, wrapped up in a bundle. People who were fit, or capable of moving on crutches, would have to walk to the Alambagh, as all the carriages and carts would be needed to carry the seriously ill and wounded. 'It will be a dreadful affair getting us off!' thought Mrs Case.[23]

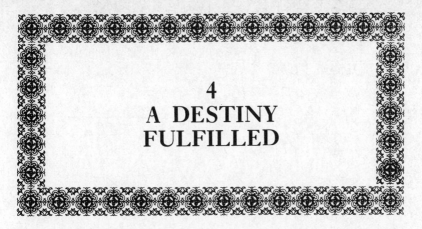

4
A DESTINY
FULFILLED

AT THE end of the first week in November his friends noticed a profound change in Thomas Henry Kavanagh. Even at times of greatest peril and exhaustion, he had always had a genial greeting for everybody. Now he seemed morose and remote. Perhaps he was ill? Perhaps even his great strength was giving out? No one guessed that Kavanagh was struggling with a sense of destiny. A few days before, his friend James May, a draughtsman in the Engineers Department had shown him the plans he had been working on for General Outram. They showed detailed routes into the city and to the Residency, for the use of Sir Colin Campbell and the relieving force. Looking at them, Kavanagh suddenly realised that only one route was being suggested, and that was one which would be difficult to follow without the aid of someone who knew it well. Havelock had been accompanied by two men who knew the city and its narrow ways, yet he had still suffered severely, so severely that the force had been unable to break out again. Under no circumstances must the same fate be allowed to overtake Campbell. And what if the action suddenly opened up an easier and safer route? Without inside knowledge, Campbell would not be able to seize an opportunity to save lives.

Kavanagh knew Lucknow as well as he knew his own house. Was it *his* destiny to cross those terrible miles of enemy territory which would separate Campbell at the Alambagh from the defenders in the Residency?

On November 8 he heard that Kanauji Lal had come in once again with despatches from Cawnpore. Kavanagh knew that it was now or never, for Kanauji would be certain to be sent back with the plans. Kavanagh sought out Kanauji Lal and told him that he had decided to disguise himself as an Indian and go back with Kanauji that night to the Alambagh. What did Kanauji think of the idea? The Indian did not hesitate. It was quite impossible. Any attempt would endanger not only Kavanagh's life but his own. Looking at Kavanagh's height, at the colour of his hair and eyes, Kanauji must have thought him mad, though he did not say so.

But Kavanagh, now committed to the fulfilling of his destiny, was very persuasive. Under pressure, and with the offer of a substantial reward, Kanauji at last agreed. But he refused to leave the entrenchment in company with Kavanagh. He would go by a different exit, and they would meet at an agreed rendezvous outside the city. This was no use as far as Kavanagh was concerned. He knew certain parts of the city very well, but his acquaintance with all the miles of narrow lanes and byways was not enough to enable him to find his way in total darkness. In any case, though his Hindustani was excellent for a European, he did not think it would stand up to a long interrogation if he were stopped—as he was sure to be—by some officious sentry. Kanauji refused to commit himself further.

Kavanagh went off to a quiet corner. If Kanauji would not go with him, was there anyone else who might take the risk? There could be no certainty of success without an Indian companion. Alone and oblivious to everything else, Kavanagh was suddenly overcome by the realisation of what he was proposing to do. For weeks he had faced death many times, but now he was contemplating going out to look for it in cold blood. His heart beat so fast that he thought it was going to burst from the ribcage. He put his head in his hands and the tears began to roll down his cheeks. He felt a great emotional release, but could remain alone no longer. He needed the company of those with whom he had fought and for whose sake he hoped he would make the right decision. By two o'clock on the afternoon of November 9, Kavanagh had decided. He would go to Outram's chief of staff, Colonel Napier, and volunteer.

Napier's surprise was total, and he could not resist a smile at the thought of this tall, light-haired, blue-eyed Irishman trying to pass himself off as a native. But he was so impressed by Kavanagh's seriousness that he agreed to go with him to Outram. Chewing on his inevitable cheroot, Outram listened to Kavanagh in silence. It was surely worth a try, Kavanagh argued, and what was there to lose? One life, against many saved, perhaps, if he were successful. The Irishman's insistence appealed to Outram. It brought back memories of his own youth. But no, he could not allow it. The chances of a European getting through the enemy lines were too remote. He could not permit himself to order an officer to try. How, then, could he ask a volunteer? But Kavanagh still persisted. Surely the chance *must* be taken, and he was not only willing but qualified to take it. At last Outram gave in—but only if Kavanagh could satisfy him that his disguise was so perfect that he would escape detection. Though he did not say so, Outram considered this highly improbable. Of all the many men inside the Residency, Kavanagh was the one who least resembled an Indian.

When he left Outram, Kavanagh returned to his quarters in the Post Office garrison. He could not rest, but lay on his bed with his back turned to his wife, who was giving the children their scanty meal, in case she saw in his face the agonies he was going through. When she offered him a chupattee to eat, he replied that he was too tired to think of food and asked only to be left alone. But his thoughts would not be quiet. What of his wife, who for thirteen years had been patient and courageous under the weight of ambitions unsatisfied and debts rising? All without complaint. And their children, of whom no father could have been more proud? Why was he proposing to risk not only his life but their future? Saying that he was needed at the mines, Kavanagh hurriedly left the room.

He went off to the Tehri Koti and found a corner in one of the underground rooms. He could not face the prospect of leaving his family destitute if he should die. There was nothing for it but to give up the idea.

On his way back to the Post Office, however, he called in at the ammunition factory near the Baillie Guard gate and chatted with Major North about the coming relief. After fifteen minutes of conversation, he had changed his mind again. He was now determined that nothing would stop him. Whatever the consequences, he would go. First he had to convince Outram, and he set about collecting the materials for his disguise.

Moving around the Residency area, seeking out servants and camp followers, he began to gather a wardrobe. From one man he acquired a short jacket of orange silk, from another a creamy-coloured turban cloth. Then a tight-fitting muslin shirt, tight trousers, also of silk. He needed and found a good dagger and a curved sabre of the kind usually carried by robbers or soldiers of fortune. To these he added—each item being borrowed from a different person, so that none would guess his plan—a white waistband, a piece of gay yellow chintz, and a pair of long-toed Persian slippers. The only thing he could not find was a supply of

265

good permanent dye.

With his clothes and arms in a bundle, he returned to his quarters and stayed with his family until six in the evening. Then he kissed them all and left, saying that he was off to the mines and would not be back till morning. Carrying his bundle, he made for the slaughter yard where another man, Francis Quieros, who knew what Kavanagh intended, was waiting to help with the disguise. Dressed in his Indian clothes, Kavanagh began to make up his face, Quieros holding the mirror. All he had been able to find to darken his skin was a mixture of oil and lampblack, which did not seem to give an authentic tone. But there was no choice, and face and hands and wrists were soon tinted almost black. Quieros had already snipped off the long curls from Kavanagh's head, and his moustache and beard were trimmed in the Indian manner. The rest of his hair had to be covered by the turban. Kavanagh thought he looked ugly, but not convincing enough. However, there was no more time to spare. He would have to keep as much in the shadow as possible and hope for the best. When Kanauji Lal joined them, he seemed much amused at the change in Kavanagh's appearance.

With Kanauji Lal following, Kavanagh made his way to Outram's headquarters. This was to be the real test, and everything depended on success. Kavanagh swaggered along with his sabre over his shoulder and his shield of buffalo hide slung on his back. But inwardly he was trembling. At Outram's house he could hear voices. He hoped that Napier, at least, would be there. He must make a dramatic entry, which would draw everyone's attention.

It was considered extremely offensive for an Indian to enter a house without first removing his shoes, and also for him to sit down without being invited. This was an Indian attitude which had been taken over by Europeans. So Kavanagh strode into the room still wearing his shoes, sat down, and made himself comfortable on one of the chairs near a wall. The officers crowded round the table asked him angrily who he was and what he thought he was doing. Kavanagh replied that he was a friend, and did they not know him? His confidence began to grow, and when Outram came into the room and also took some time to recognise him he knew that he had succeeded.

When everyone realised that this was Kavanagh in disguise, the atmosphere changed from suspicion to hilarity. Each member of the staff made his own suggestions for improvement. Kavanagh's turban was not at quite the right angle for the type of man he was pretending to be; careful hands adjusted its folds. A pair of

266

wide, pajama trousers was produced to add authenticity. Outram himself touched up Kavanagh's make-up. All the men were shaking with laughter as if Kavanagh were about to leave for a fancy dress ball. Outram's aide-de-camp, Captain Sitwell, underlined the fact that more serious matters were afoot by presenting Kavanagh with a small double-barrelled pistol, ready and loaded. Everyone knew what it was for. If Kavanagh were in danger of capture, it would be better for him to shoot himself rather than risk slow death at the hands of the enemy.

The time had come. Outram had prepared a letter written in English, French, and Greek characters.* This was handed to Kavanagh with the suggestion that, if he reached the Alambagh safely, Major McIntyre should raise a flag on the semaphore pole. It was half past eight. The laughter had stopped, and it was with serious faces that the staff shook Kavanagh's hand and wished him 'God speed'. With Kanauji Lal, and Lieutenant Hardinge—who would pass them both through the picquets—Kavanagh walked through the darkness. He could still hear Outram's last words to him: 'Noble fellow! You will never be forgotten.'

Kanauji had agreed to go with Kavanagh. Their route was across the river; it was safer that way. They intended to move along the north bank and then return across the iron bridge. The two men stripped and wrapped their clothes in bundles. The night was very dark, although there were a few stars showing and the scattered lights of the enemy positions speckled the other side. At this point the river was a hundred yards wide and not more than five feet deep. But the water was icy cold. With their bundles on their heads the men entered the water. The sharp wound of the cold, the blackness of the night, the peril perhaps waiting on the other side—all tugged at Kavanagh's resolution. If Kanauji had been by his side, Kavanagh would have grasped his arm and told him they must go back. But he was ahead, and Kavanagh had no alternative but to follow. Already Kanauji was across and clambering up the other side. Kavanagh followed in panic, keeping as close as he could when Kanauji next led him through a grove of trees to a pond.

As the two men had almost reached it, another man appeared out of the bushes and began to wash in the water. Yet Kanauji and Kavanagh succeeded in dressing again, very quietly, and the man did not hear them. Kavanagh suddenly began to feel that all was

*See 'Sir James Outram's "secret" letter', p. 307.

going well.

Moving forward, they came to a line of huts; in front was the figure of a patrolling matchlockman. Should Kavanagh hail him first and so allay suspicion?

'The night is cold,' he called out.

'It is very cold,' replied the other, 'In fact, it *is* very cold.'

Kavanagh remarked that it would probably get even colder as the night wore on, and he and Kanauji passed on to the iron bridge. There they were stopped by an officer seated on the upper verandah of a house. Where had they come from? Kanauji replied this time —they had come from the cantonment of Mariaon. All was well.

As they approached the stone bridge the number of people increased. There were sepoys and matchlockmen, some of them escorting people of obvious rank borne in palanquins, and accompanied by servants carrying torches. There was too much light for Kavanagh's comfort, and the two men kept as much to the shadows as possible. Crossing the bridge without incident, they were back in the city. The main street they now entered was not full of people, as Kavanagh remembered it, but, fortunately, neither was it as well lit as it had formerly been. There were bodies of armed men at intervals, and a guard detail of seven sepoys—who seemed too much preoccupied in bargaining with some prostitutes to have much attention to spare for anyone else.

Kanauji wanted to take to the dark alleys, but Kavanagh would not have it. It was safer, he believed, in crowds. At last they reached the outskirts of the city. For five months, Kavanagh's nose and mouth had been forever full of the stench of decay and death. It had followed him through the streets of the city. But now the clean, sweet air of the fields caught him in the throat like a fine wine. There were the smells of jasmine and lime. From a garden, he picked a carrot—the taste was indescribably beautiful. As they walked through the scented night, Kavanagh talked to Kanauji about the great fertile country of Oudh as if it were paradise. Then the dream ended. They had arrived at the Dilkusha park, miles to the north-east of their objective, the Alambagh. It was now midnight. They asked an old peasant watching over his crops if he would show them the way. He pleaded lameness. Another who came up ran off screaming when Kavanagh grasped his arm, and all the village dogs began to bark. The two men made for the shelter of the nearby canal, Kavanagh cursing as the harsh ground bit through his elegant, but thin slippers.

In the dark they could not see where they were going. They fell into ravines, ran into garden walls, but at last came to another village. Here, all was quiet. On his hands and knees, Kavanagh crawled forward and into one of the huts. His hand touched the soft thigh of a woman. He whispered urgently, and she did not scream. Would she guide them? She woke her mother and then, without further question, set them on their way.

Kavanagh was finding the going increasingly difficult. His feet felt raw, and the weeks of malnutrition now began to drain his strength. At about two o'clock the two men stumbled on a picquet of sepoys, but after only a few words of conversation they were on their way again. It was then that Kanauji Lal broke it to Kavanagh that the approach to the Alambagh was very difficult. It was honeycombed with trenches and, furthermore, Kanauji admitted that he had never been there. His contacts had been with the camp of the commander-in-chief at Bani, nearly eighteen miles from Lucknow.

There was nothing for it but to go on. The moon was now rising and at least they could see their way, though Kavanagh stumbled along on blistered feet. At three o'clock in the morning they heard a man singing as they approached a mango grove. Their appearance frightened the singer so much that he cried out—and was answered by a body of twenty-five sepoys posted in the grove. Kanauji Lal, fearful of being caught with them in his possession, threw away his copy of the despatches. But not Kavanagh. The sepoys, he explained, had startled his friend by their sudden appearance. They themselves were only two poor travellers making for a village near Bani to tell a friend of the death of his brother in Lucknow. The sepoys, who had been—Kavanagh thought afterwards—almost as frightened as he had, passed them on and even showed them the way.

Their directions led the two men into a swamp. It seemed to cover the whole of the area. Yet they had to pass through. At times, the water came up to their waists, mud sucked at their legs, the reeds were almost razor-edged. In deep water, Kavanagh had to help Kanauji. Kanauji swore at every step—at the water, at the mutineers, at the mud, the reeds, the old and lovely land of Oudh. When he had recovered from his fright, he even laughed at his own obscenities, and both men began to feel better. But by the time they had reached dry land Kavanagh felt exhausted. What was worse, the dye had completely gone from his hands, leaving them pink and freckled. He did not have the courage to ask Kanauji what his face looked like. But he had to rest for a while, whatever the danger, and however much Kanauji wanted to push on.

18 *Interior of the Alambagh*

After fifteen minutes, they moved through two of the enemy's picquets to a village where Kanauji woke a man to guide them on their way. They were, said Kanauji, sent by Raja Man Singh to find out the strength and position of the English dogs.

'Have you not heard that from the fellows who ran from them?' was the snarled reply. 'Go away and do not disturb our rest.'

Quickly the two men moved on through the lifting darkness, skirting the soft glow of the sepoy fires, listening for a moment to the murmur of many voices which meant that there was a sepoy camp nearby. There were other people on the road, too. Villagers fleeing from the battle—running for their lives, with their bullocks and chattels, from the British who, one of them said, were murdering and plundering all about them. They were too afraid to stop and tell the travellers more.

But where exactly was the British camp? It was four o'clock in the morning and time was running out. So, too, was Kavanagh's strength. He slumped down to the ground. Whatever Kanauji's objections, he must rest.

A moment later he was roused by a shout of 'Hoo cum dar?'

'Who comes there?' Were these really the British lines? Had Kanauji Lal reconnoitring the ground, stumbled upon a British Indian sentry, or was it one of the mutineers? Rushing forward, Kavanagh found Kanauji trying to be circumspect in his replies to the sentry. But it *was* a British picquet, and Kavanagh was soon able to make it clear to the Sikh officer in charge that he had come from the Residency with a message from General Outram and that he must reach the commander-in-chief as quickly as possible.

As the two men, escorted by two Sikh troopers, made their way towards the advance guard of the force, they were intercepted by an officer of the 9th Lancers. When he found out who they were he led Kavanagh to a tent, gave him dry stockings and a pair of trousers, and insisted that he should take a glass of brandy. Kavanagh thought he must be dreaming. Was he really safe? The spirits warmed his body, but his mind remained cold with the tensions of his nightmare journey. When the commander of the rearguard was roused from his bed and heard the story, he had a little Burmese pony harnessed for Kavanagh, and they set off for the main camp.

It was now 5 a.m. and the sun was rising into a beautifully clear blue sky. Before him Kavanagh could see one of the most welcome of sights, long lines of tents, guns clustered together. As they approached one of the tents Kavanagh saw by the blackboard at the flap that it was that of the commander-in-chief. At the door stood a spare, elderly man with a stern face. In reply to Kavanagh's query, he replied sharply, and in a strong Scots accent: 'I am Sir Colin Campbell, and who are you?'

Pulling off his turban, Kavanagh took from it Outram's letter. 'This, sir, will explain who I am and from whence I came.'

As Sir Colin read, he kept raising his eyes to Kavanagh's face. 'Is it true?' he asked.

'I hope, sir,' Kavanagh replied, 'you do not doubt the authenticity of the note?'

'No, I do not. But it is surprising,' was Sir Colin's answer. 'How did you do it?'

It was the moment of triumph—but Kavanagh was too exhausted to take advantage of it. All he wanted was a few hours' rest, and then he would tell everything. In the meantime, perhaps the commander-in-chief would be so kind as to send a messenger to raise a flag on the Alambagh, so that Outram would know that his trust had been justified.

As soon as Kavanagh was alone in a tent which had been carefully darkened for his comfort, he knelt down by the side of the truckle bed and thanked God for his safe journey. He could not sleep, but lay there comparing himself with the great heroes of antiquity. Would his name, too, survive into history? He hoped at least that the good, patient, and lovely women of Lucknow would remember him as the one who delivered them from the dark-skinned monsters.

At about 10 a.m. an aide-de-camp came to invite him to take breakfast with the commander-in-chief, and Kavanagh hurried to the breakfast tent. The table was so mouth-watering he could scarcely attend to the compliments and questions that were hurled at him. There was coffee, with milk and sugar. There were platters piled with bacon and eggs, and, even more exotic, white bread and golden butter and rich, chunky Scottish marmalade. Through mouthfuls of this ambrosial food, Kavanagh briefly told his story. It still seemed too improbable to be true. Even the tent, with its soft blue and buff Persian carpet on the floor, did not seem to fit. Or perhaps it was Sir Colin himself who was out of place, dressed as he was in a blue patrol jacket, brown corduroy breeches, his pith helmet at his side.

But it was certainly true that the commander-in-chief was now discussing his plans with a humble clerk, and doing so in private. Kavanagh was even more delighted when Campbell asked him not to mention the details of their discussions to his officers.

273

Once his plans were known, everyone would have his own opinion, and that was often dangerous. Kavanagh felt that he had succeeded beyond his wildest dreams. His destiny had been fulfilled and, he thought, even if he should fall on the way to the relief of the Residency, a grateful government would see that his wife and children were protected.[1]

Part 5

❧

FINAL
RELIEF

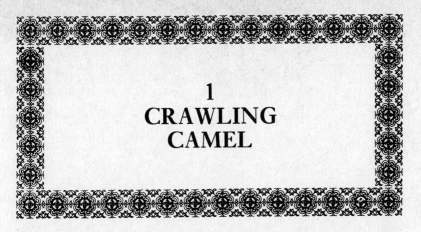

1
CRAWLING CAMEL

ON NOVEMBER 10, as soon as it was light, the lookouts in the Residency were told to keep a careful eye on the semaphore arm at the Alambagh for a signal flag that would mean Kavanagh had arrived. There was no sign by mid-morning, and as the semaphore communication system was now, in fact, working, Outram sent a message: 'Has Kavanagh arrived?' The reply that came back was: 'Unintelligible.' But at last, at midday, the lookout reported that the flag had gone up. This meant that Kavanagh was safe. The news soon flew round the Residency and the outlying posts. Everyone was delighted, not least General Outram. Mr Rees was among the many who went to congratulate Mrs Kavanagh on her husband's success. He found her 'vexed and annoyed, and yet delighted'.[1] As the poor woman had not even known until that morning that her husband had gone, her mixed feelings were hardly surprising.

But where was the salvo of guns from the Alambagh that would announce the arrival of Sir Colin Campbell and the relieving force? It had not come by eight o'clock that night. A tar barrel was lit on the roof of the Residency, and an answering blue light was seen from the Alambagh. Even if the force had not yet reached the Alambagh, it was near at hand.

It was not until November 12 that the signal came from the Alambagh that the force was ready to march and would advance on the Dilkusha on the 14th.

Outram's preparations to help Campbell were complete. Two new batteries had been constructed in the gardens of the Chuttur Munzil palace, behind the high walls, which had been mined so that they could give the guns a clear field of fire when the time came. The defenders in the Residency could hardly keep still at the prospect of rescue, and an order had to be given that no one was to leave his position until after the relief. Disease and death could not wait, however. Colonel Campbell, for whom Mrs Inglis's white hen had so suddenly begun to lay, died in great pain on the 12th. Brigadier Inglis, even, had been compelled to take to his bed for a few days but now insisted on getting up.

Towards midday on the 14th, heavy firing was heard to the south-east. Sir Colin Campbell and his men were on the move. There was, however, no firm news in the Residency until the evening, when beacons were lit both on the Dilkusha palace and the Martinière, although it had been reported earlier that British officers could be seen on the roof smoking cheroots. The enemy was extremely active that night, keeping up a strong fire from guns and muskets. But nothing, it was thought, could stop Sir Colin now.

The relieving force seemed to advance no further on the following day. The garrison was on continuous watch, ready to assist.

It was Brigadier Inglis's birthday. Mrs Inglis invited one of the officers to dinner. As it was a special occasion, there was to be a tart, an extravagance Mrs Inglis would certainly not have been guilty of if hopes of relief had not been so high. Young Johnny ran after the officer screaming at the top of his voice: 'Come to dinner! We've got a pudding!'

But it was no real substitute for Sir Colin. Some of the garrison remembered that Sir Colin Campbell had a nickname—'Sir Crawling Camel'—but others pointed out that he was also called 'Old Khabadar', which was Hindustani for 'Walk Warily'. With so much at stake, it would be wiser for him not to repeat Havelock's experience.

The lookouts on the Residency roof reported that the enemy had crossed the bridge of boats and could be seen advancing in the direction of the Martinière. Soon after, guns were heard in that direction and there were signs that the enemy was in retreat again. Everyone was anxious for news, but it was not until night had almost fallen that the semaphore on the Martinière sent the signal that Sir Colin would advance tomorrow. The guns and mortars of the relieving force that night carried out a heavy bombardment of the enemy positions. Shells lit up the sky, their long tails of flame like so many comets. It was a splendid sight.

Excitement was great next day inside the Residency. The roofs were crowded with officers, and even some of the ladies joined them, as the mutineers' attention seemed to be wholly concentrated on the attacking force.

278

From the roofs the action could clearly be seen. It was soon apparent that Sir Colin had decided on a more northerly route than the one Outram had recommended, but troops could distinctly be seen approaching the walls of the Secundrabagh, and Sir Colin's guns were soon firing on the high, loopholed walls of the park. Through the smoke, bayonets flashed in the sun. From a vantage point in the Chuttur Munzil palace Mr Gubbins could see the kilts of the 93rd Highlanders, already famous for their exploits in the Thin Red Line at Balaclava.

From the Secundrabagh, Campbell's men moved on the Shah Najaf tomb. From the palace, the tomb appeared to be surrounded by great masses of the enemy, sepoys and matchlockmen. At the Chuttur Munzil, the order came to unmask the batteries in the garden, and the mines were exploded to bring down the wall. Unfortunately, they had been laid for detonation on the 15th, and delay had allowed the powder to become damp. Part of the charges did explode, but there was still a large run of wall left standing. Through two of the holes that had been blown the enemy began a heavy fire directed at the batteries and at a garden house behind. There, Outram and a number of others—including Mr Gubbins— had been observing operations. Gubbins left, but Outram would not move, and only narrowly missed being hit by a six-pounder shot.

That afternoon, the British guns opened up on the wall in the Chuttur Munzil garden, tearing great gaps in the masonry, and finally bringing down the wall the mines had failed to break.

Other mines were more successful. At about three o'clock a breach was made in the walls of another small palace to the right of the Chuttur Munzil position and the guns made further breaches in a building known as 'the steam-engine house' directly in front. Havelock, who was in command, ordered an advance on the two points. To the sound of the bugle and the cheers of the men, both were quickly taken, despite very heavy fire from the enemy in the Kaisarbagh palace, which overlooked the positions. All that now stood between the relieving force and the advance guard of the garrison were the old Mess House of the 32nd, and the Moti Mahal palace. Havelock and Outram were very pleased with the day's work. What they did not know was that Campbell's men had suffered severely.

That night, a new battery was set up by the garrison in advance of the steam-engine house. As there were no gun-bullocks, the guns—an eight-inch howitzer and two large-calibre guns—had to be manhandled. All around, the enemy was active. They attacked the Martinière College during the night, and also the walls of the Dilkusha. A large force was reported near the Alambagh. The noise of their drums and fifes could be heard from across the river.

Inside the Residency, the day's fighting had been watched with growing excitement. Mrs Germon observed that the smoke from the mines was quite different from that of the guns. Thick yellow smoke from the mines; almost white from the guns. The watchers from the roofs could see the roundshot striking across the river, and rockets could be observed flaming into the enemy's buildings and setting them on fire. Charlie Germon's post was so unsafe as a result of earlier damage that he would not allow more than fourteen people on the roof in case it collapsed, and he was forced to place a Sikh guard outside to keep people away, or at least to persuade them to wait their turn. When six o'clock came and it was time for the evening meal, Mrs Germon was quite sorry to have to relinquish her position. The thought that Sir Colin and his men were there fighting, barely a thousand yards from the Residency, made Katherine Bartrum wonder what would happen to them. The firing had been so tremendous that she began to doubt whether the relieving force would, after all, be able to get them out of Lucknow at last.

On the morning of November 17, Sir Colin's heavy guns could be heard in action near the Shah Najaf, and the guns and rockets were next turned against the Mess House. So, too, were the garrison's guns, from the forward battery beyond the steam-engine house. At about three in the afternoon, a regimental colour was visible over the Mess House. It was soon shot down by enemy fire, and just as soon replaced. The gap between the garrison and Sir Colin's men was now less than half a mile. The two sides moved slowly towards a meeting.

The relieving force, reaching the walls of the Moti Mahal, was held up for a while until breaches were made in the strong walls. As the men drove the enemy from the palace, one of the officers met up with a party of his own regiment which had just made a sortie from the Chuttur Munzil. The two forces had at last met, and cheer after cheer ran through the rooms of the palace.

Outram, Havelock, Napier and other members of the staff had moved forward to the steam-engine house, when they suddenly saw running across a gap criss-crossed, it seemed, with musket fire, a strange figure wearing a large pith helmet. He arrived, breathless. Someone shouted: 'It's Kavanagh! Three cheers for him! He's the first to relieve us.' As they crowded together, shaking hands, Kavanagh remembered his mission. Turning to Outram, he asked: 'Are you willing, Sir James, to join the commander-in-chief at once? The road is clear, but there is that fire from the palace to be encountered.'

'Never mind it,' was Outram's instant reply. Waving his hand at the others, he invited them to join him.

As the nine men ran across the open space, enemy musket fire was heavy. Only two of them arrived at the Moti Mahal unscathed. No one could run very fast. Outram suffered from asthma, and was overweight. His heavy breathing could be heard above the sound of guns and the crunch of feet on gravel. Havelock, too, was in poor condition. Those who did try to run faster tripped and fell.

Kavanagh and Outram reached the hut near the Moti Mahal and, while Outram stopped to get his breath back, the Irishman went on to find the commander-in-chief.

'Sir James Outram is waiting to see you,' Kavanagh announced, with the formality of an English butler.

'The devil he is! Where is he? Where has he come from?'

'I have fetched him, Sir Colin, from the Residency,' replied Kavanagh, exaggerating a little, 'and he is standing yonder.'

'Well done,' Sir Colin said. 'Lead the way!'

Kavanagh introduced the two generals. 'I am delighted to meet you, Sir James,' said Campbell punctiliously, 'and I congratulate you on the successful defence of Lucknow.'

Havelock and Napier had now joined Outram, and Campbell was able to congratulate Havelock on the knighthood the queen had bestowed on him, but of which Havelock until then knew nothing. Campbell next turned to Outram and dropped a bombshell.

'Are you prepared, Sir James, to quit the Residency in two hours? Time is precious.'

Outram, startled, burst out: 'It is impossible, Sir Colin!'

'Nothing is impossible,' Campbell snapped.

Outram was surprised at this show of temper. He replied, with deliberation: 'If you will permit me to explain the reasons for considering it impracticable, you will, Sir Colin, be well satisfied that it cannot be done.'

Sir Colin relaxed again. 'Very well, Sir James, we'll discuss this as early as possible.'[2]

Suddenly there was the sound of cheering. The news that the generals were in the Moti Mahal, that the two sides had now met up on the highest level had reached the men. A party of the 53rd, Havelock's old regiment, came rushing into the room. Havelock shook hands with Brigadier Hope Grant and, turning to the men with tears in his eyes, said:

'Soldiers, I am happy to see you. Soldiers, I am happy to think you got into this place with a smaller loss than I had.'[3]

Quietly, Hope Grant asked what he thought the losses had been. Havelock said he had been told about eighty. When he heard the real figures, he was shocked. Forty-three officers and 550 men had been killed and wounded.

The party from the Residency now made its way back to the forward outposts. Again, they had to cross the bullet-swept space. Halfway across, Havelock could run no longer. Turning to his adjutant he said: 'I can do no more, Dodgson, I can do no more.'[4] Dodgson gave him his arm and the two men walked slowly on—reaching shelter without injury.

Kavanagh and a number of Sir Colin's staff were allowed to accompany the Residency party. When Kavanagh arrived back at the entrenchments he was cheered and congratulated. Only Mrs Kavanagh, weeping bitterly, asked repeatedly why he should have done such a thing.

A little later, some more officers of the relieving force came into the Residency area. For all the heavy fighting, they all looked neat and clean and properly uniformed; in comparison with the garrison, they appeared as if they had just stepped off the parade ground. There was also the unusual sight of sailors. The soldiers thought the men of the Naval Brigade very odd. Who ever heard of sailors fighting on land? The sailors wore their usual uniforms, with the addition of large straw hats with white cotton covers which hung down over the neck.

The men of the relieving force brought in with them tobacco and rum and a few other easily portable items. Mr Rees was lucky enough to be given an orange, and another received the gift of a loaf of bread and a slab of butter. Sometimes, it was difficult for the men of the relieving force to recognise old friends among the garrison, who looked, in fact, peculiarly alike. So thin, so dirty were they, so tattered their clothing, that it was difficult to tell them apart. One officer, carrying with difficulty a keg of rum for his fellow officers in the garrison, looked into a room in the Farhat Buksh palace where he had been told they were, and recognised no one. It was only as he turned to leave that someone cried out: 'Why, it's Wolseley!'[5] Then he realised how much they had been changed by the siege.

That evening, Brigadier Inglis informed the garrison and the ladies that they were to be evacuated from the Residency on the following night and taken to Cawnpore. Though relief had long been awaited, now that the time had come to leave the Residency there was gloom. The men of the garrison who had fought and held out so long—140 days—almost resented leaving the ruins to the enemy.

When he heard that the Residency was to be totally evacuated, Inglis had gone to Outram and pleaded with him that the flag must be kept flying on the Residency tower, the only place in Oudh where it had not been torn down by the mutineers. Inglis himself volunteered to stay behind, if only the commander-in-chief would give him a single regiment. Without the sick and the wounded, the women and children, the Residency could still be held. Outram passed this proposal on to Campbell, but the answer was no. The entire garrison must be evacuated.

When the news reached the ladies—with the rider that they would not be allowed to carry more than would go into a small bundle—there was consternation. Several of the ladies sat up all night stitching their personal belongings into their petticoats and making large pockets in their skirts. Mrs Germon was so shaken that she did not feel able to stay up, and sensibly went to bed. Naturally, she could not sleep. Katherine Bartrum was not upset. All she had to carry was Bobbie, and her belongings would not take up much space, for they consisted of no more than a few old clothes. That day, she heard that her kind friend, Dr Darby, had been wounded, and that it was not thought he would recover. 'He promised to take care of me on the journey to Calcutta, but now I am utterly friendless.'[6]

Sir Colin's decision to evacuate the Residency completely had been dictated by lack of numbers. The forces at his disposal were stretched to their limit. Out of between 5,000 and 6,000 men of all arms, 1,000 were needed to keep open communications at the Alambagh and Dilkusha. This left him with just over 4,000 to cover the evacuation of the Residency. Against him, according to Intelligence reports, were ranged between 20,000 and 50,000 of the enemy. The retreat would have to be made along a line four and a half miles long. And that was only the first stage, to the Dilkusha. All the way was open to enemy fire, from the Kaisarbagh which was very heavily held, and from across the river. Each part of the way would have to be covered by posts, which meant that the men would be very thin on the ground. Should the enemy attack in the rear, there was no knowing what might happen. There was also the imminent danger of the Gwalior contingent attacking Cawnpore. Campbell's decision was undoubtedly sensible, Inglis's pleas a matter of sentiment.

November 18 was spent on preparing the way for the garrison from the Residency. Heavy fire was opened on the Kaisarbagh, both from the advanced batteries at the Chuttur Munzil and from the guns of the Naval Brigade at the Moti Mahal. Engineers set to work to throw up protective embankments along the routes. A covered way was constructed between the steam-engine house and a house near to the Moti Mahal. Walls were destroyed between buildings and canvas screens erected in the exposed sections so that the enemy could not see what was going on behind them. Batteries were set up to command the north bank of the river, and the best marksmen were sent to the top of the domed roof of the Shah Najaf, from where they could fire across the river.

There was still some dispute between the generals as to what should be done. Outram and Havelock, though they did not go all the way with Inglis, believed that a successful attack on the main enemy stronghold, the Kaisarbagh, would make it possible for the British to hold the city. Some of Campbell's staff agreed with them. But Campbell would not be moved. The place for a concentration of British forces was the Alambagh, from which a highly mobile column could not only dominate the city but control the route from Cawnpore, along which the Gwalior contingent might choose to come. The argument was so hot that Campbell sent a telegram over the newly repaired line to the governor-general in Calcutta, and received a prompt reply: 'I have received your message of yesterday,' it ran. 'The one step to be avoided is a total withdrawal of the British forces from Oudh. Your proposal to leave a strong movable division, with heavy artillery, outside the city, and to hold the city in check, will answer every purpose of policy.'[7]

Campbell's temper was somewhat strained by these proceedings. He had made his intentions quite clear in a Greek-character letter to Outram on November 10. 'I shall blow up the Residency . . . You must make your arrangements for getting everyone clear . . . when I am able to give the order, abandoning baggage, destroying your guns, but securing the treasure.'[8] He had also made his point in military terms. 'Until the women and wounded are in my camp the real business of this contest cannot go on, and all the efforts of Government are paralysed.'[9] The governor-general's telegram, however, settled the matter. Nevertheless, the arrangements for evacuation had been delayed.

Inside the Residency, the old garrison had at least had a little extra time to gather its belongings together and to read some of the letters and newspapers that had been brought in. Mr Rees was extremely grateful to find a letter of credit included in his correspondence, for he was now totally without money—having been robbed, by a friend, of a bag containing a hundred rupees. Others found that reading the newspapers was like hearing of another world, long forgotten, but soon to be rejoined. Malicious rumours were going the rounds. It was said that Sir Colin had dined with Mr Gubbins and had been served with champagne and claret, *saucisses aux truffes*, vegetables, and meat in plenty. Sir Colin, went the tale, had refused to eat, with the words: 'How is it, Mr Gubbins, that these things were not given to the starving garrison?'[10] This story fitted in well with the general opinion of Mr Gubbins, though it was not in fact true.

All day on the 18th, the Residency was in turmoil. It was now conceded that more baggage could be taken after all, and those who had precipitately burned some of their belongings so that they should not fall into enemy hands were regretting their haste. Charlie Germon had managed to get hold of some men to carry boxes and bedding, and had found a horse for his wife to ride. Mrs Polehampton had decided to carry with her her dead husband's surplice, hood and stole, as well as some of his sermons. She was still hoping, too, to take away with her the harmonium which had been presented to her husband by the 32nd, and had survived the siege, unharmed, in the church.

The next day, preparations were still going on along the route the women and children and the wounded were to follow. Lieutenant Roberts was sent, that morning, by Sir Colin to inform Outram of the details and tell him that carts and other conveyances were on their way from the Dilkusha. Sir James asked Roberts whether the openings which had been made in the walls of the gardens and houses along the way were large enough. Roberts thought that perhaps some of them were rather small.

At this, Colonel Napier—who had been wounded while going to meet Sir Colin two days earlier, and was lying on a bed in the same room—asked angrily whether Roberts had measured the openings himself. Roberts said he had not, and Colonel Napier told him: 'You had better wait to give your opinion until you know what you are talking about; those openings were made by my orders and I am quite sure they are the necessary size.'[11] Roberts felt badly snubbed, though, as it turned out later, his doubts were justified.

19   *Arrival at Cawnpore of the relieved garrison of Lucknow*

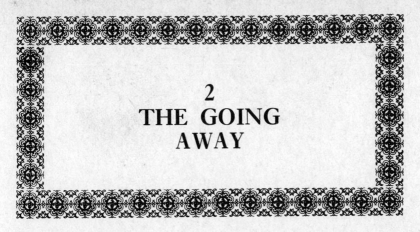

2
THE GOING
AWAY

AT ABOUT midday the exodus began. Mrs Germon had been ready
since dawn. She had expected that Charlie would accompany her,
and was distressed to find that this was not allowed. She had
dressed herself in four flannel waistcoats and three pairs of stockings, three chemises, three sets of drawers, one flannel and four
white petticoats, a pink flannel skirt, a plaid jacket, and on top
of all this a cloth dress. Around her waist was a Cashmere shawl
with Charlie's silver mug tied in it. On her head were a worsted
cap and a large hat. Stitched and hidden in various layers of this
wardrobe were a fish knife and fork which had belonged to her
mother, some jewellery, and a card-case with her diary and other
papers. When Charlie and another officer arrived with her pony,
they dissolved into fits of laughter as they tried to hoist her up
onto the unfortunate animal. But the laughter stopped at the
Baillie Guard gate when it was time to say goodbye.

The procession moved slowly along the lane that had been
broken through the palaces and gardens. There were carts and
horses, even a carriage or two, but many of the women had to
walk. As they passed the guards, there were kind words, and the
children were picked up and carried to the next post. Some of the
men of the relieving force were disappointed. The women seemed
unable to say a word of thanks for being rescued, and they looked
a very rough lot.

Mrs Case had managed to get a carriage drawn by coolies—and
did not even recognise at first that it was her own carriage, because it was riddled by shot and practically falling to bits. She and
her sister and Mrs Inglis walked while the children rode. As
escort, they had Captain Birch, Inglis's aide-de-camp. When there
was danger, he picked up the children and ran while the women

followed. The little white hen which had laid for Colonel Campbell also travelled in the carriage.

The Reverend Mr Harris and his wife rode in a carriage drawn by two half-starved horses which had a habit of stopping without warning, usually at the most exposed and dangerous spots. Eventually, the carriage had to be abandoned when the coolies who were helping by pushing it from behind were hit.

As soon as the enemy discovered what was going on, they concentrated as much fire as possible on the escape route. Grapeshot whistled overhead, and musket balls occasionally burst through the canvas-protected sections of the route. Everywhere, the guards tried to keep people moving. The men of the Naval Brigade would shout: 'What cheer, lads and lasses! Bend low and run as fast as you can!'[1] Mrs Germon dismounted at the dangerous points, but it needed the combined efforts of an orderly and anyone else who happened to be nearby to get her back on the pony again. At one spot she decided to risk it, rather than face the difficulties of remounting, and urged the pony to a gallop as shot whistled around.

As the women and children arrived at the Secundrabagh, Sir Colin decided that it was too dangerous for them to move on to the Dilkusha before nightfall. The commander-in-chief personally greeted each new arrival, and though it occurred to Mrs Inglis that he must be wishing them far away he succeeded in being very courteous. The officers and men of the relieving force had arranged tables with white cloths, and there were wine, tea, biscuits, and the luxury of bread and butter. One little girl ran to her mother, shouting: 'Oh, mama, there's a loaf of bread upon the table. I'm certain of it; I saw it with my own eyes!'[2] Mrs Germon feasted on bread and butter, cold mutton, and a bottle of beer. Another lady, asked by an officer whether he could get anything for her, replied that she would like a piece of cheese, adding, rather mysteriously, that it was for a poor sick lady. The officer ransacked the stores and finally found some strong-smelling stuff—then was unable to find the lady again. He was just about to throw the cheese away when she called out to him. As the officer later reflected, it was a very odd experience for the commander of a section of the relieving force.[3]

From the Secundrabagh to the Dilkusha turned out to be a nightmare journey for many. The confusion along the way was almost indescribable. Men and animals wandered all over the place, and there was a good deal of firing in the distance. Katherine Bartrum and Bobbie moved off at about 11 p.m. in a litter that a doctor had managed to find for them. As the bearers tramped along her mind wandered, until suddenly she became aware that she could hear nothing, no sound of men shouting, no scuffling from the rest of the convoy. Looking out, she found that she and the baby were alone with only the bearers in what seemed to be an empty plain. She asked the bearers where they were taking her, but they only shrugged their shoulders and replied that they had lost their way.

Terror jerked her into activity. Grasping Bobbie, she jumped screaming from the litter and ran and ran until she heard voices. But were they British or enemy? Fortunately, they turned out to be British soldiers who had also lost their way, but they told her they were sure that there were enemy picquets nearby. They told her not to return to the litter, but to stay with them. 'We'll do our best for you, poor girl.' With Bobbie weighing her down, Katherine found it difficult to walk through the soft sand, but the men helped her. It was almost two o'clock in the morning when the party heard a noise among some trees.

'Oh, God!' one man burst out. 'It's all up with us; we're done for now!'

But they gathered round Katherine and Bobbie and whispered: 'Don't scream, and we may be able to creep past.'

They waited, Katherine stiff with terror, and then, as they heard no other sound, crept forward. An hour later they reached the Dilkusha. Katherine was so drained and exhausted that she could do nothing but sit down and cry, but an officer came and took her to a large tent where others were sleeping on the floor. There she was given a cup of tea and some milk for Bobbie, and there they lay down and slept.[4]

The sick and wounded did not have a pleasant journey either. Their convoy did not leave the Residency until after dark. The journey was made as slowly and carefully as possible, but the tension, and the sudden movements of the bearers, placed such a severe strain on those who were most badly wounded that, in spite of everything, a number of them died on the way.

As Lieutenant Havelock left the Residency—in a litter, as he had been wounded yet again—he stopped to say goodbye to his father, who was remaining behind with the garrison until it was time for them, too, to move. He seemed tired but well, and his son left him reading a volume of Macaulay's *History* by the light of a candle. Next day, the general was suffering from dysentery and on November 21 was sent down in a litter to join the others at the Dilkusha. After the move, he seemed better.

291

The garrison did not march out of the Residency until the following day. In the meanwhile, the engineers were blowing up the guns that could not be taken along by the retiring column. Mr Rees was almost hit by a large piece of one of the guns which came flying through the roof of a shed. The Residency area was covered with articles of clothing, furniture, crockery and plate which had been abandoned by their owners. It seemed a pity to leave anything behind for the rebels, but there was a limit to what could be done. The treasure had been sent out at the same time as the women and children, as had the state prisoners. Campbell, however, did not want the enemy to know that he was proposing to evacuate the Residency completely. Heavy fire was therefore kept up from the guns of the Residency and those of the Naval Brigade. Their target was the Kaisarbagh, still an enemy stronghold. It was not until the afternoon of the 22nd that the majority of the Europeans were told that they were to move out that night. The Indian troops were kept in ignorance until the last possible moment, though most of them had guessed what was to happen.

Sir Colin's plan was that each party should retire *through* the party stationed in front. The Residency party would go first, passing through the defenders at the palaces, who would then follow, and so on until the retreating line had reached the Secundrabagh where Sir Colin in person waited with a concentration of artillery, loaded, the portfires lit, ready to sweep the enemy with shot and shell should they attempt to pursue the rearguard. The whole operation relied for success on precision and, above all, quietness.

At last the time had come. It was midnight, and the lights were left burning in the Residency so that the enemy should not become suspicious. At the Baillie Guard gate stood General Outram, and Brigadier Inglis, with some members of their staffs. Each of the separate garrisons was to march out in turn so that they could be counted. As the last man passed, some of the watchers insisted that there was still one other to come. But the Residency was empty, and Captain Birch, who was sent to look for the missing man, found the utter stillness of the deserted positions strike coldly on his nerves. He found no one, and reported back to Outram.

The General and Inglis took off their hats in honour of the long defence. Outram waved Inglis to move off, but Inglis claimed that his was the right to be last in leaving the Residency. Outram put out his hand. 'Let us go out together,' he said. The two men shook hands and, side by side, walked down the slope that led from the battered gate.[5]

Whatever compromise their senior officers might have accepted, Captain Birch and Captain Wilson was each determined to be the last man to leave the Residency. Captain Wilson, however, was still weak from the effects of the siege and was no match for Birch. As Birch wrote later, he 'could not stand the trick of shoulder to shoulder, learnt on the Harrow football fields. Prone on the earth he lay, till he rolled down the hill, and I was the last of the staff to leave'.[6]

Birch was certainly the last of the staff to go, but he was not, after all, the last of the garrison. Captain Waterman of the 13th Native Infantry was so tired that he fell asleep after he had given his name at the preliminary rollcall. In the dark, his absence had not been noticed, and Birch, searching without much conviction for a supposedly missing member of the garrison, had not looked in every corner. At two o'clock in the morning, Waterman woke up to find the Residency deserted. He rushed around the posts. The was no room for doubt—he had been left behind. Overcome with panic, he rushed out through the Baillie Guard gate and on through the row of palaces. They too were empty. By the time Waterman caught up with the rearguard, he was like a madman, and had to be restrained.

The rearguard consisted of men of the 78th Highlanders. Outram told them why. 'Soldiers,' he said, 'you had the honour of leading the advance into Lucknow, and for that reason you have been selected to form the rearguard on leaving.'[7] Outram also instructed them to break step at intervals, in case the steady tramp of a disciplined body of men should be identified by the enemy. For some reason, the enemy never suspected that the Residency and the posts in the river palaces had actually been abandoned. As one of the retreating columns passed the Kaisar-bagh, there was a heavy burst of fire, and it was thought for a moment that the enemy had grasped what was happening. One of the Naval Brigade's rocket launchers was brought up, and after a few rockets had been discharged the firing ceased. The enemy now began firing on the Residency and kept up the fire until daylight, when it became obvious that the defences had been evacuated.

The garrison, the sick and wounded, the women and children, were now concentrated at the Dilkusha. There, some of the wounded—Charles Dashwood among them—died at the very moment when all seemed safe. And there, in the pleasure park of the kings of Oudh (called by them 'Heart's Delight'), the tragedy, the pettiness, and the humour which had threaded life during the siege continued to flourish.

Sir Colin found it necessary to speak sharply to some of the ladies from the Residency. One of them had replied to a dying soldier who had asked her for water: 'There is the well, my man, and you can get the water yourself.' Others had been overheard complaining bitterly about the transport allotted to them. Sir Colin turned and said: 'Ladies—women, I mean—you ought to be thankful that you have got out with your lives, for I do not know how it might have been in two hours more with you.'[8]

General Havelock was lying in a small tent at the Dilkusha. Though the doctors said he was in no immediate danger, he had told visiting friends that he would not recover.

But, as always, there was a leaven of humour. At the Dilkusha there had been an enemy attack, and musket balls had been flying near some of the women and the wounded. A soldier had come up to Sir Colin and asked for permission to fall out and assist an English nursemaid with a child. Sir Colin, straightfaced, enquired: 'Is she pretty, man?'

'Oh, Sir Colin, I told you that she wanted me to help her!'

'Is she pretty, man?' Sir Colin repeated. 'I thought that if she was pretty you would be all the better pleased to help her!'

'There you are, Sir Colin,' the man exclaimed, 'at your old nonsense'—and permission having been granted, took himself off to help the nursemaid.[9]

On November 23, early in the morning, Gubbins went to General Havelock's tent to enquire after his health. He found Havelock's aide-de-camp and his doctor lying on the floor while Havelock occupied a litter which had been brought into the tent to serve as a bed. On one side was sitting Harry Havelock, his arm still in a sling. The doctor told Gubbins that Havelock was dying and would allow only his son to attend to him. Havelock, in fact, had known that he was dying before the doctors admitted it, and constantly, that day, repeated: 'I die happy and contented.' At one time he turned to his son and exclaimed: 'See how a Christian can die!'[10]

That afternoon, he was visited by Outram. Havelock talked of their service together and told him that he was not in any way frightened by the thought of death. 'I have,' he said, 'for forty years so ruled my life, that when death came I might face it without fear.'[11]

The next morning, in the arms of his son, Havelock died. Immediately afterwards, the troops began to evacuate the Dilkusha with the wounded and the women and children. Havelock's body was carried with them in the litter on which he had died. Escorting it were some men of the 32nd, so worn and tattered that when Sir Colin had inspected them after their arrival at the Dilkusha he had told Inglis: 'On my honour, Brigadier, you have a motley crowd to command and more like an invalid depot than the once fine regiment who fought with me in the Punjab and on the North-West Frontier.'[12] When the Alambagh was reached, a grave was dug and Havelock buried. The site was marked by a mound of earth, and the letter 'H' was carved on the trunk of a mango tree nearby. Campbell and Inglis, and as many officers and men as could be spared, attended. Outram was not present. He had been left behind in command of the rearguard.

Again, the move had been all confusion, as the stream of men and animals, carts loaded with women and children, litters bearing the sick and wounded, stretched far along the road, covered by an immense cloud of dust. Fortunately, the enemy made no attempt to attack the column. It took Mrs Inglis and her party six hours to make the short journey, and when they arrived there was no sign of their baggage cart. Brigadier Inglis managed to find some food and a small tent for them. Mrs Bartrum and Bobbie were less cared for, and spent the night in one of the carts. It was bitterly cold.

The next two days were passed in awaiting orders, while Outram brought in the rearguard. Outram was to remain at the Alambagh, with about 4,000 men and twenty-five guns, until Campbell could return and retake Lucknow.

Gubbins went up on the roof of one of the buildings. Through a telescope he could just see the enemy—on the roof of the Residency. It saddened him to think that, after all these weeks, the enemy had finally penetrated the defences.

But there were more serious things to think about than regret. Campbell was anxious to get the convoy to Cawnpore, as he feared that the Gwalior contingent might have attacked the tiny garrison which was all he had been able to spare to hold the town. There had been no news of any kind from General Windham, who had been left in command, for the last ten days. First, however, Sir Colin had to make his arrangements for the defence of the Alambagh.

At 11 a.m. on the 27th, the column set out again. By now it was nearly twelve miles long. The terrain was difficult, sometimes swampy, sometimes dry and bumpy. Everybody suffered much, especially the wounded. That day, Sir Colin was informed that heavy firing had been heard from the direction of Cawnpore. If the rebels had cut the bridge of boats across the Ganges, then not only Windham but the convoy itself would be in great danger. If Windham *was* being attacked, Sir Colin would be unable to help him if passage across the river was blocked. There was no time for delay. At 7 a.m. the next day, the column was on its way again. Soon after it had moved off, gunfire could plainly be heard, and at midday a messenger came in with a note from Windham. It was written in Greek letters and inscribed: 'Most urgent. To General Sir Colin Campbell or any officer commanding troops on the Lucknow road.'

Windham wrote that he was being attacked in great force, and if he did not receive help he would be forced to give up the town and retire into a small defensive area. The letter was dated the 26th. Two more letters followed shortly afterwards. Windham was now shut inside his entrenchment, and the bridge of boats was being threatened.

The column plodded on, the sound of guns growing louder and louder. At dusk the front of the column was halted a few miles from the river after a forced march of almost thirty miles. Everyone was tired out, and the suffering among the sick and wounded had been severe. Some had nothing to eat for the whole of the journey, and there was no time to halt to dress wounds. Mrs Bartrum did not reach the camp until three in the morning. There was no tent for her, and she sat exhausted on the wet ground until daylight, with Bobbie in her lap. No one came near her. Was there, she wondered, not a soul in all the host of her fellow creatures who cared whether she lived or died? She felt very lonely that night, as if she had been forsaken by not only man, but God.[13]

Sir Colin, with some of his staff, left the column and made for the river. To their relief, they found that the bridge of boats was still intact, though they could see flames rising from Cawnpore on the other side. What was almost a worse sight for men who had been unable to change their clothes for weeks, was the vision of their kit—which had been left behind at Cawnpore—blazing like a bonfire. Campbell and his staff passed over the bridge, and reached Windham's entrenchment without incident. After discussing the next day's operations, they recrossed the bridge and returned to camp.

By dawn on November 29, the heavy guns of the Naval Brigade were at last dragged into position by bullock and man-power. Soon, they opened up on the enemy on the other side of the river. The advance guard of the troops crossed the river and began to establish a safe line to the entrenchment. At three o'clock that afternoon the convoy began to move again, but it was not until six in the evening of the following day that Brigadier Inglis took the rearguard across.

It was almost sunset on the 29th when a young chaplain, James Mackay, went out on to the verandah of the hospital inside the entrenchment. Before him he saw a 'procession of human beings, cattle, and vehicles six miles long coming up to the bridge of boats'. The sky was shot with the colours of the setting sun, but Mackay could clearly see the bright costumes and the dark faces of the native servants, the long train of cavalry, their lances catching the dying light, the carts with the women and children, the sick and the wounded in their red-curtained litters, 'raw stumps hanging over the side like torn butcher's meat'. It seemed to James Mackay to be a subject for some dramatic painting. From where he stood, with 'the crowds of camels and horses, the rows of cannon, heaps of shot, piles of furniture in the foreground, all seen between the two pillars of this verandah', it produced 'a very picturesque effect'. But the chaplain could not linger to delight his connoisseur's eye with the panorama spread before him. The groans of the wounded on the beds and on the floor behind him dissolved the 'fascination of the scene', and he turned aside to give what comfort he could to the hurt and dying.[14]

The column continued on its way across the bridge of boats. Somewhere, in what the Reverend James Mackay had seen as another of those vast, impersonal narrative paintings which lined the walls of the Royal Academy every autumn, were Mrs Inglis and her party, worrying about her husband far behind with the rearguard, the flock of goats which had preserved the children now lost forever. Mr Rees, merchant and volunteer soldier, marching doggedly on, concerned once again about his business, the merchandise lost, the profits blown away by the winds of war, putting aside at last the fears and the excitement of the last six months. Katherine Bartrum, her thoughts only for her son. Mrs Polehampton, zealously guarding the harmonium that meant so much to her. The Reverend James Harris and his wife, Mr Harris heavy with the knowledge that, during the siege, he has conducted five hundred funerals. Beside the carriage runs the dog, Bustle, who had miraculously found his way back to them after being lost during the nightmare journey from the Residency to the Secundrabagh.

With all the survivors of the siege travelled the indelible memory of a terrible, desperate experience—already a part of history —of a time of agony and suffering, of courage and fear, of humour and pettiness, of human weakness and human strength. Of a season in hell.

EPILOGUE

CAMPBELL was anxious to get rid of the women and children, civilians, and such wounded as could be moved, as soon as possible. Without them, he could turn his attention to the enemy, some 14,000-strong, who lay only a few miles from his entrenchment. By December 3 the transport was assembled, and that night the convoy set out for Allahabad. Four days later it reached the railway, and arrived in Allahabad on the following day, to be welcomed by a cheering crowd and every possible comfort. The officers and their wives and the senior civil servants were accommodated inside the fort, in large tents which had once formed part of the governor-general's travelling camp. Some of the Lucknow veterans were not quite as well treated as others. Some of the lesser civil servants were swiftly turned out of the comfortable barracks at first assigned to them and put instead in small tents outside the fort.

From Allahabad, the intention was to ship the survivors down river to Calcutta. Mr Rees preferred not to wait for what would certainly be a tedious journey. With a friend, he left by carriage and reached Calcutta safely, where he had 'the unspeakable pleasure of again shaking' his 'dear brother by the hand'.[1] Most of the others decided to wait for the boats which were coming up river to fetch them. But the boats were a long time in arriving, and it was not until January 11, 1858 that the main party left Allahabad to join the steamers, which had been unable to come further up river because the water was too shallow.

On Christmas Day, Mrs Inglis had given a dinner for the women and children of the 32nd. But it was not a festive affair. Of the seventeen women present, nearly all were widows, and of the children, most had lost one or both of their parents. Mrs Bartrum found it 'such a sad Christmas: so different to all that have gone before'.[2] Mrs Germon and Charlie had a quiet dinner with an officer of the Fusiliers, and could think of nothing beyond getting away to Calcutta.

Calcutta was to deal a bitter blow to at least one of the survivors. Katherine Bartrum had been told by the doctors that, as Bobbie was very delicate, it would do him good to make the four-months' sea voyage to England round the Cape of Good Hope. As the time came to board the ship Bobbie became progressively weaker. On February 11, Katherine and her son boarded the *Himalaya*. There were others from Lucknow aboard.

Now, the child was very ill indeed. 'But I *cannot* spare him,' Katherine prayed. Surely God would not 'take away my little lamb when I have nothing left'. Mrs Polehampton kept watch with her over the sick child.

'Look,' she said, 'how bright his eyes are growing.'

But Katherine had turned her head away. 'I *could* not see my child die.'[3]

Next day, Katherine sailed for England alone. Later, she remarried and had three other children, but died of pulmonary tuberculosis in March 1866. Mrs Polehampton also married again, in the autumn of 1859. This time her husband was not a clergyman but an army officer, Colonel Henry Mortimer Durand, who later became one of a distinguished band of administrators on the North-West Frontier of India. Mrs Inglis, Mrs Case, and the latter's sister Caroline, embarked on the same day as Katherine Bartrum but not on the same ship, for they were going home by what was known as the Overland Route—by sea to Suez, and then across Egypt by land to Alexandria. But their vessel, the *S.S. Ava*, struck a rock off Ceylon, and though all on board were saved Mrs Inglis lost her journal of the siege. With the aid of a brief diary which survived, however, she reconstructed her journal the moment she reached land again. Her husband, now with the rank of Major-General, had remained behind at Cawnpore to take over General Windham's command. Knighted for his services at Lucknow, he died in September 1862, aged forty-seven, having never fully recovered from the strain of commanding the defence.

Sir James Outram remained at the Alambagh until Campbell was able to return in March 1858 and retake the city of Lucknow. Outram left for Calcutta in April, to become the Military Member of the Governor-General's Council until he was advised by Dr Fayrer that he should retire for the good of his health. Outram left for England in July 1860 and was welcomed as a hero at a public banquet given in honour of himself and Sir Colin Campbell, recently raised to the peerage as Lord Clyde. Outram died at Pau, in southern France, in March 1863, 'sitting in his armchair, without a struggle, his face unmoved'.[4] He was buried in West-minster Abbey. A few months later he was joined there by Lord Clyde.

For Private Henry Metcalfe the war did not end until March 1859. In the following month, he and other survivors of the 32nd embarked for home and were received on their arrival at Dover in October with a civic reception and banners which read: 'Welcome the Heroes of Lúcknow', and 'Welcome the Protectors of Women and Children'. Two years later, by now a sergeant and stationed at Aldershot, he was on duty one day when he suddenly saw the Reverend Mr Harris running across the parade ground accompanied by a dog. It was Bustle, and he rushed at Metcalfe, 'cutting all sorts of joyful antics'.[5] Mr Harris invited Metcalfe to spend the day with him and Mrs Harris, and presented him with a large pipe and a great packet of tobacco, saying: 'Now, Metcalfe, if I could not accommodate you in Lucknow, I can now.'[6] Metcalfe took his discharge from the army in 1872, but later became drill instructor to the Macclesfield Volunteers. He died in 1915, aged eighty.

The last surviving officer of those who had garrisoned Lucknow during the siege was Colonel John Bonham C.B., who as a lieutenant had invented the 'Ship' mortar which did so much damage to the enemy batteries. He died at the age of ninety-three in Ireland, in May 1928.

Among the civil servants who survived the siege, Martin Gubbins was taken ill at Cawnpore and went home to England. He returned to India at the end of 1858 and became a judge at Agra. There was an enquiry into his conduct at Lucknow, and his justifications were not regarded as convincing. Growing ill health forced his resignation, and he returned to England again in January 1863. In a fit of mental depression, he committed suicide in May of the same year at Leamington Spa. Of the doctors, Joseph Fayrer became an expert on tropical medicine, was knighted, and in 1901 was appointed physician in ordinary to King Edward VII, whom he had accompanied, as Prince of Wales, on a tour of India. Dr Brydon, the veteran of two sieges, retired to the Western Highlands of Scotland, to a sheep farm, and was described some twenty years after the Mutiny by Archibald Forbes, the war correspondent, as 'a quiet, rather silent man, much beloved among the neighbouring shepherds and crofters,

301

20 *Havelock's grave*

whose ailments he cared for professionally but gratuitously'.[7]

Time did not deal kindly with Thomas Henry Kavanagh. Awarded the Victoria Cross—the first civilian ever to receive it —the sum of £2,000, and the appointment of Deputy Commissioner in the Indian Civil Service, he was heavily in debt again by 1876. Faced with compulsory retirement on a pension of £500 a year, he maintained that he had been shabbily treated and returned his V.C. to the man who had first taken him seriously when he offered to leave the Residency for the Alambagh. Napier, now Lord Napier of Magdala—an honour he had won for the storming of the fortress of Magdala in the Abyssinian war of 1868—refused to accept the Cross and persuaded Kavanagh to take a less extreme attitude. Kavanagh died at Napier's house on Gibraltar in 1882, when he was on his way back to India.

Of Kanauji Lal, the man who accompanied Kavanagh on his famous mission, little more is known than that he was rewarded and retired to live on land given to him by a grateful government. Angad Tewari also lived comfortably on his land, and was presented to Edward, Prince of Wales, at Lucknow on January 7, 1876.

The news of Sir Henry Lawrence's death had been received in England with considerable sadness. On July 22, 1857, three weeks after his death (news of which did not reach England for some considerable time), he had been appointed 'provisionally to succeed to the office of Governor-General of India, on the death, resignation, or coming away of Viscount Canning [who then held the office] pending the arrival of a successor from England'.[8] Lawrence's simple gravestone, with the words he desired to be engraved on it, still stands among the ruins of the Residency at Lucknow.

When the news of General Havelock's death reached England in January 1858, 'one common feeling pervaded the whole land, from the royal palace to the humble cottage. There has been no example of so universal a mourning since the death of Nelson'.[9]

It was natural enough that England should honour one of her own imperial heroes, but perhaps the most unexpected tribute was paid in the U.S.A., where when the news was received the flags of the ships in the harbours of New York, Baltimore, and Boston were flown at halfmast from nine in the morning until sunset. As the *New York Times* commented:

'A mark of respect was shown yesterday to the memory of General Havelock, which was worth more than a peerage. The

304

flags of the shipping in our harbour and on our public buildings were displayed at half-mast during the day, as a token of grief for his loss. It was a purely voluntary tribute paid to his memory by a people to whom he was a stranger, who were in no way interested in his career, and to whom even his name was unknown six months since. It was a tribute of respect which even the Duke of Wellington did not command, and which we believe was never before paid to a foreigner . . . Certainly no English soldier ever before excited so marked a feeling of sympathy among the American people as has been done by General Havelock; and we may feel proud that no considerations of national jealousy prevented a spontaneous expression of such generous impulses.'[10]

APPENDIX 1

Sir James Outram's
'secret' letter

Sir,

I σενδ un σκεтch du γρουνδ ιντερυενινγ
βετωην αλυμ βαγ et cette ποσιτιον et βεγ à συγ-
εσт θη φολοωινγ μοδε d'οπερατιονς as that whereby vous may εφεκт une jυνκτιον avec nous avec le
λεασт διφικυλτη. φρομ αλυμ βαγ πασινγ ρουνδ le
σουθερν φασε de l'ενκλοσυρε et βετωην les υιλαγες
de ὑσℎτνυγρ et πορωα et προσηδινγ αλμοστ δυε
εασт pour αβουτ trois μιλες ουερ un λευελ κουντρη
de γρας λανδ et κυλτιυατιον avec un σℎαλοω jℎηλ
à κροςς σℎορтλη après ληυινγ αλυμ βαγ (προ-
βαβλη pas plus θαν ανκλε δηπ νοω et νο οβσтακλε
aux γυνς) vous will αριυε οποσιτε à la υιλαγε de
jαμαιτα sur votre λεφτ—σλαντινγ παστ wʰ pour
αβουт une μιλε à νορθ εασт vous αριυε à la διλκυσℎαρ παλασε—rien mais le παρκ ωαλ ιντερυενινγ
αβουт ειτ φℎτ ἱ, wʰ est βροκεν δοων dans μανη
πλασες et κουλδ βη νοκεδ δοων ανηωℎερε par a
κουπλε δες πιονηρς. Le παλασε ἁυινγ λαργε ωιν-
δοως en ευροπεαν στιλε n'est pas λικελη être δε-
φενδεδ, mais ιφ σο, a φευ κανον σℎοτ wᵈ σοον εμτη
ιτ et ινδηδ j'αντισιπατε λιτλε or νο οποσιτιον à
votre οκυπατιον de διλκυσℎαρ παλασε et παρκ or
des νειγℎβουρινγ μαρτινιὲρε or βιβιαπορε maisons
shᵈ vous θινκ νεσεσαρη, l'ενεμη's τρωπς βεινγ
cℎηφλη sur θις σιδε du καναλ. L'υνιον jακ ὁιστεδ
au τοπ de la παλασε et un ροψαλ σαλυτε φρομ
υος γυνς à δραω notre ατεντιον το ιτ, shᵈ vous ἁυε
ἁδ νο πρευιους φιρινγ wᵈ ινφορμ nous de votre
αριυαλ et notre υνιον wʰ nous wᵈ θεν ὁιστ sur la

307

chυτρ μανзιλ παλασε (διστανт deux à trois μιλες)
will show vous que nous sommes ινφορμεδ. A la
διλκυσhαρ vous avez un οπεν μαιδαν pour ενκαμπ-
μεντ οφ νηρλη une μιλε βετωην le παλασε & un
δηπ καναλ βετωην vous et la ville, les βριδγες
sur wʰ sont βροκεν δοων. Par ενκαμπινγ avec votre
φροντ to θη καναλ avec vos γυνς en votre φροντ
ετ φλανκς vous wᵈ κηπ δοων ανη φιρε wʰ l'ενεμη
cᵈ βρινγ αγαινστ vous φρομ λε ville σιδε pour ils
ont ονλη sept ορ huit γυνς en διφερεντ ποσιτιονς
sur cette σιδε de la γοομτη γυαρδινγ les διφερεντ
ἠγρεσσες τοωαρδς la διλκυσhαρ φρομ νοτρε ποσιτιον wʰ sont οφ διφερεντ καλιβρε et σο βαδλη
φουνδ εν καριαγες ils wᵈ have σομε διφικυλτη ιν
τακινγ θεμ αωαι à τυρν αγαινστ vous et ιφ ιλς διδ
ρεμουε θεμ πουρ θατ πυρποσε it wᵈ φασιλιτατε
notre δαση ουτ à μητ vous quand vous δο αδυανσε
à θις σιδε du καναλ where however ils ne sont pas
λικελη à στανδ εξποσεδ as ils θεν wᵈ be à αττακ
φρομ φροντ et ρεαρ. Under κουερ de vos γυνς vous
n'aurez pas de διφικυλτη εν σλοπινγ πασαγες pour
votre αρτιλερη δοων votre σιδε ιντο le καναλ et
υπ νοτρε σιδε δυρινγ θη φιρστ νιτε ρεαδη à κρος
ερλη νεξτ μορνινγ. φυρθερ δελαι, je pense, wᵈ be
ιμπολιτικ, as it wᵈ give l'ενεμη τιμε à βρινγ γυνς
φρομ δισταντ πλασες. λεστ μεσενγερς shᵈ μισ-
καρη votre σιγναλ pour ιντενδινγ à κροςς le καναλ
ιν 'θη μορνινγ might be τροις γυνς φολοωεδ par
trois ροκετς la nuit βεφορε, après une ρεκοναισανσε
ἀδ σατισφιεδ vous de la φησιβιλιτη de πρεπαρινγ
les σλοπες δυρινγ λα νυιτ. Les βανκς du καναλ
sont φρομ vingt à vingt cinq φητ ί, περαπς λεςς
τοωαρδς votre droit avec λιτλε ορ νο eau et σουνδ
βοτομ. Vous wᵈ οφ κουρσε ἀυε παρτης en οκυπατιον de la διλκυσhαρ παλασε, et après πασινγ le
καναλ en σομε des πρινςιπαλ βυιλδινγς κομ·
votre λινε de κομᵛ· mais nous shᵈ μητ vous ἀλφ ωαι

308

avec un πρετη στρονγ κολυμν d'ευροπεανς et γυνς et wᵈ θεν αρανγε τογεθερ le μοδε de μαιν-ταινινγ la κομν· βετωην votre καμπ sur le καναλ et notre εντρενςημεντ. Vous wᵈ περαπς ἀλτ deux trois jours à αλυμ βαγ et may κοντριυε à donner nous νοτισε dû jour de votre αδυανσε. Of course tous les τρωπς à αλυμ βαγ seront υνδερ vos κομανδ et un petit γυαρδ ινκλυδινγ λες κονυαλ-εσεντς will συφισε à μαινταιν θατ πλασε, θυς πλασινγ σομε cinq ou σιξ cents ευροπεανς à votre δισποσαλ—βεσιδες γυνς.

$\qquad$ True Copy. $\qquad$ J. Outram.

$\qquad$ George Couper,
$\qquad$ Secy. Chief Comr.

Sir,

I send a sketch of the ground intervening between Alambagh and this position and beg to suggest the following mode of operations as that whereby you may effect a junction with us with the least difficulty. From Alambagh passing round the southern face of the enclosure and between the villages of Essanuggur and Porowar and proceeding almost due east for about three miles over a level country of grassland and cultivation with a shallow jhil to cross shortly after leaving Alambagh (probably not more than ankle deep now and no obstacle to you) you will arrive opposite the village of Jamaita on your left—slanting past which for about a mile to north east you arrive at the Dilkusha palace—nothing but the park wall intervening about eight feet high which is broken down in many places and could be knocked down anywhere by a couple of pioneers. The palace having large windows in European style is not likely to be defended, but if so, a few cannon shot would soon empty it and indeed I anticipate little or no opposition to your occupation of the Dilkusha palace and park or of the neighbouring Martinière or Bibiapur houses should you think necessary, the enemy's troops being chiefly on this side of the river. The Union Jack hoisted on the top of the palace and a royal salute from your guns to draw our attention to it, should you have had no previous firing would inform us of your arrival and our Union [Jack] which we would then hoist on the Chuttur Munzil palace (distant two to three miles) will show you that we have been informed. To the Dilkusha you have an open maidan for encampment of nearly a mile between the palace and a deep canal between you and the town, the bridges over which are broken down. By encamping with your front to the canal with your guns on your front and flanks you would keep down any fire which the enemy could bring against you from the town side for they have only seven or eight guns in different positions on that side of the Gumti guarding the different egresses towards the Dilkusha from your position which are of different calibre and so badly found in carriages they would have some difficulty in taking them away to turn against you and if they did remove them for that purpose it would facilitate our dash out to meet you when you do advance to this side of the canal where however they are not likely to stand exposed as they then would be to attack from front and rear. Under cover of your guns you will not have difficulty in sloping passages for your artillery down your side into the canal and up our side during the first night ready to cross early next morning. Further delay, I think, would be impolitic as it would give the enemy time to bring guns from distant places. Lest messengers should miscarry your signal for intending to cross the canal in the morning might be three guns followed by three rockets the night before after a reconnaissance had satisfied you of the feasibility of preparing the slopes during the night. The banks of the canal are from twenty to twenty-five feet high, perhaps less towards your right with little or no water and sound bottom. You would of course have parties in occupation of the Dilkusha palace, and after passing the canal in some of the principal buildings communicating on your line of communication but we should meet you halfway with a pretty strong column of Europeans and guns and would then arrange together the mode of maintaining communication between your camp on the canal and our entrenchment. You would perhaps halt two or three days at Alambagh and may contrive to give us notice of the day of your advance. Of course all the troops at Alambagh will be under your command and a small guard including the convalescents will suffice to maintain that place, thus placing some five or six hundred Europeans at your disposal besides guns.

J. Outram

APPENDIX 2

Principal events in the Indian Mutiny
1857–59

The effects of the Mutiny were almost entirely confined to north, north-west and central India. The principal leaders were civilians —in the main, men who had suffered in one way or another at the hands of the British and hoped to restore their own fortunes, or those of the princely houses to which they belonged or owed allegiance.

The rebel leader at Cawnpore, held responsible—though there is considerable doubt about it—for the massacre of the women and children there, was Dandu Pant, known as the Nana Sahib, the adopted son of a former Maratha ruler. The British refused to continue paying a pension to him after his father's death in 1851. The Rani of Jhansi had seen the rights of her dead husband's son set aside—despite their legality according to Hindu law and custom—and the state of Jhansi annexed by the British. The rebels' finest general, Tantia (or Tatya) Topi, was a supporter of the cause of Maratha nationalism, which had been suppressed but by no means destroyed by the British after the third Maratha-war in 1819.

1857

January	Rumour of 'greased cartridges' started in Dum Dum
February 25	Mutiny of the 19th Native Infantry at Berhampur
March 30	Disbandment of the 19th Native Infantry at Barrackpur
April	Unrest and incendiarism in Ambala
May 3	Mutiny in Lucknow prevented by Sir Henry Lawrence. Disbandment of 7th Irregular Cavalry
May 6	Disbandment of 34th Native Infantry at Barrackpur
May 10	Mutiny and massacre at Meerut

May	Meerut mutiny followed by outbreaks in Delhi, Ferozepur, Bombay, Aligarh, Mainpuri, Etawah, Bulandshar, Nasirabad, Bareilly, Moradabad, Shahjahanpur, and many smaller stations. Disarming of sepoys in Lahore, Agra, Lucknow, Peshawar, and Mardan
June	Mutinies at Sitapur, Hansi, Hissar, Azamgarh, Gorakhpur, and Nimach. Surviving Europeans besieged in Nimach fort
	Mutinies at Gwalior, Bharatpur, and Jhansi
	Mutiny at Cawnpore, then siege of European survivors (June 4–25) and massacre
	Mutiny in Benares forestalled. Sepoys and doubtful Sikh battalions dispersed by gunfire
	Mutinies at Jewanpur, Allahabad, Jullundur, Phillaur, Nowgong, Rhoni, Fatehgarh, Aunrungabad (Deccan), Fatehpur, and Jubbulpur. Aurangabad mutiny suppressed after a few days; rebels flee
	Forcible disarming of Indian units at Nagpur and Barrackpur
	Mutinies at Faizabad, Sultanpur, and Lucknow. Order restored in the last place, but the city and surrounding countryside remain disturbed. Europeans take shelter in military lines and Residency area
	British defeated at Chinhat (June 30), near Lucknow. Siege of Lucknow begins
	Also in June:
	Battle of Badli-ke-serai (June 8). Delhi Field Force takes up position on the Ridge and begins operations to recover Delhi
	Throughout June, revolt spreads through the Ganges plain, the Rajputana, and Central India, and affects parts of Bengal
July	Mutinies at Indore and Mhow, Auggur, Jhelum, Saugor, Sialkot, Dinapur, and Agra. Europeans concentrate in Agra fort
	Siege of Lucknow Residency continues throughout July, as do the Delhi Field Force operations against the mutineers in Delhi. General Barnard, commanding at Delhi, dies of disease (July 5)

312

	General Havelock's force, advancing from Allahabad to the relief of Cawnpore, arrives on July 17, one day too late to save the women and children from massacre
	Indian units in Rawalpindi disarmed. Sialkot mutineers defeated by General John Nicholson at Trimmu Ghat (July 16)
August	Mutinies at Kolhapur (Bombay Presidency), Poonamali (near Madras), Jubbulpur, Bhopawar (near Indore), Mian Mir (near Lahore). During August rebellion spreads through Saugor and Narbada districts
	Also in August:
	Surprise disarmament of Indian units in Berhampur (August 1)
	Continuation of siege of Lucknow. Havelock's first attempt at relief fails
September	Outbreak forestalled in Karachi (September 14)
	Further outbreaks in Saugor and Narbada districts
	Beginning of siege of Saugor
	Delhi assaulted and recaptured (September 14–20)
	Lucknow relieved by Havelock and Outram (September 25). New siege of reinforced garrison begins
October	Mutiny at Bhogalpur (near Dinapur). Unrest in Bihar, North Bengal, and Assam
	Mutiny in Bombay city forestalled (October 15)
	Revolt in Kotah state (October 15). Major Burton, the Political Agent, murdered
November	Lucknow relieved by Sir Colin Campbell (November 17). Garrison evacuated and Residency and city temporarily abandoned
	General Windham defeated outside Cawnpore (November 28). Line of retreat from Lucknow threatened by mutineers
December	Decisive battle at Cawnpore (December 6). Armies of the Rao Sahib—nephew of the Nana Sahib—and of Tantia Topi routed by Sir Colin Campbell
	Campaign in the Doab. Capture of Fatehgarh

313

1858

January	Beginning of Sir Hugh Rose's Central Indian campaign
	Sir Colin Campbell begins campaign to retake Lucknow. Gurkha army of Nepal comes to assistance of British in Lucknow campaign
February	Saugor relieved by Sir Hugh Rose (February 3)
	Campbell's 'Army of Oudh' assembled along Cawnpore-Lucknow road
March	Lucknow recaptured (March 21) and rebel armies dispersed into the countryside
April 1	Battle of Betwa. Tantia Topi defeated
April 3	Jhansi stormed. On the following day, Rani of Jhansi flees
April 6	Final capture of Jhansi
	Azamgarh recaptured and garrison relieved
April 25	Sir Hugh Rose resumes advance on Kalpi
	Also in April:
	Sir Colin Campbell begins reconquest of Rohilkhand
	Fresh rising in Bihar, led by Koer Singh. He finally retreats to his stronghold of Jagdispur, where he dies of his wounds
May 5	Battle of Bareilly
May 7	Bareilly recaptured
	Battle of Kunch. Defeat of Tantia Topi
May 10	Jagdispur recaptured
May 23	Kalpi reoccupied by the British
May 24	Battle of Mohamdi. End of resistance in Rohilkhand
May 27	Rebels begin guerrilla warfare in jungle
	Tantia Topi and Rani of Jhansi at gates of Gwalior
June 1	Gwalior ruler's army deserts to rebels
	Tantia Topi and Rani of Jhansi seize Gwalior
June 6	Sir Hugh Rose's army marches from Kalpi, arrives Gwalior June 16
June 17	Battle of Kotah-ke-serai. Rani of Jhansi reputedly dies on this day
June 19	Battle of Gwalior
June 20	Capture of the fortress and flight of Tantia Topi
	Also in June:
	Continuation of campaign to suppress scattered

	guerrilla forces in Oudh, Bihar, and along Nepalese frontier
July until December	Guerrilla bands gradually suppressed everywhere except in the Rajputana and Central India, where Tantia Topi remains free and continues active resistance

1859

April 7	Tantia Topi betrayed to British and captured
April 15	Trial of Tantia Topi
April 18	Execution of Tantia Topi

BIBLIOGRAPHY

Unpublished records and narratives

National Archives of India, New Delhi

Foreign Consultations 104–5. ⎫ Martin Gubbins's
February 26, 1858 ⎬ conduct during
Foreign Consultations 104–8. ⎭ the siege
July 15, 1859

Foreign Consultations 200–3. T. H. Kavanagh's debts
January 11, 1856

Secret Consultations, 531.
October 20, 1857.
Outram's views on the position of the garrison in the
Residency

British Museum, London

Add. MS 39922, fol. 12.
Letter of Sir Hugh Wheeler to Sir H. Lawrence, June 4, 1857
Add. MS 43993. Outram's despatch of October 13, 1857

India Office Library, Foreign and Commonwealth Office, London

Home Miscellaneous, vols. 724–7.
Kaye Papers, containing notes, diaries, letters, narratives,
etc.

MSS Eur. C 190. Letters of Ashton Crowell Warner

MSS Eur. D 581. Narrative of the Indian Campaign by
T. S. M. Palmer

MSS Eur. E 241. Letters and papers of George Hutchinson

Published records

CROMMELIN, Captain W. A.
*Memorandum of the Three Passages of the River Ganges at
Cawnpore during the rainy season of 1857 by the Oude Field
Force under the command of the Late Major-General
Sir Henry Havelock.* Calcutta 1858

FORREST, G. W. (ed.)
*Selections from the Letters, Despatches and other State Papers
in the Military Department of the Government of India. 1857–8.*
4 vols. Calcutta 1893–1912

*General Orders and Despatches relating to the Relief of the
Garrison of Lucknow, etc.* Calcutta 1859

Parliamentary Papers. Mutinies in the East Indies. vol. iv.
London 1857

Privately printed letters and narratives

DANVERS, R. W.
Letters from India and China during the years 1854–58.
London and Aylesbury 1898

FULTON, G. W. W.
  Biographical Memoirs of the late Captain G. W. W. Fulton of the Hon. East India Company's Bengal Engineer Corps. Napier, New Zealand 1913

[HUXHAM, Mrs]
  A Personal Narrative of the Siege of Lucknow during the Indian Mutiny of 1857. London n.d.

INGLIS, Hon. Julia
  Letter containing extracts from a Journal kept by Mrs Inglis during the Siege of Lucknow. London 1858

OUTRAM, Sir James
  Outram's Campaign in India 1857 to 1858. London 1860

PALMER, H.
  Indian Life Sketches. 1816 to 1866. Mussoorie 1888

Published works

ANDERSON, R. P.
  A personal Journal of the Siege of Lucknow. London 1858

[BARTRUM, Mrs Katherine]
  A Widow's Reminiscences of the Siege of Lucknow. London 1858

BONHAM, John
  Oudh in 1857: Some Memories of the Indian Mutiny. London 1928

BOURCHIER, G.
  Eight Months' Campaign Against the Bengal Sepoy Army. London 1858

BROCK, Rev. William
  A Biographical Sketch of Sir Henry Havelock. London 1858

CAMPBELL, Sir Colin
  A Narrative of the Indian Revolt from its outbreak to the Capture of Lucknow. London 1858

CASE, A.
  Day by Day at Lucknow. London 1858

DASHWOOD, A.F.
  'Untimely Arrival at the Siege of Lucknow', in *The Listener,* December 2, 1936

DODGSON, D.
  General Views and Special Points of Interest in the City of Lucknow. London 1860

EDWARDES, H. B. and MERIVALE, H.
  Life of Sir Henry Lawrence. London 1873

EDWARDES, Michael
  Battles of the Indian Mutiny. London and New York 1963; and London 1970

EDWARDES, Michael
  Bound to Exile: The Victorians in India. London 1969, New York 1970

EDWARDES, Michael
*The Orchid House: Splendours and Miseries of the
Kingdom of Oudh.* London 1960

FAYRER, Sir Joseph
Recollections of My Life. Edinburgh 1900

FORBES, Archibald
Colin Campbell, Lord Clyde. London 1895

FORBES, Archibald
Havelock. London 1891

FORBES, Mrs Hamilton
Some Recollections of the Siege of Lucknow. Axminster 1905

FORBES-MITCHELL, W.
The Relief of Lucknow, ed. Michael Edwardes. London 1962

FORREST, Sir George
History of the Indian Mutiny. 3 vols. Edinburgh 1904

GERMON, Maria
Journal of the Siege of Lucknow, ed. Michael Edwardes.
London 1958

GOLDSMID, F. J.
James Outram. 2 vols. London 1880

GRANT, Sir J. H. and KNOLLYS, Sir H.
Incidents in the Sepoy War. Edinburgh 1894

GROOM, W.H.
With Havelock from Allahabad to Lucknow. London 1894

GUBBINS, Martin
*An Account of the Mutinies in Oudh and the Siege of the
Lucknow Residency.* London 1858

[HARRIS, Mrs G.]
A Lady's Diary of the Siege of Lucknow. London 1858

HILTON, E. H.
The Tourist's Guide to Lucknow. Lucknow 1916

HUTCHINSON, G.
Narrative of the Mutinies in Oude. Calcutta 1859

INGLIS, Lady
The Siege of Lucknow. London 1892

INNES, J. J. McLeod
Rough Narrative of the Siege of Lucknow. Calcutta 1857

JOCELYN, J. R.
*The History of the Royal and Indian Artilllery in the Munity
of 1857.* London 1915

KAVANAGH, T. H.
How I won the Victoria Cross. London 1860

LANG, Lt. Arthur
'Diary and Letters 1857–8', in *Journal of the Society of
Army Historical Research,* vols. 9–11. 1930–2

LOW, C. R.
A Memoir of Lieut.-General Sir Garnet Wolseley. London 1878

MACKAY, Rev. James
From London to Lucknow. 2 vols. London 1860

MACPHERSON, A. G.
'The Siege of Lucknow', in *Calcutta Review*, September 1858

MARSHMAN, J. C.
Memoir of General Sir Henry Havelock. London 1860

MAUDE, E.
Oriental Campaigns and European Furloughs. London 1908

MAUDE, Col. F.C. and SHERER, J. W.
Memories of the Mutiny. 2 vols. London 1894

MECHAM, C. H. and COUPER, G.
Sketches and Incidents of the Siege of Lucknow. London 1858

METCALFE, Private Henry
The Chronicle of Private Henry Metcalfe, ed. Sir Francis Tuker.
London 1953

MORISON, J. L.
Lawrence of Lucknow. London 1934

NAPIER, Colonel Robert
Report on Engineering Operations at the Siege of Lucknow.
Calcutta 1859

NORMAN, Sir Henry
A Lecture on the Relief of Lucknow. Simla 1867

NORTH, Major
Journal of an English Officer in India. London 1858

POLEHAMPTON, Rev. Henry
A Memoir, Letters and Diary, ed. E. and T. S. Polehampton.
London 1858

RAMSAY, B. D. W.
Rough Recollections of Military Service and Society.
2 vols. Edinburgh 1882

REES, L. E. Ruutz
A Personal Narrative of the Siege of Lucknow. London 1858

ROBERTS, Field-Marshal Lord
Letters written during the Indian Mutiny. London 1924

ROBERTS, Field-Marshal Lord
Forty-one Years in India. London 1898

RUGGLES, John
Recollections of a Lucknow Veteran. London 1906

RUSSELL, W. H.
My Indian Mutiny Diary, ed. Michael Edwardes. London 1957

SHADWELL, Lieut.-General L.
Life of Sir Colin Campbell, Lord Clyde. 2 vols. Edinburgh 1881

[SOPPITT, E. S.]
'The Diary of an Officer's Wife', printed as an Appendix in
Fitchett, W. H. *The Tale of the Great Mutiny.*
5th edn. London 1912

320

[SWANSTON, W. O.]
My Journal, by a Volunteer. Calcutta 1858

SWINEY, G. C.
*Historical Records of the 32nd (Cornwall) Light Infantry
1702–1892.* London 1893

THORNTON, Lt. Col. L. H.
'Some Lucknow Memories', in *The Army Quarterly*, vol. 25. 1932

TROTTER, L. J.
The Bayard of India. London 1910

VERNEY, Lt. E., R.N.
The Shannon's Brigade in India. London 1862

WATSON, E. S.
Journal with H.M.S. Shannon's Naval Brigade. Kettering 1858

WICKENS, Private Charles
'Journal of the 90th Light Infantry', in
Journal of the Society of Army Historical Research. 1957–60

[WILSON, T. F.]
The Defence of Lucknow by a Staff Officer. London 1858

WOLSELEY, Field-Marshal Viscount
The Story of a Soldier's life. London 1903

WYLLIE, McLeod
The English Captives in Oudh. London 1858

WYLLY, H. C.
Neill's Blue Caps. Aldershot 1925

NOTES ON SOURCES

Preface
1   Rev. J. P. Harris
    in HARRIS, p. 192

PART ONE: Prelude
Chapter 1
Mutiny at Mariaon
1   Based on MS of
    Colonel Wilson in
    EDWARDES and MERIVALE,
    vol. 2 p. 332
2   REES pp. 12 and 14
3   MORISON p. 306
4   *ibid* p. 307

Chapter 2
Escape to Lucknow
1   ANDERSON p. 16
2   BARTRUM p. 8
3   *ibid* p. 10
4   *ibid*. p. 11
5   *ibid*.
6   *ibid*.
7   *ibid*. p. 12
8   *ibid*.
9   *ibid*. p. 14
10 *ibid*. p. 15

Chapter 3
Conflicts and preparations
1   MORISON p. 290
2   *ibid*. p. 283
3   RUSSELL pp. 57–58
4   Wilson in EDWARDES and
    MERIVALE, vol. 2 pp. 346–47
5   EDWARDES and MERIVALE,
    vol. 2 p. 336
6   MORISON p. 313
7   *ibid*.
8   ANDERSON pp. 25–26
9   REES pp. 29–30
10 EDWARDES and MERIVALE,
    vol. 2 p. 353
11 *ibid*. p. 354

12 REES p. 31
13 *ibid*. p. 32
14 *ibid*.
15 INGLIS, Lady pp. 40–41
16 MORISON p. 317
17 Wilson in MORISON p. 319
18 *ibid*.
19 *ibid*. p. 320

Chapter 4
Disaster at Chinhat
1   John Lawrence in REES p. 88
2   *ibid*.
3   *ibid*.
4   *ibid*.
5   REES p. 75
6   *ibid*.
7   *ibid*.
8   INGLIS, Hon. Julia p. 52
9   EDWARDES and MERIVALE,
    vol. 2 p. 361

PART TWO: The first siege
Chapter 1
Retreat to the Residency
1   INGLIS, Lady p. 45
2   ANDERSON p. 54
3   *ibid*. p. 55
4   REES p. 116
5   *ibid*. p. 117
6   CASE p. 79
7   REES p. 119
8   *ibid*.
9   BARTRUM p. 30
10 *ibid*.
11 ANDERSON p. 57

Chapter 2
Sir Henry, are you hurt?
1   MORISON p. 326
2   HUTCHINSON pp. 168–69

Chapter 4
Chupattees and Sauterne

1 BARTRUM p. 23
2 *ibid.* p. 22
3 *ibid.* p. 24
4 *ibid.* p. 25
5 REES p. 166
6 *ibid.*
7 METCALFE p. 36

Chapter 5
Waiting for attack
1 ANDERSON p. 39
2 *ibid.* p. 41
3 REES p. 135
4 *ibid.*
5 *ibid.* p. 141
6 CASE p. 118
7 REES p. 139
8 *ibid.* p. 138
9 *ibid.* p. 140
10 POLEHAMPTON p. 68

Chapter 6
Assault
1 REES p. 149
2 *ibid.* p. 151
3 *ibid.*
4 *ibid.* pp. 152–53
5 ANDERSON p. 68
6 REES p. 158
7 GUBBINS p. 225

Chapter 7
Mine and counter-mine
1 FULTON p. 82

Chapter 8
Hope deferred
1 WILSON p. 68
2 REES p. 168
3 INGLIS, Lady pp. 92–93
4 *ibid.* pp. 93–94
5 *ibid.* p. 101
6 REES p. 170
7 BARTRUM p. 33
8 *ibid.*
9 FORREST *History*, vol. 1 p. 259
10 REES p. 170

Chapter 9
Assault renewed
1 ANDERSON p. 64
2 *ibid.* p. 79
3 METCALFE p. 43
4 *ibid.* pp. 41–42
5 HARRIS p. 86
6 *ibid.*
7 METCALFE p. 45
8 *ibid.* p. 46
9 *ibid.* pp. 49–50
10 *ibid.* p. 50

Chapter 10
Will Havelock never come?
1 REES p. 183
2 *ibid.* pp. 185–86
3 ANDERSON p. 84
4 INGLIS, Lady p. 119
5 *ibid.* pp. 119–21

Chapter 11
Auctions and alarms
1 REES pp. 201–2
2 WILSON p. 107
3 METCALFE p. 49
4 GUBBINS p. 268
5 ANDERSON p. 97
6 MARSHMAN p. 383
7 WILSON p. 111
8 MARSHMAN pp. 392–93
9 PALMER fol. 40
10 *ibid.* fol. 17

PART THREE: *The first relief*
Chapter 1
A partial eclipse
1 KAVANAGH p. 36
2 FULTON p. 80
3 INNES p. 147
4 REES p. 218
5 *ibid.* p. 220
6 *ibid.* p. 115
7 SOPPITT, in Fitchett
   'Appendix'
8 *ibid.*
9 MARSHMAN p. 400

Chapter 2
The battered gate
1 INGLIS, Lady pp. 151–52
2 *ibid.* p. 152
3 GUBBINS p. 298
4 WILSON p. 140
5 GOLDSMID vol. 2 p. 161
6 WILSON p. 152

Chapter 3
Good news and sad
1 GERMON p. 98
2 REES p. 186
3 RUSSELL, p. xv
4 EDWARDES *Battles*, p. 95
5 *ibid.* p. 100
6 GOLDSMID, vol. 2 p. 216
7 *ibid.* p. 250
8 PALMER fol. 52
9 INGLIS, Lady p. 160
10 REES p. 226

Chapter 4
Outram takes command
1 FAYRER p. 162
2 Based on Dr Home's narrative
   in GUBBINS pp. 323–332
3 METCALFE p. 53
4 *ibid.*
5 *ibid.*

Chapter 5
Dilemmas and decisions
1 REES p. 253
2 BARTRUM pp. 45–46
3 TROTTER p. 170
4 Based on description by
   Lieutenant Edmondstone
   in METCALFE pp. 113–15
5 METCALFE p. 59
6 *ibid.* p. 60
7 *ibid.*
8 OUTRAM pp. 314–15
9 *ibid* p. 315
10 GOLDSMID, vol. 2 p. 282

PART FOUR: *The second siege*
Chapter 1
Reorganising the Residency
1 OUTRAM pp. 320–21
2 REES p. 281
3 GERMON p. 103
4 *ibid.*
5 *ibid.*
6 *ibid.* p. 104
7 REES p. 285
8 *Home Miscellaneous* vol. 724
9 REES p. 293
10 *ibid.*
11 *ibid.*
12 *ibid.* p. 294
13 *ibid.* p. 296
14 *ibid.* p. 294
15 *ibid.* p. 290
16 MAUDE and SHERER,
   vol. 2 p. 63
17 OUTRAM p. 320
18 GOLDSMID, vol. 2 p. 270
19 GUBBINS p. 367

Chapter 2
Food, clothes and Victoria Crosses
1 METCALFE p. 60
2 *ibid.* p. 61
3 REES p. 262
4 *ibid.* pp. 262–63
5 *ibid.* p. 264
6 BARTRUM p. 49
7 *ibid.*
8 Letter of Ashton Crowell
   Warner
9 INGLIS, Lady p. 194
10 SOPPITT, in Fitchett
   'Appendix'
11 OUTRAM p. 345
12 *ibid.* p. 331
13 KAVANAGH p. 45
14 *ibid.*
15 OUTRAM pp. 328–29
16 GOLDSMID, vol. 2 Appendix I
17 KAVANAGH p. 123
18 GERMON p. 110
19 OUTRAM pp. 333–34
20 *ibid.* p. 334

Chapter 3
Underground and overground
1 MARSHMAN p. 308

2 *ibid.* p. 434
3 Letter of Ashton Crowell
   Warner
4 *Foreign Consultations* 203
5 KAVANAGH p. 32
6 *ibid.* p. 35
7 Based on KAVANAGH
   pp. 68–72
8 OUTRAM pp. 352–53
9 *ibid.* p. 353
10 OUTRAM pp. 359–60
11 GOLDSMID, vol. 2 p. 336
12 OUTRAM p. 361
13 *ibid.* p. 375
14 *ibid.* p. 369
15 *ibid.* p. 373
16 REES p. 296
17 *ibid.*
18 BARTRUM p. 51
19 *ibid.*
20 INGLIS, Lady p. 191
21 CASE p. 266
22 OUTRAM p. 375
23 CASE p. 283

Chapter 4
A destiny fulfilled
1 Chapter based on
   KAVANAGH's *Narrative,*
   written at the Alambagh on 24
   November 1857, and
   KAVANAGH pp. 75–97

PART FIVE: *Final relief*
Chapter 1
Crawling Camel
1 REES p. 311
2 Based on KAVANAGH
   pp. 116–18
3 FORBES *Havelock,* p. 161
4 *ibid.* p. 163

5 WOLSELEY p. 113
6 BARTRUM p. 53
7 FORREST *Selections,* vol. 2
   p. 186
8 *ibid.* p. 146
9 *ibid.*
10 REES p. 340
11 ROBERTS *Forty-one Years,*
   p. 192

Chapter 2
The going away
1 GERMON p. 127
2 *ibid.* p. 128
3 GRANT and KNOLLYS p. 141
4 BARTRUM pp. 55–56
5 INGLIS, Lady p. 207
6 *ibid.*
7 GOLDSMID, vol. 2 p. 339
8 CAMPBELL, pp. 102 and 113
9 GUBBINS p. 411
10 MARSHMAN p. 445
11 *ibid.*
12 METCALFE p. 62
13 BARTRUM p. 59
14 MACKAY, vol. 2 p. 285

Epilogue
1 REES p. 361
2 BARTRUM p. 62
3 *ibid.* p. 70
4 TROTTER p. 221
5 METCALFE p. 90
6 *ibid.*
7 FORBES *Havelock* p. 34 f/n
8 EDWARDES and MERIVALE,
   vol. 2 p. 383
9 MARSHMAN p. 454
10 *ibid.* pp. 461–62

NOTE ON ILLUSTRATIONS

Illustrations 4, 6, 7, 8, 9, 10, 11, 12, 13, 14, 17, 18 and 20 are from *Sketches and Incidents of the Siege of Lucknow* by C. H. Mecham and G. Couper (London 1858); 3, 5, 15 and 16 from *General Views and Special Points of Interest in the City of Lucknow* by D. Dodgson (London 1860); 1 from *The History of the Indian Mutiny* by C. Ball (London 1858, 1859); 2 from *The Campaign in India 1857–58* by G. F. Atkinson (London 1859); and 19 from *Views in India Taken from Drawings* by D. S. Greene (London 1859). The plans on pp. 70, 72, 78, 80, 84, 86, 88 and 90 are adapted from *Lucknow and Oude in the Mutiny* by J. J. McLeod Innes (London 1896). The three maps have been specially drawn by Patrick Leeson.

INDEX